Ethics at the Center

The Jewish Publication Society expresses its gratitude for the generosity of the sponsors of this book.

The Dorothy K. and Myer S. Kripke Institute (Dr. Ron Wolfson, president), in honor of our beloved colleague, Rabbi Elliot Dorff, for his decades of superb teaching and personal *menschlikhkeit.*

Bill and Sandy Goodglick, with admiration and fondness for our dear friend and teacher Rabbi Elliot Dorff.

Elliot N. Dorff

UNIVERSITY OF NEBRASKA PRESS | LINCOLN

Ethics at the Center

Jewish Theory and Practice for Living a Moral Life

Elliot N. Dorff

Foreword by Louis E. Newman

THE JEWISH PUBLICATION SOCIETY | PHILADELPHIA

Library of Congress Cataloging-in-Publication Data
Names: Dorff, Elliot N., author.
Title: Ethics at the center: Jewish theory and practice
for living a moral life / Elliot N. Dorff; foreword by
Louis E. Newman.
Description: Philadelphia: Jewish Publication Soci-
ety; Lincoln, Nebraska: University of Nebraska Press,
[2024] | Includes bibliographical references and
index. | Summary: "Ethics at the Center culls the best
of Rabbi Elliot Dorff's pioneering thinking in Jew-
ish ethics over the course of nearly five decades"—
Provided by publisher.
Identifiers: LCCN 2023034939
ISBN 9780827615656 (hardback)
ISBN 9780827619166 (epub)
ISBN 9780827619173 (pdf)
Subjects: LCSH: Jewish ethics. | Jewish way of life. |
BISAC: RELIGION / Ethics | PHILOSOPHY / Ethics &
Moral Philosophy
Classification: LCC BJ1285.2 .D667 2024 |
DDC 296.3/6—dc23/eng/20231122
LC record available at https://lccn.loc.gov
/2023034939

Set in Minion Pro by L. Welch.

Ethics are first learned from, and most importantly practiced within, one's family, and so this book is dedicated to my family:

To the memory of my parents, Sol and Anne Dorff, who demonstrated to me in word and deed what it means to be a morally sensitive and communally involved person and Jew, all with a sense of humility, humor, and joy.

To Marlynn, my wife since 1966, the love and light of my life.

To Tammy, Michael, Havi, and Jonathan, our children, whom we love dearly and who make us exceedingly proud for the people and Jews they are and for how they contribute to the betterment of society.

To Tanya, Adam, and Mara, our children-in-law, wonderful partners for three of our children, and children to Marlynn and me too.

To our grandchildren—Noa, Zachary, Ayden, Amiel, Zoe, Shira, Miles, and Lev—who reinvigorate their parents and Marlynn and me and who show us that there is indeed hope for the future.

"May you live to see your children's children. May there be peace for the people Israel."

—Psalm 128:6

Contents

Foreword LOUIS E. NEWMAN

I no longer remember precisely when I first met Elliot Dorff, but I remember distinctly the first impression that he made on me. The place was probably a meeting of the Academy for Jewish Philosophy, the time roughly the early 1980s. Elliot was then already an established scholar of Jewish ethics and a leading figure in the Conservative movement whose reputation I knew and whose work I respected. By contrast, I was fresh out of graduate school, as green as they come, utterly unprepared by my graduate training in rabbinics to begin pursuing my interest in Jewish ethics. So, meeting Elliot felt a little like being introduced to your idol, the person who embodies what you wish you could be, who inhabits some exalted realm that you can only dream of. I fully expected him to be too engaged with his peers—Steven Schwartzschild, Norbert Samuelson, and other prominent scholars—to pay any attention to someone with no reputation and not a single publication to his name. Nothing could have been further from the truth. Instead, he seemed to be genuinely interested in me. He talked to me as if I had something of value to contribute to our conversation. He invited me to share my work-in-progress with him. I could not know it then, but this towering figure in the field of Jewish law and ethics was to become first my mentor, then my colleague, and finally my friend. And so I welcome this opportunity to honor you by writing this foreword to your new book, Elliot, for it is no exaggeration to say that my academic career has been shaped more decisively by my interactions with you than by anyone else.

I want to begin by summarizing as best I can the extraordinary scope of Elliot's scholarship in our field. I should note at the outset that Elliot has always been something of an overachiever. His first book, *Jewish Law and Modern Ideology*, was published the same year he graduated from rabbinical school. Just a year later he received his PhD in philosophy from Columbia, where he wrote his dissertation on moral theory. In very short order, he became the leading thinker of Conservative Judaism, widely respected for his ability to articulate the guiding philosophy of the movement in both intellectually compelling and readily accessible terms. He did this in his *Conservative Judaism: Our Ancestors to Our Descendants*, first published in 1977, and he has continued to offer articulate and thought-provoking Conservative positions on a wide range of moral and theological issues throughout his career.

His voluminous list of publications includes twenty-nine major responsa (legal position papers) for the Rabbinical Assembly's Committee on Jewish Law and Standards; scores of articles in *Conservative Judaism* and United Synagogue publications; hundreds of legal commentaries and essays on justice, revelation, and law in the Conservative movement's *Etz Hayim* Torah commentary; theological reflections in Lawrence Hoffman's *My People's Prayer Book* series; and fourteen books that he wrote and an equal number he either edited or coedited; to say nothing of over two hundred articles in diverse periodicals and in the popular press. His copious writings alone place him among the most influential and widely read religious thinkers of the past half century. One reviewer's assessment of *A Living Tree: The Roots and Growth of Jewish Law* could equally well apply to much of his oeuvre: "[*A Living Tree*] simply possesses no competitors in terms of depth, description, and clarity of explanation. It will undoubtedly serve as the most comprehensive and accessible introduction to Jewish law for a generation to come in the American university."

It is worth highlighting, in particular, Elliot's contributions to discussions of bioethics, both within the Jewish community and nationally. His *Matters of Life and Death: A Jewish Approach to Modern Medical Ethics* is the only comprehensive Conservative Jewish statement on bioethics and a very welcome corrective to the Orthodox Jewish voices who have dominated that field. His volumes, *To Do the Right and the Good: A Jewish Approach to Modern Social Ethics* (which, incidentally, won a coveted National Jewish Book Award), *Love Your Neighbor and Yourself: A Jewish Approach to Modern Personal Ethics*, *For the Love of God and People: A Philosophy of Jewish Law*, and *Modern Conservative Judaism: Evolving Thought and Practice*, are further fruits of his decades-long commitment to developing a distinctly Conservative Jewish approach to contemporary ethical issues.

Yet Elliot's reputation extends far beyond the Jewish community. His standing as one of the country's leading Jewish ethicists has earned him invitations to address several national commissions and bioethics task forces, including the National Bioethics Advisory Commission, where he has testified on human cloning and stem cell research; the Surgeon General's Commission on Responsible Sexual Behavior; and the National Human Resources Protections Advisory Commission. He also served, in 1993, on the Ethics Committee of Hillary Rodham Clinton's Health Care Task Force. In addition, Elliot has participated in several other collaborative projects through the American Association for the Advancement of Science and the Carnegie Foundation. In all these contexts, Elliot offers a distinctively Jewish voice, yet one capable of speaking to a diverse audience. And in each of these settings, he has earned a reputation for the depth of his learning, the respectful way he listens to others, and the incisive way he frames the key issues. It is no wonder that whenever people are looking for a Jewish authority on major moral issues, Elliot's name rises to the top of the list.

But Elliot's influence in this field is hardly confined to his published work. He has shaped the education of two generations of rabbis, Jewish educators, and lawyers through his courses at the American Jewish University (formerly called the University of Judaism) and UCLA law school. As a teacher he is known for his clear and engaging lectures, his ability to make classical texts come alive, and his insistence that students take the teachings of this tradition seriously, which means that they must be applied in a spirit of creativity commensurate with that which created them in the first place. His reputation as a brilliant teacher accounts for the invitations he regularly receives to lecture at synagogues throughout North and South America and in England. For many years, he also served as rabbi-in-residence at Camp Ramah in California, where he taught campers and staff members alike to both respect and challenge this tradition.

In short, Elliot is not only a prolific and widely respected scholar but an enormously gifted and popular teacher. Indeed, one of the trademarks of his life's work is that he so successfully bridges the worlds of the academy, the pulpit, and the broader Jewish community.

Most scholars would be satisfied to be prolific writers, renowned in their religious community and respected in the world of social policy makers. But, in addition to all this, Elliot has also taken on leadership roles in both academic and communal organizations. He has chaired or served as president of the Academy of Jewish Philosophy; the Rabbinic Assembly's

Committee on Jewish Law and Standards; the Academy of Judaic, Christian, and Islamic Studies; the Jewish Law Association; the Society of Jewish Ethics; the Jewish Hospice Commission of Los Angeles; and the Jewish Family Service of Los Angeles. He has also taken on leadership roles in the Center for Jewish Learning and Leadership and the National Conference of Christians and Jews. He has served on the ethics committees of both the Jewish Homes for the Aging and the UCLA Medical Center. He has long co-chaired the Priest-Rabbi Dialogue, cosponsored by the Los Angeles Archdiocese and the Board of Rabbis of Southern California, and he has served on the editorial boards of numerous publications. All this is in addition to a full-time job as rector and Distinguished Professor of Philosophy at American Jewish University. It is no exaggeration to say that the creative work outlined here—and this is far from an exhaustive list—is surely worthy of several lifetimes.

Yet the *quantity* of Elliot's work, impressive as it is, is not what distinguishes his contribution to the fields of law, religion, and ethics. Rather, the distinctive *quality* of his mind animates everything he does, from the books and articles he writes to the courses he teaches, from his contributions to interreligious dialogue to those on public policy, from his academic work to his community leadership. That razor-sharp mind is in no small way what makes his writing and teaching so insightful and accessible. To illustrate, allow me to quote from the appendix to his *Matters of Life and Death: A Jewish Approach to Modern Medical Ethics*, where he lays out the methodological foundations of his approach:

[This approach] bespeaks the Jewish tradition's long-standing insistence that individual cases must be decided on their own merits; that general rules may not substitute for careful consideration of the particular circumstances of the people involved; and that, more generally, law and morality are, and must remain, intertwined. Making decisions in specific cases does not eliminate the importance of articulating general standards—that is, commonly used principles and policies; one must just know when and how to use them. In the technical terms of contemporary ethicists, I am arguing neither for an exclusively situational ethic nor for a solely rule-based one. . . . I am arguing instead for a character-based ethic, in which both rules and contexts combine with moral moorings in philosophical/religious sources and moral education to produce moral sensitivity. This approach represents a much richer—and, I think, much more realistic—view of how moral norms evolve and operate than the exclusive attention to principles that has characterized much of moral theory until this century.[1]

As I see it, there are several virtues evident in this sort of approach, and they bespeak the qualities that distinguish Elliot's work in the fields of ethics and religious thought more generally. Let me highlight just three.

First, there is the sheer depth and breadth of Elliot's learning. He is equally at home in the pages of the Talmud and the discourse of modern philosophers. He knows and values the religious insights of Christians and Muslims and can relate them to those in his own tradition. Pick up any of his published works and you will immediately discover that his presentation of every issue is fully synthesized. Here the sharp (one might say, facile) distinctions between law, religion, and philosophy give way to a more organic approach to seeking religious and moral guidance. It is Elliot's primary insight that the guidance we find in Jewish tradition (and, by implication, I think, in every other) must be holistic, encompassing the full range of resources at our disposal—classical and contemporary, legal, scientific, philosophical, and theological. There are surely many voices within the tradition, and yet they are all of a piece. To pretend that we can neatly divide law from ethics or theology is really to misrepresent the tradition we claim to be interpreting. More importantly, to limit ourselves to one genre or one period is to impoverish our repertoire of moral insight, which does a disservice to our traditions and, most especially, to ourselves.

Second, Elliot's work is consistently clear and accessible. He will tell you that this has something to do with being the son of a high school English teacher, but I know plenty of English teachers who could learn something about clear prose from reading Elliot's work. He manages to communicate positions of remarkable subtlety, built from multiple interpretations of numerous texts, without losing the reader in a mass of detail.

His clear prose is essentially the external expression of extraordinarily clear thinking. Sit with Elliot at a conference, as I have done on many occasions, and you will quickly see what I mean. After many speakers have tackled an issue from multiple, often incompatible perspectives, Elliot will quietly raise his hand and, in one decisive move, bring conceptual order to the entire debate. The first few times I watched him do this, I was truly amazed. Over the years, I have just come to expect that, if Elliot is in the room, he will invariably cut to the heart of an issue and, in doing so, move the whole discussion to a new plane. And, when he is not in the room, I frequently find myself wondering what Elliot would say if he were there. That razor-sharp mind is in no small way what makes his writing and his teaching so insightful and so accessible.

Finally, Elliot's broad learning and incisive thinking are always tempered with his deep commitment to people living in community with one another, facing the real problems of daily life. In this respect, he is a rabbi above all else. His reading of the tradition is never an intellectual exercise; his learning is entirely in the service of making this world a better place. That is why his involvement with Jewish communal service agencies, hospital ethics committees, and government task forces is no diversion from his scholarship. Quite the contrary—it is an integral part of his intellectual life, providing him with an opportunity to apply legal and moral principles to the real world and, of course, to bring the lived experience of those who are suffering and needy back into his reflections on the tradition. So it is that his writings on violence, poverty, sexual orientation, and bioethical issues never lose touch with the people for whom these are pressing issues. This is engaged scholarship at its very best.

If I were to summarize these qualities in a word, it would be that Elliot's life work is about building bridges—between the world of classical Jewish sources and the contemporary world in which Jews live; between the legal, moral, and theological components within Jewish tradition itself; between the wisdom of the tradition and the real-life needs of people; and between Jews and non-Jews. In everything he does one finds evidence of this desire to integrate, bring people together, cross-fertilize ideas, bring the past and the present into conversation with one another. This quality, above all, I think, is what makes Elliot's teaching and writing so compelling. We sense that the person addressing us is fully present, that he has not shut himself off to any source of religious or moral insight, nor turned his back on any segment of the community or any social issue. He brings not only all his learning, but also all his sensitivity and human experience to his engagement with the tradition and with his readers. That is why I always feel so nourished when I read Elliot's work: he honors his own humanity and ours.

To all this, I would like to add a few personal reflections.

Nearly thirty years ago, as I prepared to teach a class on Jewish ethics, I became aware that the standard anthology of articles on the subject was then both out of date and out of print. I resolved to put together a new volume that would showcase the best work of contemporary Jewish ethicists, highlighting both the methodological and substantive diversity in this field. I knew I would need a partner in this project, someone whose broad knowledge of the field, sophisticated understanding of the underlying issues that needed to be presented, sound judgment, and editorial skills were commensurate to the task. Moreover, I needed to find someone I would enjoy working with. There was only one candidate for the job. Thankfully, Elliot agreed to join me in this project, and, for me, our collaboration was truly a labor of love. Producing a reader of this sort is notoriously difficult, since judgments about what to include, scope, and level of difficulty must be made at every point, to say nothing of writing the essays that will frame the whole volume. But making those decisions with Elliot was virtually effortless, not only because of the many intellectual gifts he brought to the table, but because he is, above all, a mensch of the highest order. His generosity of spirit and willingness to compromise when we disagreed, his dedication and uncommon common sense, made this work rewarding, to say nothing of making the final product far better than anything I could have done alone. Indeed, the collaboration was so enjoyable and fruitful that just a few years later we put together a second anthology, this time of essays in contemporary Jewish theology. And, again, I benefited from the opportunity to learn from Elliot, not only about aspects of Jewish theology or even about how best to introduce readers to this material but, most of all, about how to be a colleague. Simply put, Elliot is the colleague every teacher and scholar dreams of having, and few are fortunate enough to experience. I consider the opportunities I have had to learn with him and from him to be the greatest blessing of my academic career.

Over these years, Elliot has been my idol, mentor, colleague, and conversation partner—and, in no small way, my best editor. Who else would have found time amid such a busy schedule to read the full manuscript of my *Introduction to Jewish Ethics*, much less comment, longhand, on virtually every page?

Above all, he has been a model of the sort of teacher, scholar, and colleague I strive to be. Our sages admonish us: *aseh l'kha rav, u'knei l'kha* _haver_, "select for yourself a rabbi/teacher, and acquire for yourself a friend/colleague." In Elliot, I have found all these things.

This volume of collected essays, drawn from Elliot's vast collection of writings, stands as yet one more testimony to his stature as a leading Jewish scholar of our time, as an influential and beloved teacher, and as a person whose deep humanity shines through in everything he does. Readers of this volume will likewise experience the unique pleasure of exploring issues of enormous significance, guided by one of our most distinguished scholars and most beloved teachers.

Acknowledgments

As Professor Louis Newman so kindly wrote in his foreword for this volume, my interests and writings have ranged across a wide gamut of topics. When Rabbi Barry Schwartz, then editor in chief of The Jewish Publication Society (JPS), first suggested that I write a volume that goes to the core of what I have tried to contribute to the thinking and action of Jews of all affiliations as well as people of other faiths and those who see themselves as secular, I realized that ethics has always been my focus. So thank you, Barry, for first suggesting that I write this volume, and for providing important guidance in considering which of my many writings should be included and how to shorten them to comprise a book of reasonable length. Through her many questions and suggestions, Joy Weinberg, the JPS managing editor, has helped me immensely in shaping both the contents and form of the selections, and in making this manuscript more cogent than my proposed text. I am also indebted to Ann Baker, managing editor, and Stephanie Marshall Ward, copyeditor for this book, at the University of Nebraska Press, JPS's copublisher, who skillfully saw this project through to publication. Thank you also to Jessica Freeman for preparing the index for this volume.

Much of my thinking on moral issues has taken shape in the form of responsa written for the Rabbinical Assembly's Committee on Jewish Law and Standards (CJLS), of which I have been privileged to be a member since December 1984 and to serve as its chair from 2007 to 2022. I thank all the CJLS members for their many questions and suggestions responding to early drafts of my responsa, especially those with whom I wrote responsa: Marc Gary and Rabbis Susan Grossman, Aaron Mackler, Daniel Nevins, Joel Roth, Elie Kaplan Spitz, and Gordon Tucker. I also want to thank the Rabbinical Assembly more broadly for all the important ways that it helps rabbis serve the Jewish community and tradition, thereby enabling the tradition I love to enrich the lives of Jews and give us moral guidance in generations past, present, and future.

Thank you, Dr. Ron Wolfson, my longtime friend and colleague at American Jewish University, who as executive director of the Kripke Fund agreed to help fund the publication of this book. Thank you also, Bill and Sandy Goodglick, longtime personal friends who supplied the additional funds necessary to publish it.

I would also like to thank Professor Michael Berenbaum, my longtime friend and colleague at American Jewish University, and my son Professor Michael Dorff for creating and co-editing a collection of essays in my honor (a Festschrift), presented to me, as a complete surprise, in the celebration of my eightieth birthday. The book, *Hesed V'Emet Nashaku, Loving Kindness and Truth Embraced: The Life and Thought of Rabbi Elliot Dorff*, whose title is based on Psalm 85:11, includes essays by twenty-five scholars, each of whom I also want to thank for the honor and pleasure of knowing you and for your contribution to the volume.

Finally, as I begin my eighties, I wish to thank the members of my family, who have been a major source of meaning and joy throughout my life and who have exhibited amazing tolerance and patience with me as I spent hours upon hours writing essays and books. First and foremost is my wife of fifty-seven years, Marlynn, who typed the 312 pages of my PhD dissertation in 1970–71. As a mark of amazing love and patience, she even retyped the first hundred pages when it became clear that I needed to organize the material by topic rather than by thinker. (This was all before computers and even before Wite-Out.) That project convinced her that philosophy was not for her, but she continually supported me in following my rabbinic and philosophic interests. Our children—Tammy, Michael, Havi, and Jonathan—have been a deep source of meaning and joy for us from the moment they were born to the present day, and I am really glad that they each have pursued interests of their own. Three of them are married, and Tanya, Adam, and Mara are wonderful additions to our family and amazing people in their own right. And then there are our eight grandchildren—in age order: Noa, Zachary, Ayden, Amiel, Zoe, Shira, Miles, and Lev—some of whom actually study with me by Zoom on Sunday mornings and tolerate my philosophical meanderings, and all of whom are a sheer delight to have in our lives. Some have even told me that they do not mind being asked whether they are my grandchild. What love! I truly thank God for the blessings of Marlynn, our children, our children-in-law, and our grandchildren, and I thank them for being the people and Jews they are. They all exemplify a strong sense of moral values and compassion and empathy for others intuitively and constantly, which makes someone like me—both a scholar of the theory and practice of ethics and a loving and doting father and grandfather—immensely proud.

Quoting Rabbi Ḥanina: "I have learned much from my teachers and even more from my friends, but from my students I have learned more than from all of them" (B. *Ta'anit* 7a), and, I would add, even more from the members of my family. Thank you to each and every one of you for the multiple blessings with which you have enhanced my life and my thinking about the subject of *ethics at the center*.

Introduction

A notable 72 percent of American Jews think that living a moral life is an important part of their Jewish identity. What is more, the 72 percent of Jews scoring ethics as Judaism's core is far higher than the 45 percent who chose "caring about Israel," the 33 percent who prioritized "being part of a Jewish community," and the 15 percent who replied "observing Jewish law"; indeed, for American Jews, only "remembering the Holocaust" scored higher (76 percent).[2]

They are correct in believing that ethics is central to Judaism. Consider the implications of the following three classic Jewish texts:

Thus said the Lord:
Let not the wise man glory in his wisdom;
Let not the strong man glory in his strength;
Let not the rich man glory in his riches;
But only in this should one glory:
In earnest devotion to Me.
For I the Lord act with kindness,
Justice, and equity in the world;
For in these I delight, declares the Lord. (Jer. 9:22–23)

Rabbi Ḥama, son of Rabbi Ḥanina, says: What is the meaning of that which is written: "After the Lord your God shall you walk, and Him shall you fear, and His commandments shall you keep, and unto His voice shall you hearken, and Him shall you serve, and unto Him shall you cleave" (Deuteronomy 13:5)? But is it actually possible for a person to follow the Divine Presence? Has it not already been stated: "For the Lord your God is a devouring fire, a jealous God" (Deuteronomy 4:24)? Rather, the meaning is that one should follow the attributes of the Holy Blessed One. Just as God clothes the naked, . . . So too, should you clothe the naked. Just as the Holy Blessed One visits the sick, so too, should you visit the sick. Just as the Holy Blessed One consoles mourners, so too, should you console mourners. Just as the Holy Blessed One buried the dead, . . . So too, should you bury the dead. (B. *Sotah* 14a)

Rabbi Simlai continued: King David came and established the 613 mitzvot upon eleven mitzvot, as it is written: "A Psalm of David. Lord, who shall sojourn in Your Tabernacle? Who shall dwell upon Your sacred mountain? [1] He who walks wholeheartedly, and [2] works righteousness, and [3] speaks truth in his heart. [4] Who has no slander upon his tongue, [5] nor does evil to his neighbor, [6] nor takes up reproach against his relative. [7] In whose eyes a vile person is despised, and [8] he honors those who fear the Lord; [9] he takes an oath to his own detriment, and [9] changes not. [10] He neither gives his money with interest, [11] nor takes a bribe against the innocent. He who performs these shall never be moved" (Psalms, chapter 15). . . . Isaiah came and established the 613 mitzvot upon six, as it is written: "He who walks righteously, and speaks uprightly; he who despises the gain of oppressions, who shakes his hands from holding of bribes, who stops his ears from hearing blood, and shuts his eyes from looking upon evil" (Isaiah 33:15). Micah came and established the 613 mitzvot upon three, as it is written: "It has been told to you, O man, what is good, and what the Lord requires of you; only to do justly, and to love mercy, and to walk humbly with your God" (Micah 6:8). . . . Isaiah then established the 613 mitzvot upon two, as it is stated: "So says the Lord: Observe justice and perform righteousness" (Isaiah 56:1). Amos came and established the 613 mitzvot upon one, as it is stated: "So says the Lord to the house of Israel: Seek Me and live" (Amos 5:4). . . . Habakkuk came and established the 613 mitzvot upon one, as it is stated: "But the righteous person shall live by his faith" (Habakkuk 2:4). (B. *Makkot* 24a)

Notice that in all three of these classic texts, especially the last one, although rituals are easily more than half of the 613 commandments, *not a single ritual commandment appears on the list of their essence.* When push comes to shove, I believe, although rituals and family and communal connections are very important parts of what Judaism adds to the lives of Jews, ethics is at the center of Judaism.

Ethical Discernment

Sometimes in life, the ethical issues we encounter are obvious, so our task is to take, or motivate others to take, the moral action. Many other times, the issues are more complex, requiring our sensitivity, knowledge, moral vision, and discernment, and the task is to learn the relevant facts before making a hard decision. Acting morally and wisely may require specialized knowledge of science, technology, mathematics, medicine, economics, literature, sociology, politics, and education—much more knowledge than any of our ancestors had in those fields—as well as the entire Jewish tradition! Of course, nobody has that breadth of knowledge but, thankfully, we human beings can consult with others to learn enough about those areas to resolve moral quandaries as best we can.

The harder skill to achieve is the *judgment* necessary to balance conflicting claims wisely. This requires the skills to listen attentively to others to determine the facts of the situation and the needs of the people directly involved as well as those in the larger society. It also requires the ability to discern when a particular claim is not correct or moral, and skill in balancing correct but conflicting moral claims.

If the tradition is properly interpreted and applied, I believe our Jewish knowledge and commitment can enable us to bring the wisdom of Jewish tradition to bear on hard moral questions, and then the Jewish tradition will add to our own insights and help to bear the moral burden of whatever decision is made.

That has been my experience in the nearly fifty years I have spent grappling with moral issues alongside people from diverse walks of life. These include the Conservative movement's Committee on Jewish Law and Standards; federal government commissions on health care, reducing the spread of sexually transmitted diseases, and research ethics; the state of California's commission to govern stem-cell research within the state; the ethics committees of UCLA Medical Center and the Jewish Homes; and the boards of directors of Jewish Family Service and the Jewish Federation Council of Los Angeles. It also includes many interfaith activities, including Intersem (the annual conference of seminarians in Southern California); the Priest-Rabbi Dialogue; the Academy of Judaic, Christian, and Islamic Studies; the Anti-Defamation League's Bearing Witness program; World Council of Churches conferences and publications; Fuller Theological

Seminary programs; and much more. These discussions have sharpened my thinking on a range of issues in bioethics, including infertility, abortion, end-of-life care, and the distribution of health care; and on sex and family issues, including the ethics of human intimacy and parent-child relations. These also include new issues prompted by the availability of the internet, including how to preserve privacy and modest communication and avoid harmful communication in this new setting; responding to poverty and homelessness; business issues such as intellectual property and employer-employee relations; and environmental protection. In all these areas of moral concern, many of which are treated in this volume, Judaism has much to contribute, but so do other religious and philosophical traditions. Seeing what other traditions have to say on complex and complicated moral issues sometimes shows me how Jewish perspectives and norms can and should be supplemented by those from other traditions (e.g., Judaism's focus on our duties to our community complemented by Western liberal philosophy's focus on individual rights). At other times, that investigation sheds light on how different Judaism is from those other traditions and why, prodding me to evaluate the strengths and weaknesses of each approach. At the very least, seeing issues from the perspectives of other religious and philosophical traditions makes it clear that not everyone thinks and acts as Judaism would have us do, and that should enhance Jews' understanding of their own tradition. As Fredrich Max Muller, often credited with founding the study of comparative religion, said about religion, "He who knows one, knows none."[3]

In other words, I am a pluralist. As Professor Diana Eck of Harvard University defines it, pluralism has four components: (1) the energetic engagement with diversity; (2) the active seeking of understanding across lines of difference; (3) not relativism (that every claim to truth or goodness is as good as any other), not syncretism (seeking to combine insights from all perspectives), and certainly not the demand to renounce one's own beliefs, but the encounter of commitments; and (4) dialogue and encounter as its mode of learning about other people's traditions and, in the process, about one's own as well.[4]

Foundational Commitments of My Life's Work

Zooming out to look at my life's work in this regard, I would say that two foundational commitments have guided it:

1. *Epistemological humility:* the realization that even though God may be omniscient, no human being is, so each of us should understand one's own beliefs about what is true and good and those of others with a high degree of humility about what anyone can know. Consider that throughout the vast majority of human history, even the smartest people thought the world was flat. In asserting anything, we should be open to challenges and even changes in what we believe based on new evidence and what we learn from others. Along with many others who similarly changed their views on these issues, that certainly has been the case for my understanding of the proper role of women in Jewish life as it evolved in the 1970s and 1980s and of the status of gay and lesbian marriages as it evolved in the 1990s and early 2000s. More recently, as one chapter in this book describes, in 2019 I wrote a rabbinic ruling that would allow aid in dying in specific circumstances, in contrast to the rabbinic ruling I wrote in 1997 that banned assisted suicide altogether.

2. *Gratitude as the central religious response to life and foundation for ethics:* Rabbi Abraham Joshua Heschel thought that the central Jewish response to life should be awe and wonder, and indeed many of the psalms and other parts of the Jewish liturgy express awe about the world. But as much as awe is an important feeling to have so that we do not take life or anything in it for granted, one can have awe and wonder about the world and treat people terribly. In contrast, for me the central Jewish response to life is one of gratitude, voiced as the first thing we are supposed to say when we get up in the morning and through all one hundred blessings the Talmud tells us we are supposed to proclaim each day.[5] When you praise someone for something, you are acknowledging the significance of that achievement, that it is important for your own life and should not be taken for granted. In mandating that we utter one hundred blessings of God each day, then, the tradition is helping us get out of ourselves (our "egocentric predicament," as philosophers call it) to recognize the degree to which we depend on God and, by extension, on God's creation (including humans) to live and even thrive. Similarly, the sentence we are supposed to say first each day is: "I thank You, living and eternal Sovereign, for Your

kindness in restoring my soul to me. How great is Your faithful-ness." Although Hebrew grammar permits the reverse (*ani modeh*), the sentence begins with *modeh*, thank you, and only then says *ani*, I, so the very first utterance each morning is "thank you."[6] Fur-thermore, we thank God in the *Amidah* three times each day "for our lives that are in Your hands, for our souls that are under Your care, for Your miracles that accompany us each day, and for Your wonders and Your gifts that are with us each moment—evening, morning, and noon." Here "miracles" clearly does not mean inter-ruptions in the order of nature, but just the opposite—the normal structure of nature that enables us to live. People whose conscious-ness is filled with gratitude for their very lives and for these nor-mal "miracles" may certainly vary in personality but, in my view, gratitude is a much stronger foundation than awe for sensitivity to other people and hence moral conduct. One can, of course, recite one hundred blessings each day mechanically and ignore their import for how one should live life and treat other people, but con-sciously seeing life as filled with blessings that should not be taken for granted and making gratitude to God and people a central fea-ture of your life should motivate you to appreciate and care for oth-ers. As Warren Buffet says, "If you're in the luckiest 1% of humanity, you owe it to the rest of humanity to think about the other 99%,"[7] a principle on which he has acted dramatically by giving away almost all of his fortune—and his principle is true, I contend, even if one has far less money than he has amassed.

About This Book

In *Ethics at the Center: Jewish Theory and Practice for Living a Moral Life*, I have endeavored to cull the very best of my ethical insights over the course of nearly five decades, in large part to stress these essential ideas:

Whether each of us is conscious of this or not, how we view moral issues ultimately depends on our own foundational conceptions about the nature of both human beings and God.

Jewish law, theology, prayer, history, and community all play roles in defining and motivating Jewish responses to moral issues, for they are all part of the organic whole that is the Jewish tradition.

Western philosophy and other religions offer important and honorable but also divergent ideas about morality that are best understood in contrast to Judaism's foundational stances.

Because, as we will see, Judaism roots its moral convictions in its understandings of God and human beings, the book begins with how Judaism views God and humans, and the interactions between them. Part 1, "Zooming Out: Thinking Theologically about God and Human Beings," zooms out to see God and humanity from thirty thousand feet up, as it were, so that Judaism's fundamental convictions about God and humanity can be understood as the basis for Judaism's views of specific moral issues. Although many Jews may think of these conceptions as obvious, most other religions and secular philosophies begin with very different conceptions of humanity and ultimate reality. The chapters in this section explore some of these comparisons.

The goal of part 2, "Getting Down to Earth: Methods for Converting Thought into Practice," is to alert readers to the multiple aspects of the Jewish tradition that can be called into play as we seek to apply the tradition wisely, authentically, and creatively to the moral realities of contemporary life. First up is a statement of the many sources to be called into play when considering moral issues, especially difficult or new ones. Because Jewish law has been the primary way to address moral issues in the Jewish tradition, my own theory of Jewish law follows, and, afterward, concrete guidelines about how to use Jewish law in addressing moral issues. Because Jewish theology also plays a critical role in any authentic Jewish response to a moral issue, the next chapter describes one example—how theology is important in addressing physical and mental health issues. The subsequent chapter, devoted to how prayer can play a role in our moral lives, may seem strange to Jews, although it is obvious to Evangelical Christians who, when faced with a moral dilemma, will not just say "I will think about it" but often "I will pray on it." Prayer, I believe, can remind us of our place in life and the moral goals for which we ought to strive, and it can thereby clarify our moral vision and motivate us to do what we should. We conclude this section on methodology with a wonderful exchange of letters between Rabbi Eugene Borowitz and me in which we weigh the relative roles of autonomy and community in deciding moral issues.

After these theological and methodological discussions, we arrive at part 3, "The Real Deal: Personal and Social Ethics," explorations of how to apply Judaism's ethics to real-life circumstances. What does Judaism's understanding of abortion add to the debate after the U.S. Supreme Court overturned *Roe v. Wade*? How are we to understand human dignity and apply it to how gay and lesbian individuals and couples should be treated and their unions publicly celebrated?

Then there are several issues that the internet has made much more acute, including how to avoid harming other people (e.g., bullying or sharing negative information) or violating reasonable rules of modesty in language. A related issue is playing violent or defamatory video games. If the vast majority of people who play those games do not then cause harm to other people, what, if anything, is wrong with playing such games? As readers will see, it is less a matter of one's actions and more a matter of what doing so says about one's character.

Then I tackle actual instead of virtual violence—namely, a modern Jewish approach to the ethics of war when the instruments of war are far more lethal than our ancestors ever imagined and when the establishment of the State of Israel means that, for the first time since the end of the Hasmonean period in 63 BCE, Jews have the power and responsibility to determine when to go to war and how.

Additionally, how should charities identify and avoid donations of ill-gotten gain and respond to them after the fact? Furthermore, does "ill-gotten" mean only money made illegally, or does it include money earned legally but in morally questionable ways, such as investments in companies that pollute the environment or depend on oppressive working conditions?

An analysis of Jewish moral guidelines for providing references for schools and jobs follows. What seems obvious—that you should simply tell the truth about what you know of the person's skills and work ethic—can be complicated by the Jewish norm that one should not speak ill of another person. If the reference-seeker has been problematic, how should one balance the moral teaching not to speak ill of another with concern about causing harm to the potential school or employer by rendering an overly positive reference? And what about the concern that telling negative truths about the person might subject you to being sued in civil law?

Because the essays in this volume were written at a variety of times and for varying audiences, each chapter begins with an introduction that explains when and for whom I wrote the essay, why I wrote it, why I think it is still relevant today, and if and how I would now change what I wrote earlier. I hope that these personal introductory reflections enable you, the reader, to experience not only my evolving ethical thought but many facets of the person, and the Jew, I am today.

I conclude with "Final Thoughts," reflections on how many other rich components of the Jewish tradition—family and community, holidays and rituals, theology, study, and law—have moral import as well.

All in all, *Ethics at the Center* explores the multiple ways in which the Jewish tradition addresses morality. It looks at how to apply this tradition to old issues that are significantly different in modern circumstances, as well as how to apply it to substantially new issues in authentically Jewish ways, while being attuned to the realities and sensitivities of contemporary life.

Of course, in the effort to provide the best examples of my thinking over time, this volume could not possibly include all the moral issues discussed in my previous books, including those published by The Jewish Publication Society: *Matters of Life and Death: A Jewish Approach to Modern Medical Ethics, To Do the Right and the Good: A Jewish Approach to Modern Social Ethics,* and *Love Your Neighbor and Yourself: A Jewish Approach to Modern Personal Ethics.* I chose the texts in this volume for several reasons:

1. They illustrate how the philosophical foundations of a Jewish approach to life (described in part 1) and the methodology (described in part 2) can and should affect Jewish thinking about specific moral issues.

2. Part 3 and chapter 7 speak to a wide range of moral issues that most of us confront, from questions in bioethics (abortion, aid in dying, sexual orientation) to the ethics of language (norms to define and avoid harmful communication and uplift modest communication) to moral norms governing forms of violence (playing violent and defamatory video games, formulating a Jewish ethic of war), to issues in business ethics, including managing nonprofit organizations (responding to donations of ill-gotten gain, providing references for schools or jobs). In this context they serve as examples of the theoretical approach I describe in parts 1 and 2.

3. Furthermore, neither the chapters in part 3 nor chapter 7 have been published in book form before, and I believe they are worthy of a wider audience.

To learn more about my discussions of a wide range of other moral issues, readers are encouraged to turn to the bibliography of published works in this volume.

Space limitations precluded inclusion of many responsa (rabbinic rulings) I wrote or cowrote for the Rabbinical Assembly's Committee on Jewish Law and Standards (CJLS), which decides matters of Jewish law for the Conservative/Masorti movement. Readers can see the list of my responsa in the bibliography and access them on the Rabbinical Assembly's website here: rabbinicalassembly.org/rabbinic-resources/committee -jewish-law-and-standards.

This website is organized according to the four sections of the Shulhan Arukh, Joseph Karo's sixteenth-century code of Jewish law. Karo was a Sephardic (Spanish-Mediterranean) rabbi. Moses Isserles, a Polish rabbi, wrote what he called a *Mappah* (tablecloth) to Karo's Set Table (the literal meaning of the name, "Shulhan Arukh") to note where the practices of northern and eastern European (Ashkenazic) Jewry differed from those of the Sephardic community. As a result, the combined work gained widespread authority because it represented the Jewish practices of both Sephardic and Ashkenazic Jewry at the time. We in the Conservative Movement, in turn, want to indicate that our rulings are a continuation of traditional Jewish law, effectively a new *Mappah* on the Set Table, and that is why the website for the Committee on Jewish Law and Standards of the Conservative Movement retains the organizational pattern of the Shulhan Arukh. Those unfamiliar with these works may simply scroll through the table of contents of each of the four sections or use the search engine at the top of the page.

Now on to placing ethics at the center of our thought and action!

Notes about the Cover

The artwork gracing the cover of this book, *Micah 6:8–Love Mercy #3*, is one in a series of paintings of the biblical verse Micah 6:8 by Reverend Eric Bagwell, a United Methodist minister currently serving as a hospice chaplain in Huntsville, Alabama. On his website (ericbagwellart.com), Reverend Bagwell describes the context of this verse: "In the 6th chapter, [the prophet] Micah reproaches unjust leaders, defends the rights of the poor against the rich and powerful, all while looking forward to a world at peace. The heart of his instructions to the leaders is to 'do justice, love mercy, and walk humbly with God'" (his translation from the 2011 update of the New International Version of the Bible).

Reverend Bagwell describes his abstract interpretation of that verse: "A small moon is shepherded through space, embraced and held in relationship by the gravitational field of its planet." Expanding on these ideas in conversation with JPS, he writes: "I paint to capture the Spirit trying to connect with us. In the Micah 6:8 series of paintings, doing justice requires disruption or correction of what is wrong. Mercy must be extended to those less powerful who are wronged. Humility is essential, because all of us belong to the Creator, and therefore to one another, no matter our place in the order of things. One must act to bring justice, while remembering one's role as an actor is not that of the playwright."

All of us, in other words, should be guided through the space and time of our lives by the gravitational pull of what God wants of us—"to do justice, love goodness, and to walk modestly with your God" (the New JPS translation of that verse). Justice is vital both for the moral reason that fairness is required in our dealings with others and for the practical reason that we need social order. At the same time, the Talmud (B. *Bava Metzi'a* 30b) says that one reason the Second Temple was destroyed was that Jews acted only in accord with the demands of the law and not the moral demands beyond the letter of the law. Thus, in addition to justice, we must, as Micah says literally in this verse, "love *hesed*"—that is, be committed to acts of loyalty and kindness to one another. Finally, walking modestly with God is ultimately the basis for both justice and morality, for humility is the quality of a person who realizes that nobody, least of all oneself, is the be-all-and-end-all of life; that we depend on and owe many others for the necessities and enhancements of our lives; and that we all, as traditional Jewish liturgy has us say three times a day in the *Amidah*, must "thank You . . . for our lives that are in Your hands, our souls that are in Your charge, for Your miracles that are with us each day, and for Your wonders and kindnesses at every time, evening, morning, and afternoon."

I have chosen this painting as the cover for several reasons. First, as the title of this book, *Ethics at the Center*, indicates, I am claiming, as Micah did, that ethics is at the center of what God wants of us. I think that we Jews are immensely fortunate that our tradition includes numerous other components that enrich our lives, but, as I demonstrate in "Final Thoughts," many of these other parts of the Jewish tradition—family and community, holidays and rituals, theology, study, and law—have moral import as well.

Second, I love the fact that the colors are bright, for life itself is not neutral: it presents us with many choices that will have great import for us individually and communally and, indeed, for the very planet on which we live. So we dare not sleep through life! We must instead be alert to the significance of the choices we make.

Third, the colors blend into each other, and for me that symbolizes the importance of paying attention, as we shape our moral character and make moral judgments and decisions, to a multitude of factors. These include the most abstract—like how we understand God and human beings and how we should apply the many resources within Jewish tradition to modern moral questions. They also include the most concrete, including how Jewish law can plausibly be interpreted to guide us in new contexts and how Jewish legal decisions, in turn, must be influenced not only by legal sources but also by Jewish moral norms, history, and theology. It must also be influenced by contemporary science, medicine, technology, and social and political concerns ("what's good for the Jews," for humanity in general, and for the planet).

Fourth, I love that this painting is by a United Methodist minister, for I took college courses in both Abrahamic and east Asian religions, earned a PhD in philosophy to probe and learn from secular Western philosophical traditions, and have spent much of my life engaged in interfaith relations. I strongly believe that people of all religions and none can be both smart and moral, and therefore it is vitally important for each of us to learn from religious and philosophical traditions other than one's own. For me, doing so sheds light on my commitment to Judaism, and strengthens it. So thank you, Reverend Bagwell, for bringing readers into this book with a painting that symbolically communicates many of its central messages.

Ethics at the Center

PART 1

Zooming Out

Thinking Theologically About God and Human Beings

1

A Philosopher Explains What Belief in God Means

In my teenage years at Camp Ramah, I loved our serious discussions of moral issues, as camp was shaping me as a Jew. Immediately apparent, though, was that Jewish contributions to those discussions, and to prayer and ritual life at camp, were filled with references to God.

This was the 1950s, before American Jews were trying to figure out the import of the Holocaust on belief in God, so my problem was not that. I just did not know how to understand what was being asserted about God, let alone why I should believe it. The traditional images of God as Father and King who was not a human father or king had given me a sense that the Jewish tradition was asserting the existence of something beyond the level of sensory experience, but I did not know how to imagine that other level of experience or how to understand why and how it mattered for my life. Furthermore, the traditional Father and King images clearly intended to convey a sense of authority, but for what? And why should I obey that authority?

Even with those doubts, Ramah had made Jewish religious life meaningful and even joyous for me, so I began observing the dietary and Sabbath laws and praying each morning, leaving it to the future to discern exactly why I felt drawn to do them. This came at a social cost, for none of my Jewish friends back home in Milwaukee were doing these things. They were my friends despite these commitments, not because of them.

In college, I majored in philosophy to explore how we come to know things and justify our convictions to ourselves and others, and I took courses in Christianity, Islam, and the East Asian religions as well. My questions about God remained, however. In the rabbinical school admission essay that asked about your belief in God, I wrote a lot about the human side of our Covenant with God, hoping that nobody would ask me what I believed about the divine side—and, thankfully, they did not! This was the 1960s, when even rabbinical students were talking about civil rights, the

Second Vatican Council, the Six-Day War, and Vietnam, so it was easy to avoid probing what God meant.

It was not until my midthirties, then, that I finally decided that I needed to confront head-on what I meant by "God" and connect this meaning to my Jewish moral and ritual commitments. My 1992 book, *Knowing God: Jewish Journeys to the Unknowable*, first told the story of my developing Jewish commitment. Simply assuming that "God" meant what the Jewish traditions said it did—a being with a personality and will that interacts with human beings and with Jews in a particular way—I then used my background in analytic philosophy to examine why anyone might believe in such a God intellectually. Specifically, I argue that it is *not* appropriate to try to know God through reason in the mode of *hypothetical discovery*, characteristic of science, in which a person begins with a hypothesis, knows what kind of evidence will confirm or disconfirm it, searches for such evidence, and then comes to a conclusion as to whether the hypothesis is true or false. Instead, to know God we need to use *non-hypothetical discovery*, in which we already know all the relevant evidence, do not seek more, have no piece of evidence that will demonstrate something with certainty, but make a discovery by seeing the evidence in a new pattern. For example, by the time a jury begins deliberations, it knows all the information it is going to have, and the question before it is whether to see in that evidence a pattern of actions that amounts to guilt or innocence.[1]

The core insight of the book, though, is that the Jewish tradition's image of God is as a person, and we do not come to know other people by creating proofs for their existence. Instead, the apt way to know God is the way we come to know other people—by speaking with them and by doing things with them. So there are chapters about God talking to us (revelation), our talking to God (prayer), God doing things with us (God acting in history), and our doing things with God (the life of following the commandments). In each case, I ask what this form of interaction with God tells us about the nature of God and why we should trust that there is a God in the first place. Finally, I discuss how we can best construct and test our images of God to reflect, as adequately as possible, what we learn about God from our experiences with the Divine in mutual speech and action.

More recently, it occurred to me that *Knowing God* should have also explained what it means *not* to believe in God and, conversely, what it means *to believe* in God. That is, I just assumed that everyone had a sense of the transcendent and thus the only questions were how and why to think about it and live in light of it. (There is a reason why philosophers are sometimes called "Luftmenschen," people who live in the air!) Many people, though, think and live their lives exclusively—or almost so—in terms of what we can experience with our five senses because, in their view, only that is true and important. Yet, whether we are conscious of this or not, how we respond to the most concrete moral issues ultimately depends on more abstract but foundational conceptions—how we understand the nature of human beings and, in religious thought, of God. The following essay, "A Philosopher Explains What Belief in God Means," written and published in 2022 in the newly revived journal of the Conservative movement, *Masorti*, and updated for this volume, explores what belief or disbelief in God may truly entail.

One important way in which Judaism differs from its daughter religions, Christianity and Islam, is that the latter are creedal religions while Judaism is not. That is, they have official statements of belief that one must affirm to be a Christian or Muslim. Specifically, unless you believe that Jesus is Christ in some understanding of that term, you cannot be a Christian (and unless you believe a specific version of that belief, you cannot be a Catholic or Protestant). Similarly, unless you believe that there is only one God and Mohammed is his primary prophet, you cannot be a Muslim. You may have been raised in a family or country in which most people believe those things, and you may share ethnic characteristics with such people, but you are not a Christian or Muslim unless you personally affirm each of those religion's beliefs.

Judaism is not like that. There are certainly Jewish beliefs about God, human nature, the relationships between God and human beings, and the relationships of both God and human beings to the world, but there is no one accepted formulation of those beliefs. In fact, Rabbi Louis Jacobs, z"l, cataloged multiple versions, among later Jewish thinkers, of each of the thirteen beliefs that Maimonides listed.[2] Later Joseph Albo wrote that only three beliefs were at the heart of Judaism.[3] Similarly, Hasdai Crescas thought that only one conviction, the love and fear of God, was at the core of Jewish belief.[4]

More to the point, Jewish identity is not a function of belief; it is determined by being born to a Jewish woman or reborn into the Jewish religion and community through the rites of conversion. This raises its own problems, but clearly beliefs are not at the heart of that question. Because of this, in fact, Jews have managed only with difficulty to exclude as Jews those born to a Jewish woman but who believe in Jesus as Christ.

Even with these difficulties, most Jews are happy that Jewish identity is not defined by belief, for that would be restrictive. It would also undermine the deep humility that Judaism embraces about what any one person—or, for that matter, all of us together—can know about anything. We definitely must seek whatever we can know, but the approved way of gaining as much knowledge as we can is not by simply accepting any particular formulation, but by arguing about what to believe with our fellow Jews and with those outside our faith. As my colleague at American Jewish University Michael Berenbaum is fond of saying, "We Jews believe in at most one God!"

And yet, Judaism is filled with references to God, and Jews from the Bible to our own time have done their best to articulate their understandings of God.[5] In what follows, I want to zoom out, as it were, to explain the philosophical status of all the understandings of God that Jews have proposed. In doing so, I hope to make clear what, in philosophic language, the "truth-functional status" of any such beliefs is—the way in which, and the degree to which, any claim to affirm or deny a belief in God can claim to be the truth.

Beginning with Ludwig Wittgenstein and, especially, A. J. Ayer in his book *Language, Truth, and Logic*, analytic philosophers in the mid-twentieth century sought to distinguish what they called the "truth-functional" goals of some forms of language—language whose goal is to describe reality—in contrast to the emotional functions of language, under which, they first asserted, moral and religious language fit.[6] (There are also, of course, forms of sentences that are questions or commands, and later another British philosopher, J. L. Austin, identified yet another function of language, "performative utterances," in which language is used to perform a task—e.g., "I hereby declare you married.")[7]

Ayer's criterion for truth-functional language was that it could be subjected to the "verifiability criterion"—it could be tested empirically. In subsequent decades, though, it became clear that even some scientific terms, like atoms and quarks, could not fit that criterion, so his definition of "truth" was too narrow. In what follows, my explanation of what constitutes truth is, as readers will see, much wider. It includes an accurate description of anything that we experience, through our five senses or otherwise, as long as many human beings experience the same phenomenon (to distinguish truth from fantasy or even insanity). For example, egregious violations of justice are clear to many people, so we can assert that norms of justice are real, however much we might argue as to what they are and how they should apply to a given case. What will constitute truth in this essay, then, is the description of a portion of our experience that most adequately describes it. Because human beings are not omniscient, many such statements will be only partial takes on the full truth.

Levels of Experience

We human beings experience the world on three different levels. The first is the concrete level that we experience through our five senses. This includes such diverse things as tables, songs, and people.

Even on this level, it is harder than we might first think to precisely define what is, for example, a "table." Is it a flat surface with legs? But so is a chair! And what about the tables in restaurant booths that are screwed into the wall and have no legs? If instead of defining a table in terms of its form we want to define it in terms of its function—for example, a table is a surface on which to put things—how is that different from a desk? Or even a floor?

At this point we are talking only about a table, where we are pretty confident that we know what we are talking about. What if instead we are talking about a song? How would you differentiate a song from noise, especially given people's diverse tastes in music and the existence of atonal music?

So even on the concrete level, being able to describe precisely what we mean can be difficult. When asked to define many elements of the concrete world and finding it impossible to be precise, one is sorely tempted to give up and fall back on Justice Potter Stewart's comment about obscenity (in *Jacobellis v. Ohio*, 1964) when he could not define that precisely: "I know it when I see it."

Defining precisely what we mean becomes even harder on the second level of experience we humans have: the first level of abstraction. This level includes some very important aspects of life that have major impacts on its shape and quality but which we do not experience directly with our five senses, although we do see concrete examples of them, such as justice, goodness, truth, beauty, and all our associations (e.g., family, friendship, nationhood). Defining "justice" is the subject of one of the very first books of Western philosophy, Plato's *Republic*, and philosophers, jurists, and legislators have struggled to define it in both theory and practice ever since. There are similarly varying theories of truth (e.g., the correspondence theory vs. the coherence theory) and an even broader set of theories about what constitutes beauty. Modern DNA testing has revealed that some of us are related to people we never would have guessed are members of our family. Adopted children and children created through donor sperm or eggs need to differentiate those who are their family genetically from those who are their family socially, including the ones who put in the time, effort, and resources to raise them. So defining "family" is also more complicated than one might imagine.

It should not be surprising, then, that precise definitions are even more difficult when it comes to the third level of human experience: the second level of abstraction. Sometimes described as "the transcendent," or "ultimate reality," it is often conceived as the container of all our experiences. Philosophers try to describe it in the area of philosophy known as metaphysics, which Aristotle, in his book *Metaphysics*, called "the queen of the sciences." As is typical for philosophy, the goal of those thinking and writing in metaphysics is descriptive and analytic: what is the phenomenon that we experience, how does it function, and how is it different from, and related to, other phenomena that we experience?

How Religions Differ from Philosophies in Their Approach to the Levels of Experience

Like philosophy, the religions of the world think deeply about all three levels of human experience, but they do so with a different goal, which is captured in the very word "religion." The "lig" in that word comes from the Latin word *ligare*, which means to connect, tie, or bond. That Latin root also appears in the English word "ligament," which can be any connection but in medicine is specifically the connective tissue that binds one bone to another. Similarly, when a woman has had as many children as she wants, she sometimes has her tubes tied, called medically a "tubal ligation."

Religions, then, etymologically and in practice, are interested not so much in *describing* and *analyzing* the three levels of our experience (the central goals of philosophy), but in fostering our *connections* to all three levels. Religions concern themselves with creating and shaping our interactions with the environment and the people within it. Some of the ways that religions do this are: (1) rituals to call our attention to, and mark the change of, the seasons and the life cycle and to bring us together as families and communities; (2) art, music, literature, and dance to help us make an art of life; (3) stories to articulate our sense of historical connection to our past, present, and future; and (4) moral norms to guide our interactions with each other and motivate us to help ameliorate the moral problems of everyday life, including poverty, illness, and prejudice.

On the first level of abstraction, religions provide both materials and formats to bring us together to discuss what a given religious group's stance should be on moral issues. Among the issues discussed most in religious settings these days are climate change; poverty; prejudice; inequity in housing, education, health care, and jobs; immigration; sexual and business ethics; the proper and improper use of social media; and medical issues at the beginning and end of life. Grappling with such issues in light of each religion's visions of what is a good human being and a good society, as well as more concrete articulations of what that vision entails in practice, is a major function of religion.

Another issue on this first level of abstraction is the relationships that a particular religious group should have with other religious and secular groups. Putting it starkly, if we believe that x is true and good, do we have enough humility to believe that other groups, who see things differently, can nevertheless consist of smart and moral people and deserve to be respected as such—hopefully to the point of entering into respectful dialogue and, if not mutual action, at least friendly disagreement?

It is on the second level of abstraction that the word "God" appears in religious language. That word is defined in many ways, but two common ones are these: a separate being with a will and personality who created and sustains the universe and who actively interacts with it and cares about it ("theism"); or, alternatively, the force that created the world and sustains it, or that is the world ("deism"). Each of these two major groups has subsets. So, for example, there are rationalists and existentialists among theists, and among deists there are those who think that the world has been created in a particular time and is static (e.g., Platonists) and those who think that the process of creation is dynamic and ongoing (Aristotelians, including, but not limited to, "process theology" adherents). Religions use the word "God" or some other name or metaphor, rather than just saying "the transcendent" or "ultimate reality," because, again, they aim to help us *relate* to that reality, not just describe or analyze it, and it is much easier to relate to the world if it is imagined in an anthropomorphic image or some other concrete term.

Precisely because we are talking about the second level of abstraction, precise descriptions of that ultimate reality, let alone precise definitions of it, are not just difficult, but impossible. That is expressed in theological language as God being "holy"—that is, wholly other than anything we human beings can comprehend. Importantly, recognizing God as holy should not stop us from learning whatever we can about the world on all three levels of experience, or from trying to live in it more robustly through whatever changes we make to it. On the contrary, if God created the world, learning more about it through the various relevant sciences is also learning more about God's plan for us who live in it. As we do that, the recognition of God's holiness should make us aware of the awesome nature of the universe, our dependence on it, and our inability to comprehend it all, thus fostering a sense of humility and gratitude.

God's holiness should also inspire us to live a righteous life. Leviticus 19 makes this clear: one of the opening verses, with "you" and "shall be" in the plural and so addressed to the entire People Israel, asserts: "You shall be holy, as I, the Lord, your God, am holy" (19:2). That verse serves as a header for the rest of the chapter, which defines at least part of what holiness entails, including respect for parents, taking care of the poor, having honest weights and measures, rescuing those in distress, observing one day a week as the Sabbath so that work does not become an idol, refraining from vengeance and bearing grudges and instead reproving someone who needs rebuke, and, ultimately, "Love your neighbor as yourself" (Lev. 19:18). As a society, we should strive to become "a kingdom of priests and a holy nation" (Exod. 19:6). So the point of relating to God is to model ourselves after God and thus become better individuals and communities.

We find it easier to relate to God—that is, the transcendent element of our experience, ultimate reality—through metaphors, so the Bible refers to God in many ways. One is the generic word "god" (*el* or *elohim* in Hebrew) and God's proper name (the tetragrammaton of four Hebrew letters, *yod, heh, vav, heh*, but pronounced as *Adonai*, my Lord, as a matter of respect, much as we call our parents "Mother" and "Father," or the affectionate "Mom" and "Dad," rather than by their proper names). In addition to these generic and proper names for God, the Bible refers to God through multiple metaphors, as, for example, Father and Creator (Deut. 32:6), Sun and Shield (Ps. 84:11), and eight metaphors in two consecutive verses (Ps. 18:2–3): "I adore you, O Lord [the tetragrammaton], my strength, my crag, my fortress, my rescuer, my God, my rock in whom I seek refuge, my shield, my mighty champion, my haven." Then, of course, there is the famous verse "the Lord is my shepherd" (Ps. 23:1). These are all partial windows into the nature of God. The classical Rabbis aptly name this higher level of abstraction "the Place" (ha-makkom), asserting that "The Holy Blessed One is the place of His universe, but His universe is not His place" (Gen. Rabbah 68:9): that God encompasses space, but space does not encompass God.

What Belief in God Means

What does it mean, then, *not* to believe in God? It could mean that one is blind to the third level of abstraction altogether, that one lives one's life on the concrete level alone and perhaps on the first level of abstraction. Alternatively, it could mean that one experiences the second level of abstraction, but it does not matter much in their life. Most often, it means that certain individuals identify God with a particular metaphor or vision of God that has not panned out in their lives, and they became an agnostic or atheist because that particular understanding of God did not materialize. In those cases, one may want to rethink the ways one understands God rather than ignore or deny one's experience of transcendence. As the classical Rabbis assert, a prayer to reverse something that has already happened is a vain prayer (M. *Berakhot* 9:3). They also assert that we may not depend on miracles in the sense of violations of the laws of nature (B. *Kiddushin* 39b), and therefore we should not expect prayers that such miracles occur to be fulfilled. (That is very different from Jews' daily prayer in the *Amidah* to thank God for "Your miracles that are daily with us," where the "miracles" are the very laws of nature that enable us to live and function and the word "miracle" in this context means something that is awesome and should not be taken for granted.)

Conversely, what does it mean to believe in God? It is to be aware of the second level of abstraction and to make it an important part of how one understands oneself and lives one's life. The metaphors by which one refers to that level of experience (how one conceives of God) and the patterns of action motivated by that experience will undoubtedly change over time.

Martin Buber made an important distinction between "belief *that*" something is the case, which he called p-faith (from the Greek word *pistis*, knowledge), and "belief *in*" something or someone, which he called e-faith (from the Hebrew word *emunah*, trust).[8] Adopting his distinction, I would say that in Christianity and Islam, belief in God, while involving matters of trust, is primarily a matter of assertions *that* the world and anything beyond it is of a particular nature. This is articulated in their beliefs, respectively, that Jesus is Christ or that Mohammed is God's ultimate prophet. In contrast, as discussed above, Judaism does not define itself or who is a Jew by an official statement of beliefs that one must assert to be Jewish. In Judaism e-faith is dominant, so that belief in God is primarily a statement that one's experience of the transcendent, the second level of abstraction, can be trusted to be real and true, and that one should therefore live one's life with humility, gratitude, morality, and aspirations for holiness.

2

God as the Source of Moral Norms

Having described the philosophical status of belief in God—that is, what kind of assertion people are making if they say that they either do or do not believe in God (see chapter 1)—the question now becomes: what am I willing to assert about God, what are the justifications of that assertion, and how is that related to morality?

In my teenage years, because I could not see the traditional God with my five senses and yet found references to God throughout the Bible and liturgy, Mordecai Kaplan's understanding of God was helpful for a while. God, Kaplan taught, is the power in nature and in human life that actualizes potential for good—the power, for example, that turns an acorn into an oak tree, or gives you a good idea, or enables you to love. For me, the chief asset of Kaplan's view was that you didn't have to believe very much to believe in that God. After all, sometimes an acorn does become an oak tree, and sometimes you do get a good idea or fall in love. Furthermore, because these were all experiences anyone could have, and all part of the observable world, the word "God" referred to completely observable phenomena too. Kaplan's conception of God as the forces in nature favorable to humanity and to making human life worthwhile, thus worthy of worship, was helping me to connect to the tradition.

Yet there were problems with my embracing this view. I was praying daily throughout the year, and try as I might, I could not pray to a force. Moreover, Kaplan taught, because God is a force, God cannot command: Judaism's moral demands are built into nature, and Judaism's ritual requirements are "folkways." My Jewish friends, though, were not observing Jewish practices like Shabbat or the dietary laws, and they were definitely part of the Jewish people. So to say that I should observe these practices to be part of the Jewish folk did not ring true.

I knew, therefore, that Kaplan's view was insufficient for my prayer and ritual practice, but I did not know how to replace it. I also did not know how God was related to morality.

My first attempt to address those questions was in my book *Knowing God: Jewish Journeys to the Unknowable* (1992), and much of this chapter is taken from there. But this updated version of "God as the Source of Moral Norms," first published in 2013 and revised for this volume, expands upon that. In addition to explaining how we must think about God in images for lack of any direct experience of God, I have emphasized the degree to which, and the ways that, Jewish images of God claim moral authority and demand morality of us, in line with the focus of this book.

Already in Genesis 18:25, in the story of Sodom and Gomorrah, Abraham challenges God: "Shall the Judge of all the earth not do justice?" Later, Moses proclaims:

> The Rock—His deeds are perfect,
> Yea, all his ways are just;
> A faithful God, never false,
> True and upright is He. (Deut. 32:4)

Similarly, in a psalm Jewish liturgy has Jews say three times a day, the Psalmist proclaims, "God is good to all, and His mercies are over all His works" (Ps. 145:9). So from its earliest sources, Judaism portrays God as being inherently just and good, even if some of the stories in the Bible and some events thereafter raise questions about that. Moreover, this moral God demands goodness and justice of us: "Do what is right and good in God's eyes" and "Justice, justice shall you pursue" (Deut. 6:18, 16:20). Thus, that morality is part of God's nature is a fundamental element built into the Jewish understanding of God. Furthermore, human beings, created in God's image (Gen. 1:26; 5:1; 9:6), have God's ability and therefore the responsibility to discern the difference between right and wrong and to act on that knowledge (Gen. 3:22; Deut. 30:19). How, though, do we know this about God sufficiently to motivate us to act morally?

Avoiding Idolatry in Describing God

How should we picture God? To some prominent medieval philosophers, we can be certain of God's existence, but the limitations of human intelligence and the infinite character of God make it impossible for us to know the nature of God altogether. Maimonides, for example, claimed that we can only know that God is *not* characterized by any finite attributes such as the ones that humans possess.

One does not have to adopt Maimonides' position to appreciate the problem that motivates it. If we depict God, either physically or mentally, as having human form, are we not engaging in an act of human hubris and divine diminution at one and the same time? God, after all, must be infinite and omnipotent in order to be God, or so it would seem, and that effectively precludes God's having any shape, human or otherwise.

On the other hand, if we cannot picture God in some form, how are we to conceive of the Eternal at all? Moreover, what is to distinguish a believer from a nonbeliever if both assert that God cannot be conceived? Surely the belief in God must have *some* cognitive content for believers to assert it so strenuously and for nonbelievers to deny it just as vigorously. More-over, God becomes awfully abstract and distant if we can only say what God is not. The anthropomorphic images of God in the Bible and rab-binic literature are so much more alive and emotionally real for us than any intellectual abstraction.

We gain knowledge of God through discovering God in our experience (non-hypothetical discovery), talking to God (prayer), God talking to us (revelation), God doing things with us (God acting in history), and our doing things with God (the life of living by the commandments), and this knowledge presumably suggests that certain understandings of God are more apt reflections of such experiences than others. Because both the Jewish tradition and personal experiences attest to a God who is infinite, though, we can never gain a total understanding of the Divine. Instead, we must formulate images of God based on our own limited experience of the world and of God. Our epistemological position—our capacity to know and the limitations on that ability—gives us no choice in this. We simply have no other way to make sense of the knowledge our experiences give us of God. The same, of course, was true of the authors of the Bible and rabbinic literature: they too had to translate their experiences into images they could understand, feel, and communicate to others.

How, then, do we judge whether we have done this as appropriately and accurately as possible? And how do we avoid mistaking our image of God—whatever it is—for God? That is, how do we protect against idola-try in our very conception of God?[1]

How Images Mean

Because we have no choice but to use images to describe God, we need to examine the ways in which religious images convey meaning. Paul Tillich claimed that everything we say about God is symbolic.[2] But, as Wilbur Urban has maintained, without "some literal knowledge of divine things, symbolic knowledge is an illusion."[3] Without the ability to translate, however inadequately, the meaning of images to more literal language, we have no way of determining whether they refer to anything at all, and we certainly cannot discriminate between more and less adequate images for a given datum of experience.[4]

Tillich and many others who speak of the symbolic nature of our discourse also neglect the difference between the meaning of religious images when contemplated philosophically and when used in religious acts. Theologians have worried about limiting God through anthropomorphic images, hence some have sought to interpret religious images allegorically. The classic Jewish instance of this among the rationalists is, as I mentioned earlier, Maimonides, but Jewish mystics were at least as reticent to depict God in anything but metaphors. They claimed that even while their descriptions of the Godhead, as divided into specific spheres, told us some important things about the nature of God and how we should interact with God, these depictions did not actually describe the Infinite, the *Ein Sof*.

When religious people use images, however, they *want* to depict God in concrete language to make the experience of God vivid and at least partially intelligible in their daily lives. They also want to *relate* to God, and anthropomorphic images make that easier and more powerful. Moreover, they are generally not bothered by seeming conflicts in their images of God. Is God a just or merciful judge, hard like a rock or flexible and vibrant like water, majestically transcendent or affectionately imminent? God may be all these things.

God may manifest one characteristic on one occasion and its opposite on another, just as parents can appear as almost different people to their children depending upon the child's age and how the parent is interacting with them on a given day. Moreover, religious people assume that no ascription of a characteristic to God can possibly be adequate in describing the Eternal. Not only is our knowledge limited; our very language, drawn from human experience, is inevitably incapable of capturing that which is beyond it.

The Truth of Images

Even if we can discern what an image means, how shall we determine its truth or falsity? If all human understandings of God's image are limited, how can we know whether a given image reflects reality more than it distorts it? That is, how can we decide whether a particular image is helpful or harmful in revealing the truth to us?

Some thinkers believe religious images should be treated as metaphors expressing hypothetical claims awaiting further confirmation. Their truth value would then be assessed according to the usual procedures for testing scientific propositions.[5] So, for example, God pictured as a rock might be construed as a claim that God is strong. That claim would then be confirmed if our experiences of God showed that to be true.

This approach, however, misconstrues the meaning of the images in the first place. They are not stated in the hypothetical mood; on the contrary, those who use them want to make declarative statements about their faith. Moreover, one wonders how scientific methods would apply to the analysis of religious images. How, for example, can you definitively determine on scientific grounds whether or not God is a rock, water, or fire?

At the other end of the spectrum, other thinkers assert that religious language, presumably including religious images, never intends to describe. Instead, it is used to evoke emotions or moral behavior.[6] Emotionally, the image of God as a rock, for example, is not meant to describe God in any way, but to make us feel overawed by God's power and comforted by God's ability to protect and sustain us. Morally, the image is intended to confirm our assurance that we must be moral because the divinely ordained moral standards that govern the world are as reliable and unchangeable as bedrock and because God, like a rock, will steadfastly enforce them.

As Dorothy Emmett has said, however, religion "loses its nerve when it ceases to believe that it expresses in some way truth about our relation to a reality beyond ourselves which ultimately concerns us."[7] While images of God sometimes reenforce our desire to act morally, they can do this only if *we believe* that they describe a reality of God. Moreover, people who use them *intend* to describe such a reality. The people of the Bible and the Rabbis who used images certainly wanted to convey the truth about the world—or at least their perception of it—and the same is true for religious people today.

Denying these extreme positions, though, brings us back to our original questions: how do religious images carry a truth value (that is, make a claim that is either true or false), and how are we to judge that claim? As an initial description, we can say that determining whether a given image by which God is described is true would amount to deciding whether ultimate reality is, at least in some way, as the image describes. "God is our Father" would then be true if ultimate reality is, indeed, providing, protective, and so on, and false if it is not. Similarly, "God is our Mother"—one of the feminine images of God that have taken on new meaning with the rise of feminism—is true to the extent that reality as we know it manifests characteristics that we associate with human mothers. In both cases, of course, human fathers and mothers differ among themselves in their nature, and the very project of identifying some characteristics as fatherly and others as motherly is fraught with difficulties—although not, I think, ultimately meaningless.

The problem, of course, is that ultimate reality is many things, including contradictory ones. That is why God is described in conflicting images.

This has an immediate effect on the truth of images. Thomas Hobbes and anyone who shares his view of life might say that the image of God as a rock does not ring true, for life is "nasty, brutish, and short," as Hobbes said, and there seems little surety in it, even from God. For Hobbes and the like, the image of fire to describe God might come closer to the truth, but only in fire's destructive aspects and not in its warm and enlivening character.

For John Dewey and like-minded people, in contrast, God depicted as a rock would convey the confidence one can have in God and in objective moral standards. Yet the rock image would hide the dynamic character of God and of life in general. It would thus articulate only a partial truth—but so do many, if not all, images and propositions—so it would still be valuable for the truth it communicates but must be used with its limitations in mind. God described as a fire, by contrast, would correctly disclose the warm and enlivening character of life, together with its potential for destruction, but would not reveal life's stationary, dependable aspects as the rock image does, so we would need both to transmit a relatively full picture of reality.

Consequently, we must modify our criterion for the truth of an image to read as follows: determining whether a given image by which God is described is true would amount to deciding whether ultimate reality is as the image describes *from the perceiver's perspective at this time.* Albert Einstein showed us that we must take perspectives into account when assessing our sense perceptions of objects and forces, and what I am describing is a parallel process for evaluating our images of God.

Moreover, like descriptive sentences, some images may even mask some truths while revealing others. Nevertheless, I believe one *should* speak of the truth of specific religious images to emphasize that in religion one is still, after all, focusing on reality, and that religion's claim to truth is no weaker than that of any of the social sciences and humanities, where broad perspectives influence what one sees and assesses.

Furthermore, language, like rituals, laws, and customs, is a *social* phenomenon. A large part of the power of images is a function of how they are understood and used in a community, and some images communicate effectively only in the context of a community's vision of the world. God imagined as a rock, for example, is generally appealing to Jews, Christians, and Muslims, and would make less sense, if any at all, to Hindus, Buddhists, Taoists, and Jains, for whom God is too manifold or fluid to be characterized as a rock. Similarly, the East Asian religions and Islam would not relate to the Rabbis' description of God plaiting Eve's hair in preparation for her wedding and serving as Adam's best man.[8] The East Asian religions never speak of Adam and Eve, and for Islam (except, perhaps, for Sufi Islam), God is too unequivocally transcendent to be involved in the wedding of any couple, even the original one. Therefore, our criterion of truth in God images depends on *both* the intersubjective experiences we all have *and* the communal, metaphysical glasses through which we see and understand our experiences.

Finally, there is one other important component in evaluating the truth of images. It is indicated, in part, by the fact that religious people in the West do not generally speak of "ultimate reality," but rather of "God" and even of God's proper name, YHVH, usually pronounced in Hebrew "Adonai" and translated "My Lord" as a way to honor God, much as people refer to their parents not by their proper names but by their relationship, "Mother" or "Father" or the affectionate "Mom" or "Dad." In religious practice "God," especially "Adonai," signifies that the speaker is not just *contemplating* ultimate reality, but *relating* to it personally, usually in the context of a *convictional community.*[9] This is in line with the point made in chapter 1 that the ongoing practice of religion involves not just intellectual, theological thought but actions, prayer, and other forms of relationship with God. As the Torah teaches, one is to love God "with all one's heart, all one's soul, and all one's might."[10]

Thus, we encounter God's transcendence most not in the context of theology but in worship, where we encounter God's continuing judgment against our false centers of loyalty (idolatry), and God's call for us to demonstrate proper awe and gratitude in response to the intricacy and grandeur of our own being and the world God has created. In this setting, God's transcendence is referred to as God's holiness, and, as such, it takes on implications for action. The proper responses to God's holiness are not only recognition of the limits of our intellectual understanding of God and appreciation of the world God created, but also commitment to fix the brokenness of the world, to education, to family, and to community, along with humility and repentance, for all these taken together are the means by which one gains a proper center for one's life and a proper appreciation of one's own being in the larger context of God's world.[11]

The truth of a religious image, then, will depend not only on its ability to reflect an aspect of our experience, but also on its coherence with a communal framework of belief *and action* to which the particular experience is linked and through which it is understood. As I discuss more fully in my book *Knowing God*, experiences and actions are revelatory of God if, and only if, a given community perceives and interprets them to be so and acts accordingly. Issues of truth in religion are thus ineluctably and indissolubly connected with issues of authority.

The Moral and Legal Authority of Images

How does an image become authoritative for a community—say, the Jewish one? In particular, how can the images of God as moral and demanding morality of us sway us to act morally?

In essence, images of God function in much the same way as a moral norm or law does. Although the Bible acts as an original source for Jewish images and laws, it is not the final authority. What ultimately matters is *how the community has interpreted and applied the Bible in their lives*. To determine that, one must pay attention to all of the following: what the community has, over time, selectively chosen to ignore and, in contrast, to emphasize in its educational and liturgical life; how passages are narrowed or extended in the community's interpretations of them in the face of new circumstances or sensitivities; what new images or practices are added by the legal and literary leaders of the people; the extent to which all of this affects the actual thinking and practice of the masses; and, conversely, the extent to which the conceptions and customs of the masses affect the decisions and creativity of the leaders. While this process may seem strange to fundamentalist Protestants, it should be familiar to Jews, for it is nothing but the ongoing work of midrash, the biblical interpretation and expansion that is at the heart of rabbinic Judaism.

The authority of images, then, like the authority of law, rests upon an *interaction* between the constitutive text (in the case of Judaism, the Bible and the Oral Tradition that accompanies it) and the community that lives by it. The text gives all subsequent discussion a focus and a coherence. Interpretations may vary widely, but they can still be Jewish if they are based on the Bible. As the classical Rabbis maintain:

> Lest a person say, "Since some scholars declare a thing impure and others declare it pure, some pronounce a thing forbidden and others pronounce it permitted, some disqualify the ritual fitness of an object while others uphold it, how can I study Torah under such circumstances?" Scripture states, "They are given from one shepherd" (Ecclesiastes 12:11): One God has given them, one leader [Moses] has uttered them at the command of the Lord of all creation, blessed be He, as it says, "And God spoke *all* these words" (Exodus 20:1). . . . Although one scholar offers his view and another offers his, the words of both are all derived from what Moses, the shepherd, received from the One Lord of the Universe.[12]

An image or a law must also gain social confirmation to become authoritative for the community. Even in highly centralized communities like that of Roman Catholics, the authority of a law or image ultimately depends upon the degree of the community's acceptance of it as a factor in their thought and lives. Both old and new images are subject to continuing evaluation of their rationality, truth, theological coherence, adequacy, ethical probity, effectiveness, and practicality. This process may last for a long, indeterminate period of time, or it may be rapid and final. In the first century CE, most of the Jewish community quickly rejected the image of Jesus as the Messiah, and likewise in the 1960s, most Jews generally ignored or roundly rejected the image of God as dead because of its heavy Christian connotations.[13] On the other hand, the rabbinic image of God as one who studies and teaches the Torah and the kabbalistic image of God as the *Shekhinah*, a warm presence with a distinctly feminine feel—neither of which is in the Torah—are examples of how new images can become implanted in community consciousness.[14]

Ultimately, the authority of an image of God rests in its ability to evoke experiences of God. An image may have impeccable biblical or rabbinic authority, but if it fails to link people with God, it will not influence thought and behavior for long. Then it is a broken image, one that no longer functions to remind individuals and the community of the facts and values embedded in their perspective of reality and to motivate them to try to actualize their vision of what that reality should be.

What, then, is inherent in traditional Jewish images of God that make them relevant to human morality? It is the recurrent depiction of God as moral and demanding morality of us, as in the biblical verses cited at the beginning of this chapter and in passages like these:

Thus said the Lord:
Let not the wise man glory in his wisdom;
Let not the strong man glory in his strength;
Let not the rich man glory in his riches.
But only in this should one glory:
In his earnest devotion to Me.
For I the Lord act with kindness,
Justice, and equity in the world;
For in these I delight
—declares the Lord. (Jer. 9:22–23)

Hallelujah.
Praise the Lord, O my soul!
I will praise the Lord all my life,
sing hymns to my God while I exist.
Put not your trust in the great,
in mortal man who cannot save.
His breath departs;
he returns to the dust;
on that day his plans come to nothing.

Happy is he who has the God of Jacob for his help,
whose hope is in the Lord his God,
maker of heaven and earth,
the sea and all that is in them;
who keeps faith forever;
who secures justice for those who are wronged,
gives food to the hungry.
The Lord sets prisoners free;
The Lord restores sight to the blind;
the Lord makes those who are bent stand straight;
the Lord loves the righteous;
The Lord watches over the stranger;
He gives courage to the orphan and widow,
but makes the path of the wicked tortuous.
The Lord shall reign forever,
your God, O Zion, for all generations.
Hallelujah. (Ps. 146)

Good and Bad Images

Ultimately, as we have seen, we have no recourse but to think of God in images. The only real question is how we choose the images we use. In that process we must be on guard against images that are ineffective because they do not touch us; those that distort or falsify our experience; those that undermine the community's cohesiveness; and, perhaps most importantly, those that prompt us to do bad things or to shirk our responsibility to do the good things that need to be done. We must also make sure that our images are not idolatrous, that they do not represent the part for the whole, for that would distort or even undermine their truth and lead us to abandon Jews' mandate to be a people true to God.

Instead, we must seek images that have an immediately clear meaning (in contrast to creeds and symbols, which can be more enigmatic and lend themselves to multiple interpretations); that evoke the emotions and actions that powerful images should; that are true to our experience, even if they cannot be totally so; and that enjoy the community's validation in thought and action, motivating us to do morally good things. Indeed, they should motivate us to fix the world as much as we can, and in as many ways as we can.

3

How Judaism Understands
Individuals and Communities

To discuss the moral values that should govern our interactions with each other, it is first important to know the nature of the human beings who are to be governed by such values. Otherwise, the values would not fit the very people they are intended to influence.

Growing up in Milwaukee, I attended public schools, where I had many Christian friends. Additionally, my mother, who had graduated from Marquette University, a Jesuit school that required coursework in Catholic moral theology for graduation, told me about some Catholic moral doctrines that impressed her. As a result, from an early age I was keenly aware that Christians understand the nature of human beings and communities very differently from the way I was being raised and taught.

In college, I aimed to learn how other presumably smart and moral people thought about human nature and the kind of individuals and communities we should strive to be. I majored in philosophy to learn the variety of ways secular thought conceived of human individuals and communities, and I took courses in Christianity, Islam, and East Asian religions to learn how religious communities responded to these same questions.

In this chapter, adapted from my books *To Do the Right and the Good* (2002) and *Love Your Neighbor and Yourself* (2003), I explain the Jewish conception of the individual and community in contrast to Christian and American secular views. I also discuss the import of these varying conceptions of individuals and communities for how they formulate moral norms to govern our relationships with other people.

American ideology views human beings as individuals with rights. This includes the right to join or leave a community, so all communities are supposed to be voluntary. Thus, while it is hard to become an American citizen, one may renounce one's American citizenship at any time (so long as one has not committed a felony) by submitting a form to do so at any American embassy or consulate outside the United States, and some Americans living outside the United States do that each year, primarily to avoid American taxes.

In contrast, Christianity sees human beings as inheriting original sin—that is, we are sinful in our very origins, in our DNA, as it were—and we have no ability to redeem ourselves from our sinfulness through any of our actions. Only belief in a supernatural intercessor, Jesus, can redeem us from our sins and from the punishment for them, hell. It is the individual who is saved or damned; communities certainly exist, but they have no theological import.

These brief descriptions of how American ideology and Christianity understand human individuals and communities will hopefully make it clear that Judaism's view of human beings and communities, as described below, is not obvious. Moreover, as we will see, these differences in conceptions of who we are and who we should strive to be will have an immense effect on specific moral questions.

Judaism's Perceptions of the Individual

Judaism has unique ideas about human worth, free will, and the responsibility that goes with it.

Human Worth

Jewish tradition places strong emphasis on the value of each and every human being. Human worth derives not from having inherent rights, as in American ideology, but from being created in God's image—a conception the Torah repeats three times in the opening chapters of Genesis (1:27, 5:1–2, 9:6) to ensure we take note of it.

Exactly which feature of the human being reflects this divine image is a matter of debate within the tradition. The Torah itself seems to tie it to humanity's ability to make moral judgments—that is, to distinguish good from bad and right from wrong, to behave accordingly, and to judge one's own actions and those of others on the basis of this moral knowledge.[1]

Another human faculty connected by the Torah and by the later tradition to divinity is the ability to speak.[2] Maimonides claims that the divine image resides in our capacity to think, especially discursively.[3] Locating the divine image within us may also be the Torah's way of acknowledging that we can love, just as God does.[4] Or it may be acknowledging that we are at least partially spiritual and thus share God's spiritual nature.[5]

In chapter two of Genesis, humanity is created initially in the form of one human being, Adam. When the Rabbis later describe how the judges in a capital case are to be warned, they spell out several implications of God's first creating a single human being.[6] Two of these ramifications add further to the worth of each individual.

First, killing one person is also killing all of this individual's potential descendants—indeed, "an entire world." Conversely, someone who saves an individual "saves an entire world." That makes the murder of any one individual all the more serious—and, conversely, saving a human life all the more praiseworthy. It also ascribes value to each of us as the possible progenitor of future generations.

Second, when people use a mold to create coins, the image on each coin is exactly the same. According to the Mishnah, however, God's creativity is different, for God used the divine image first implanted in Adam to create every other human being as a unique individual. In accordance with the laws of supply and demand, a one-of-a-kind thing demands a far higher price than something plentiful on the market. Think, for example, of the comparative value of a Picasso original, each of a few hundred prints of that work, and, finally, a photograph of that work; the more unique the product, the greater its value. The Mishnah thus concludes that because each of us is unique, "every single person is obligated to say: 'The world was created for my sake.'"[7]

Thinking that the world was created for your sake can, of course, produce more than a little arrogance. The following lovely Hasidic saying introduces an appropriate balance: "A person should always carry two pieces of paper in his/her pockets. On one should be written, 'For me the world was created,' and on the other, 'I am but dust and ashes'" [quoting Gen. 18:27].[8]

The Rabbis, like the Torah before them, invoke the doctrines that God created human beings in the divine image and uniquely—not only to *describe* aspects of our nature, but also to *prescribe* behavior. Specifically, the Rabbis maintain that because human beings are created in God's image, we affront God when we insult another person.[9] Conversely, "one who welcomes his friend is as if he welcomes the face of the Divine Presence."[10] Moreover, when we see someone with a disability, we are to utter this blessing: "Praised are you, Lord our God, *meshaneh ha-briyyot*, who makes different creatures," or "who created us different." Precisely when we might recoil from seeing that person's limitations, or thank God for not making us like that individual, the tradition instead bids us to embrace the divine image in such a person—indeed, to bless God for creating some of us so.[11] Finally, the nonutilitarian basis of the Rabbis' assertion of human worth is graphically illustrated in their ruling that no one person can be sacrificed to save even an entire city unless that person is named by the enemy or guilty of a capital crime—and, according to an alternative rabbinic source, maybe not even then.[12]

Free Will and the Responsibility that Goes with It

Another aspect of the Jewish conception of the individual, also important for our understanding of Jewish ethics, is that humans are born morally neutral, with the ability to discern right and wrong, to make moral choices, and to act on them. All the biblical commandments—and the rewards and punishments attached to them—make logical and moral sense only if we humans have the ability to obey or disobey them. Thus, this assumption of free will and the responsibility that goes with it run very deep in Jewish thought.

The Rabbis articulate this in graphic ways, including that we each have two impulses, one for good and one for evil.[13] We inherit the evil impulse, *yetzer ha-ra*, at birth and gain the good impulse, *yetzer ha-tov*, at age thirteen, by which time we have presumably learned the Torah's norms and become responsible for obeying them.[14] The good impulse controls the righteous, the evil impulse governs the wicked, and most of us are subject to both.[15]

That simple typology, though, does not tell the whole story. The Rabbis note that in the Creation story (Gen. 1), God declares each day's creation "good," but the sixth day's work, in which the human was created, "very good," because while animals have no moral sense and hence no evil impulse, human beings have both.[16] But then, it is asked, is the evil impulse good—indeed, very good? Yes, is the answer, for "were it not for that impulse, a man would not build a house, marry a wife, beget children, or conduct business affairs."[17] Similarly, the Rabbis say, "Come let us ascribe merit to our ancestors; for if they had not sinned, we should not have come into the world."[18] Clearly, "sinned" here cannot be taken literally, for it is not a sin, but rather a very good thing for married couples to fulfill the commandment to procreate and to do what is necessary to house and support children. Thus, the Talmud there must mean that the couples engaging in sexual intercourse were under the influence of "the evil impulse."

"The evil impulse," then, simply refers to self-serving instincts, including our sexual urges, while "the good impulse" refers to our altruistic instincts. That makes the differing ages at which we inherit the two impulses completely understandable. Infants are completely self-oriented, to the extent that they think of their parents, in the early months of life, as extensions of themselves designed to serve them. To the Rabbis, it takes thirteen years for children to develop a mature sense of their responsibilities to others. Hence, they become a bar or bat mitzvah (a son or daughter of the commandments) at age thirteen, when they become fully responsible for their actions.

The "evil instinct" is called that because we are much more likely to harm other people out of our self-serving motives than from our altruistic ones, even though our self-serving instinct is also the motivation for some very good things. Conversely, the Rabbis recognize that an overabundance of altruism is also not good. They tell the story of a man who was so altruistic he would give away any money he had; as a result, the court had to send people to accompany him to his daughter's wedding, lest he relinquish her dowry on the way.[19] Similarly, friendships and marriages require reciprocity; they are often in danger of dissolving if only one party gives and the other party consistently receives.

The trick in adulthood, then, is to balance both impulses. Hence the Rabbis could understandably say that the Torah's commandment to "Love the Lord your God with all your heart" (Deut. 6:5), where the word for "heart" is spelled unusually with two of the Hebrew letter *bet* rather than just one, refers to loving God "with both impulses—the good and the evil."[20]

For most of us, too much altruism is not the problem; our challenge is to control our self-serving instincts and channel them to good purpose, as defined by the Torah. The Rabbis harbor no illusions that that is easy; indeed, rabbinic literature abounds in descriptions of how difficult it is to live a moral life.[21] They also prescribe a variety of methods for overcoming temptation when it occurs, including, but not limited to, engaging in Torah study, God's "antidote" to the evil impulse.[22] Moreover, when we do something wrong, the Jewish tradition prescribes a specific path of *teshu-vah*, literally, "return," to the proper moral path and to the good graces of God and those we have wronged.[23] Thus, in the end, the moral life, with its choices, its responsibilities, its missteps, and its modes of repair, is an integral part of what it means to be human.

These foundational convictions embedded in the Jewish concept of the individual have a direct impact on issues in ethics. If we are inherently worthwhile as unique creations of God in the divine image, we must respect ourselves and each other, regardless of anyone's age, gender identity, race, ethnicity, creed, sexual orientation, or level of abilities. We must seek the welfare of others as part of our respect for the divine image within them. We must also establish and enforce just laws and moral norms, and when individuals violate such norms, an inherent respect must underlie our corrective treatment of them.

At the same time, because every person is created in the image of God and has free will to shape many aspects of one's life, each of us has the duty to use our free will to preserve our own well-being. In fact, the Talmud says, "your life comes first," both because you have inherent worth that you have a duty to preserve and also for the pragmatic reason that if you cannot function yourself, you cannot help others.[24] (The latter reason is very much like what we are told on airplanes, "First put the oxygen mask on yourself, and then help others.") This is part of the necessary balance between the *yetzer ha-tov* and the *yetzer ha-ra* described above. Care of others must be preceded by, and balanced by, self-care.

The Relationship between the Individual and the Community

The relationship between the individual and the community is also quite different in Christianity and in American ideology than it is in Judaism.

In Christianity

The individual is very much the focus of Christianity. The individual, after all, is either saved or damned, just as an individual, Jesus, died on the cross. Missionary activities are therefore directed at converting not only the leaders of nations, but each and every person. What, then, happens to the community in Christian thought and action? The earliest Christian community was tight-knit:

The faithful all lived together and owned everything in common; they sold their goods and possessions and apportioned the proceeds among themselves according to what each one needed. They went as a body to the Temple every day but met in their houses for the breaking of bread; they shared their food gladly and generously; they praised God and were looked up to by everyone. Day by day the Lord added to their community those destined to be saved. (Acts 2:44–47)

Similar Christian communities exist to this day, in monasteries and the various orders of Catholic clergy, but the vast majority of Christians experience Christian community through what goes on in their churches. Some churches foster a strong sense of camaraderie among members through a broad range of religious, educational, social, and recreational activities, and a number of Christian communities have a proud record of achievement in social thought, ethics, and activism. Even if one disagrees with their stance on contraception and abortion, one cannot help but be stimulated by the thoughtful pastoral letters issued by the United States Conference of Catholic Bishops on social issues such as preserving the environment, caring for the poor and for loved ones at the end of life, and opposing capital punishment; and some Protestant groups have produced similar documents.[25] Moreover, Catholic and Protestant social service agencies and hospitals provide a wide range of social and medical services to the community. Many Christian denominations also sponsor programs to aid the poor. Especially in developing countries, these community efforts are often intertwined with missionary programs, but whatever the motive, these undertakings must be appreciated for the social good they do. Nonetheless, the Christian conception of community is solely as an administrative entity, designed to organize the faithful so that very important functions—including Christian worship, education, and social action—can go on.

Yet it is the exception to the rule for these efforts to be linked theologically to the purposes of Christianity. One such exception was the "social gospel" movement at the end of the nineteenth century and the beginning of the twentieth, driven primarily by liberal Protestant leaders who believed that Jesus's Second Coming would not happen until Christians put the Lord's Prayer (Matt. 6:10) into practice by working to resolve the social ills of their time, including poverty, crime, poor schools, child labor, slums, environmental degradation, and alcoholism.[26] Another is liberation theology, especially as developed by Catholics in Latin America in the 1960s and 1970s but adopted later by groups in other places as well, which calls on Christians to fight against political oppression and poverty.[27] Protestant and Catholic leaders' negative reaction to these efforts as being unduly political and, in any case, theologically misguided stems from the fundamental Christian doctrine that salvation comes from faith, not deeds. Nevertheless, Jesus's own acts of charity have served as a model and goad for such Christian social thinking and service.

On the whole, however, Christian activities do not impart any theological status onto the community. After all, in Christianity, in the end, the individual, not the community, is the one who is either saved or damned.

Differences between Jewish and American Ideology

The clashes between Judaism and American democratic theory in their views of the relationship between individuals and their community appear in several forms.

1. Duties to the Community vs. Rights Secured by the Community. The first, as noted above, concerns the assumptions that I, as a human being and a citizen, make about myself and others. If rights are the primary reality of my being, as in American legal theory, the burden of proof rests upon anyone who wants to restrict me from exercising those rights. Because other Americans are born with these same rights, there are times when my rights are legitimately restricted. For example, I do not have the right to kill anyone I choose, to physically abuse them, or to steal from them. I even have positive duties to others, such as my duty to pay taxes, to submit to the military draft when that is in place, and to provide an education for my children. In each case, however, the duty arises out of a consideration of the other person's or entity's rights to their person, property, or welfare, and is defined by ongoing American legislation and court decisions, where the debate is often about whether individuals' rights should be limited in a given way to augment someone else's welfare.

In contrast, the Jewish tradition begins by stating multiple duties—613 of them in the Torah, according to traditional count, and many, many others imposed by the later Jewish tradition.[28] Any rights I have are not inherent in me, but derive from the duties of others not to harm me or my property and to act for my welfare, as embedded in Jewish law, beginning with the Ten Commandments. So, for example, my right to the Jewish community's assistance if I am poor derives from its duty to assist me as established in a number of biblical and rabbinic laws, not from any right that I have by birth.[29]

More broadly, the way in which a person views oneself and others in the two systems of thought is different as well. In one, I owe God and other people; in the other, the world, or at least the government, owes me. Put another way, in Judaism I begin with the assumption that things can be expected of me; in the American system, I begin with the assumption that I have "an unalienable right" to "life, liberty, and the pursuit of happiness" that the government was established to secure. President John F. Kennedy said, "Ask not what your country can do for you; ask what you can do for your country," but those inaugural lines are memorable precisely because they are so surprising in an American context.

2. The Source and Purpose of One's Obligations to the Community. The source and purpose of one's obligations also divide Judaism from American democracy. "We, the people" created the United States Constitution, so the government must be "of the people" and "by the people," in President Lincoln's words, not just for them. The reason for that is the underlying assumption already articulated in the Declaration of Independence: "To secure these rights, Governments are instituted among Men, deriving their just powers from the consent of the governed." Rules are instituted to secure rights. American individualism can be set aside only by American pragmatism, in this case the practical need to ensure that all can enjoy what is theirs by right. The preamble to the Constitution adds other practical needs regarding forming a government that will make demands of its citizenry, but all in the name of securing liberty: "to establish Justice, insure domestic Tranquility, provide for the common defense, promote the general Welfare, and secure the Blessings of Liberty to ourselves and our Posterity."[30]

For Judaism, on the other hand, the author of the commandments is God, not the governed. The Bible delineates several reasons to obey God's laws—to avoid divine punishment or receive divine reward; to fulfill our ancestors' promises to abide by the Covenant, promises to which we too are subject; to have a special relationship with God, thereby becoming "a kingdom of priests and a holy nation" (Exod. 19:6); and, ultimately, to express our love for God—yet none of these objectives is to secure rights.[31]

Furthermore, some communal goals of the Jewish tradition are pragmatically designed to secure the ongoing, peaceful, and just operation of the contemporary community and further its welfare. Other aims, though, such as becoming a holy nation, are aspirational and ultimately aimed (with God's help) at bringing about the Messianic Era, which Maimonides describes as the culmination of Judaism's social and theological goals:

> At that time, there will be no starvation; there will be no hunger, no war; nor will there be any jealousy, nor any strife. Blessings will abound, comforts within the reach of all. The single preoccupation of the entire world will be to know the Lord.[32]

These theological goals—to be a holy nation and to know the Lord—are not left as obscure and abstract concepts. On the contrary, how to become such a nation and how to know and imitate God are spelled out in detail in the many laws of the Torah that define what it means to be a holy nation and to imitate God. These include, for example, the rules to avoid gossip, vengeance, or bearing a grudge; to rescue those whose lives are threatened; and, ultimately, to "love your neighbor as yourself."[33] Judaism and American democracy differ completely, then, in the initial assumptions of the legal system (rights vs. obligations), the source of the law (the people vs. God), and its goals (securing rights vs. participating in the Covenantal relationship with God, becoming a godly nation, and bringing about the Messianic Era).

3. The Assumptions about the Individual's Relationship to the Group. All these differences between Jewish and American ideology derive at least in part from disparate basic assumptions about the individual's relationship to the group. In American ideology, all individuals are independent agents who may or may not choose to associate themselves with others for specific purposes. Religious congregations, for example, are voluntary associations to which individuals belong and from which they may dissociate themselves at any time. That is one manifestation of the enduring individuality of existence in the Enlightenment system of thought, for even when people join groups, they do not lose their primary identity and privileges as individuals. Locke's and Jefferson's rights are "unalienable" even by any government. A corollary of this focus on individual rights is that even if other people happen to belong to a group to which

I too belong, what they do is none of my business unless it has a direct effect on me.

This metaphysic stands in stark contrast to the traditional Jewish view, shared with most Western pre-Enlightenment theories, in which the individual is defined by membership in a group, membership is not voluntary but organic, and it cannot be terminated at will, any more than your ankle can decide to dissociate itself from your body.[34] A Jew's membership in the Jewish People is a metaphysical fact over which born Jews and adult Jews-by-conversion have no control. God speaks to the entire People Israel at Sinai. God makes the Covenant with the people as a whole, who will be rewarded or punished as a group according to their adherence to that Covenant. The community's leaders, not each individual, bear the responsibility and have the right to interpret and apply God's word in each generation; and ultimately the People Israel as a whole will be redeemed in Messianic times. Thus, contrary to the concept of the group in Christianity or American secular thought, in Jewish thought the community has not only practical but theological status.

These tenets have important implications in practice. For example, because membership in the People Israel is not voluntary, Jews who convert to another religion lose their *privileges* as Jews—they cannot be married as a Jew, count as part of a prayer quorum (minyan), etc.—but even as apostates (*meshumadim*) they retain all the *responsibilities* of Jews! Moreover, this indissoluble linkage between the individual and the group means that each Jew is responsible for every other, and that virtually everything one does is everyone's business.[35] As the Talmud puts it:

> Whoever is able to protest against the wrongdoings of his family and fails to do so is punished for the family's wrongdoings. Whoever is able to protest against the wrongdoings of his fellow citizens and does not do so is punished for the wrongdoings of the people of his city. Whoever is able to protest against the wrongdoings of the world and does not do so is punished for the wrongdoings of the world.[36]

At the same time, the communal view of traditional Judaism does not swallow up the individual's identity. It actually enhances it by linking it to the larger reality of the group. Law professor and legal philosopher Milton Konvitz has expressed the resulting viewpoint well:

The traditional Jew is no detached, rugged individual. Nor is his reality, his essence, completely absorbed in some monstrous collectivity which alone can claim rights and significance. He *is* an individual but one whose essence is determined by the fact that he is a brother, a *fellow Jew*. His prayers are, therefore, communal and not private, integrative and not isolative, holistic and not separative. . . . This consciousness does not reduce but rather enhances and accentuates the dignity and power of the individual. Although an integral part of an organic whole, from which he cannot be separated, except at the cost of his moral and spiritual life, let each man say, with Hillel, "If I am here, then everyone is here."[37]

Similarities in Jewish and American Ideology

These legal and philosophical differences between American democracy and Judaism can make it difficult for those of us who are American Jews to integrate the two parts of our identity, and similar considerations apply to Jews living in other nations governed by Enlightenment principles of individual rights. We are grateful for the many liberties we enjoy as full citizens of the United States, including our rights to choose where we live, what we do for a living (within legal bounds), and whom to marry if we so desire, as well as our freedoms of speech, assembly, press, and religion. At the same time, we may also feel, as Jews, that sometimes American individualism does not pay adequate attention to our communal duties to each other, such as providing an adequate social safety net of housing, food, clothing, education, and medical care for those who cannot afford them on their own.

These divergences, though, should not be exaggerated. In a number of ways American Jews' Jewish and American identities converge and reenforce each other. The following factors speak to the high degree of comfort Jews feel in America.

On a practical level, Jews have fared much better politically and economically under American democracy than under the corporate, stratified societies of the Middle Ages and most of the dictatorships of past or present. Jews in America have been legally protected from infringement of the free exercise of their religion, and they have enjoyed unprecedented political, cultural, and economic opportunities. The open, pluralistic view of community inherent in American ideology, however markedly different from Judaism's view, has provided a welcoming, nurturing context for Jews, and many other minorities as well.

Theoretical affinities also link the Jewish and American visions of community. Although Judaism places strong emphasis on community solidarity, it also calls for protecting individuals and minorities. Rabbinic Judaism respects the right of non-Jews to live as such, as long as they obey the seven laws given, according to tradition, to the descendants of Noah.[38] In many passages the Bible boldly proclaims equality in law between Jews and non-Jewish residents; for instance, "There shall be one law for you and for the resident stranger; it shall be a law for all time throughout the ages. You and the stranger shall be alike before the Lord; the same ritual and the same rule shall apply to you and to the stranger who resides among you."[39] Although Jews' attitudes toward non-Jews have varied through the generations according to the specific conditions of their interactions, and although there have been exceptions to the general principle of equal treatment, the Rabbis applied this principle not only to the ritual context in which it appears most often in the Bible, but to broad areas of civil legislation as well.[40] Furthermore, Judaism does not missionize, except by example.[41] It even reserves a place for righteous gentiles in the World to Come.[42] In all these ways, Jewish law and theology protect the rights of individuals and minorities and bear similarities to the protections offered by American law and ideology.

Jewish law also protects the rights of individual Jews and minorities within the Jewish community. For example, the Tosefta, edited in the second century, requires Jews to support the poor and sick of the non-Jewish community, even though the Romans certainly did not do the same for Jews at the time, and that became Jewish law as reflected in the primary codes of Jewish law and in actual practice.[43] Maimonides, writing in the twelfth century, said he did not know a single Jewish community that lacked a charity fund to support the poor.[44] Lancelot Addison, describing the Jews of seventeenth-century Barbery, felt the need to dispel the impression that "Jews have no beggars" by attributing that error to "the regular and commendable" methods by which Jews supported the poor and "much concealed their poverty."[45] In our day, as a board member and past president of Jewish Family Service of Los Angeles, I am proud to say that this Jewish ethic of caring for the poor continues through the multiple Sova food pantries that JFS sponsors throughout the city as just one of its many types of social services open to all people in Los Angeles. Jewish law also treats Jews who are disabled like everyone else (with the exception of a few functions that specific disabilities make impossible to perform), and Jews are enjoined, for example, from insulting people who are deaf or placing a stumbling block in front of people who are blind.[46] American government programs such as food stamps for the poor and laws such as the Americans with Disabilities Act (1990) articulate the same concerns and communal duties, even if presidential administrations have carried them out to varying degrees.

Additionally, Jewish law, like American law, safeguards individuals' rights to express their opinions, however unpopular these may be. The Talmud is a prime example of Judaism's high degree of tolerance for questioning and disagreement. Ultimately a rule of law had to be established, but individuals were free to question it and argue against it, and all "were the words of the living God."[47]

These similarities between Judaism and American ideologies are rooted in a broader, shared doctrine, specifically, that we are human beings first and citizens second. The Declaration of Independence refers to "all men," and the Bill of Rights applies to all "people," not just to citizens. Similarly, in the Bible, God creates the progenitors of all human beings in the divine image long before establishing a special relationship with the Jewish people through the Covenant. Both traditions are thereby asserting the inherent dignity of all human beings independent of membership in a nation. Their shared moral affirmation is that people are not merely means for some social or theological goal; they are ends and are to be treated as such.[48] It is no accident, then, that both traditions seek to protect individuals and minorities, and both cherish and vigorously exercise individual freedoms.

Another important manifestation of individual over group sanctity in both ideologies is the overpowering emphasis the two put on the rule of law. Kings, presidents, military leaders, legislators, and judges are all subject to the law.[49] Thus, in a poignant passage, the Torah requires the king to own a copy of the Torah, to keep it nearby, and to "read it all his life. . . . Thus he will not act haughtily toward his fellows or deviate from the Instruction to the right or to the left" (Deut. 17:18–20). Similarly, to ensure that judges are not lured into thinking that they are the source of the law, the Mishnah counsels them not to judge cases on their own. As

Rabbi Ishmael, son of Rabbi Yose, said, "Do not judge by yourself, for there is only One who [appropriately] judges by Himself."[50]

There are even some similarities in the sources of the law. Although, as we have seen, one major distinction between American democracy and Judaism is the source of the law—namely, the people and God, respectively—one should not exaggerate this difference. After all, according to the Declaration of Independence governments are instituted among men to secure rights given them by their Creator. Government in this theory is thus not only a pragmatic mechanism to care for practical needs in society; it is also an instrument to accomplish divine purpose. Conversely, while classical Judaism understands God to be the author of the law, the judges of each generation have both the right and the obligation to interpret and apply it—even to the extent of revising it outright. Over the centuries those judges have been guided significantly, and sometimes openly, by the needs and customs of the people.[51] All in all, then, American law cannot be reduced to populism, and Jewish law cannot be reduced to divine governance. Both traditions involve both human and divine elements, albeit in significantly different degrees and forms.

Ultimately, however, what many American Jews *want* to believe—that their Jewish and American identities fit neatly together, with no contradictions or even tensions—is untrue. American ideology depicts community in a "thin" sense: membership is completely voluntary and may be revoked by a given individual at any time. In contrast, Judaism's sense of community is "thick": members are organically part of the communal corpus and cannot fully sever themselves from it. In America, community holds an essentially pragmatic purpose, whereas in Judaism, it may be partially pragmatic, but it is essentially moral and theological.

As we will see, these distinctions affect how both the Jewish and American traditions see their roles in defining and motivating morality, including the roles of law, theology, prayer, individual choice, and relevant communal norms. This is the subject of part 2, to which we turn next. These distinctions will also affect many of the specific moral issues addressed in part 3.

Getting Down to Earth

Converting Thought into Practice

4

Traditional Jewish Means of Inculcating Morality

How does a group determine the correct way to respond to moral questions and then inculcate that moral stance into the members of that group? Lawrence Kohlberg was among the first to research moral development across cultures, and others have furthered our understanding of how we learn how to be moral and gain the motivation to live morally.[1] For our purposes, suffice it to say that children learn what behavior is acceptable, prohibited, or praiseworthy first from their parents, subsequently from their teachers and peers, and then from what they observe while growing up and learning about the culture to which they belong.

The way this happens varies widely from one group to another. To take just a few examples, Roman Catholics, at least in theory and often in fact, depend on their priests, bishops, and ultimately the Pope to determine what is moral. Protestants instead trust their individual consciences as guided by their Bible study and the traditions of their particular denominations. Muslims largely use the Koran and the legal precedents (shari'a) of their particular form of Islam (Sunni, Shiite, Sufi, etc.). Then each group uses a combination of theological belief and communal pressure to motivate its adherents to behave accordingly. In many places during the Middle Ages and thereafter, and in some nations yet today, governmental authorities have buttressed this process by enforcing a particular religion's view of morality.

The remainder of this chapter on inculcating morality is adapted from my 2003 book *Love Your Neighbor and Yourself: A Jewish Approach to Modern Personal Ethics.*

Although Judaism primarily uses Jewish law to discern the moral path when it is not clear, many other parts of the Jewish tradition—the moral precepts articulated in the Torah and later Jewish literature, stories, theology, Jewish leaders, Jewish historical experience, prayer, and text study—come into play in educating and motivating Jews to act morally.

Moral Precepts

The Torah urges us to perform many actions grounded in moral values, such as pursuing formal and substantive justice, saving lives, caring for individuals who need assistance, demonstrating respect for parents and elders, acting honestly in business and in personal relations, telling the truth while being tactful, and educating both children and adults. Other ancient reservoirs of Jewish moral precepts include the biblical book of Proverbs and *Pirke Avot* (Ethics of the fathers) (a tractate of the Mishnah, ca. 200 CE), which describe different ideal types of living morally, with concrete instructions about how to attain those ideals. Medieval and modern Jewish writers have produced other such works. For example, Moses Hayyim Luzzato's *Mesillat Yesharim* (Paths of the righteous) (1738) is widely studied in rabbinical academies to augment study of Jewish law with a deep consideration of how to acquire moral traits, following Pinchas ben Yair's teaching: "Torah leads to watchfulness; watchfulness leads to alacrity; alacrity leads to cleanliness; cleanliness leads to abstention; abstention leads to purity; purity leads to piety; piety leads to humility; humility leads to fear of sin; fear of sin leads to holiness; holiness leads to prophecy; prophecy leads to the resurrection of the dead."[2] Luzzato explains what can aid, and what can impede, each step of Pinchas ben Yair's description of moral development. Over the centuries, other Jewish thinkers have had very different concepts of the ideal person and how to accomplish that ideal—hence the variety of works on morality, ethics, spirituality, and social justice from the Bible to our own time.

Morals in Stories

Stories are concrete, so they tend to be easier to remember than rules or maxims. As such, when stories portray real-life situations—including what can happen when moral norms are broken—they can effectively educate and motivate people to act morally.

For example, the core Jewish story encompassing the Exodus from Egypt, the revelation at Mount Sinai, and the trek to the Promised Land proclaims that we as the Jewish people can and must work together with God to redeem ourselves and others from slavery of all sorts. It also teaches us to live our lives in accordance with the moral norms revealed at Sinai, and to continue to work for the real Promised Land, the State of Israel, and the Promised Land of the Messianic Age.

Theology: Aspiring to Be Like God

In Judaism, God is central to morality by defining the good and the right, enforcing these norms, and serving as a model for us. Although the Bible itself raises questions about God's morality—at times, God appears to act arbitrarily and even cruelly—nonetheless, Jewish texts trust that God is good.[3] We, then, should aspire to be like God: "As God clothes the naked, . . so you should clothe the naked; as God visited the sick, . . so you should visit the sick; as God comforted those who mourned . . . so you should comfort those who mourn; as God buries the dead, . . so you should bury the dead."[4]

Even more so, God serves to shape moral character by entering into a loving relationship with each of us. Just as we hopefully treat our beloved life partner according to whatever the norms of morality require and more, "beyond the letter of the law" (*lifnim m'shurat ha-din*), we are asked to do as much for God.[5] In moral terms, then, we become the kind of people who seek to do both the right and the good, not out of hope for reward, but simply because that is the kind of people we strive to be and the kind of relationships we try to have, reflecting God as our model and our covenantal partner.

Moral Leaders

The Torah warns extensively against idolatry, making any person or thing instead of God the center of one's concerns and values. Even Moses was buried in an unknown place to prevent his contemporaries from worshiping him (Deut. 34:6). Some groups, such as the followers of Shabbtai Tz'vi and some followers of various Hasidic rabbis, have come dangerously close to such worship of an individual. That danger notwithstanding, many Jews find moral role models in some of their rabbis, teachers, or lay leaders who exemplify for them what it means to be a person living in accord with Jewish moral values.

Jewish Historical Experience

Through living in multiple countries, Jews have learned how to live with people of other faiths. Unfortunately, that often has meant how to survive under oppressive conditions, but it has also meant how to learn from other cultures. So, for example, many of the business norms found in the Talmud were borrowed from the Romans.[6] On the other hand, the Talmud specifically rejects as immoral the Roman gladiator games and other parts of Roman culture.[7] In more modern times, although Jews are heavily involved in medical research, we—and Western society generally—have learned, from the cruel Nazi medical experiments on Jews and others, that research on human beings must be governed by many protections for the participants.[8]

Prayer

The fixed liturgy draws our attention to Jewish values, including knowledge, forgiveness, health, justice, hope, and peace. It can reorient our focus from everyday distractions onto the fundamental, important things in life. Prayer can help us muster the courage to recognize what we have done wrong and go through the process of *teshuvah*, returning to the proper path, repairing whatever harm we have done and taking steps to act justly in the future.

Study

One goal of text study is to inform us about what constitutes right and wrong. Beyond this, when done correctly—when study enables us to understand Judaism's deeper philosophy as embedded in its moral rules—it can guide us ethically in new situations not covered by existing laws.

In real-life encounters, values often clash, making good judgment in resolving conflicts a necessary asset. Studying dialectic texts that demonstrate moral argumentation helps sharpen our ability to navigate these moral challenges.

Studying within a community of learners to which we want to belong can also give us a communal reason to sacrifice our immediate, perhaps immoral wants for Judaism's long-term ends. Learning with others reminds us that we are part of a community to whom we have moral obligations. Then there are the moral values attached to group study, among them responsibility, care, self-control, punctuality, exactitude, circumspection, sociability, friendliness, and team spirit.

Law

At the basic level, a minimal moral standard enacted into law enables everyone to know what is expected of each person and what each person can expect of others. This provides a level of security for everyone (contrast Kafka's depiction of the absolute terror that ensues when you do not know this in *The Trial*), and it also enables society to secure cooperation for that standard. Law can also impel us toward higher levels of morality by requiring us to uphold higher standards of behavior than we otherwise would think is required of us. And when the law requires us to do good, the hope is that ultimately, once educated, we will do the good for its own sake.[9]

On the communal level, a goal of law is social peace. When disputes arise, law provides a forum for weighing conflicting moral values, adjudicating disputes, and setting moral priorities. A system such as Jewish law also delivers ways to make amends, repair moral damage, and reconcile with God and community.

5

My Own Theory of Jewish Law

Having been part of the intensive Talmud study program at the Jewish Theological Seminary and having completed a PhD in philosophy at Columbia
University, with a dissertation in moral theory and a course in philosophy
of law, from very early in my career I have been interested in how to identify what moral norms and Jewish law require of me, the sources of such
norms, how moral and legal norms interact, how they change over time,
and their claims to authority for us in the first place. The legal part of my
interests was greatly stimulated by team-teaching a course on Jewish law
with Professor Arthur Rosett at the UCLA School of Law from 1974 to 2002.
His service as part of the Judge Advocate General Corps in Japan and his
major field of expertise, international business transactions, led him to a
keen interest in the differences between American law and Japanese, Chi-
nese, and German law, and he pushed me to grapple with the kinds of
philosophical questions about Jewish law that arise in that kind of comparative analysis. Furthermore, engaging in deeply probing discussions on
issues of Jewish law as a member of the Conservative Movement's Committee on Jewish Law and Standards (CJLS), from December 1984 to the
present, has made it crystal clear to me that legal decisions on specific
issues depend not only on what relevant previous legal sources say, but
on the particular legal theory that the rabbi writing the ruling embraced
and whether or not that person was cognizant of the role that specific legal
theory played in the decision.

In 2007 I wrote a book on my own theory of Jewish law, *For the Love
of God and People: A Philosophy of Jewish Law*, from which this chapter is
adapted. It is important for readers of this book to know at least the broad
parameters of my theory of Jewish law to understand my legal rulings on
specific issues, some of which compose part 3 of this book.

In my 1992 book, *Knowing God: Jewish Journeys to the Unknowable*, I
described Jewish law as a way to *know* God.[1] Here, I would like to go
further: Jewish law is perhaps even more clearly a way to learn how to

relate to both God and human beings in action. Specifically, I view Jewish law as *an expression of the love that we Jews have for both God and other human beings.* Like all forms of human love, our love of God and other human beings and God's love of us ideally involve all of our being—body, mind, emotions, will, interactions with others, and the contexts in which we live. Putting this another way, our love is best expressed in both body and soul, for then it can be both physically active and intellectually and emotionally compelling.

To be a meaningful expression of both forms of love—the mutual love among people and that between God and us—Jewish law must, therefore, have both a body and a soul. I consequently see Jewish law very much like a human being, the entity that we most associate with the capacity to love. Some features of Jewish law resemble a human body, and some are like a human soul—that is, the mind, emotions, will, and ability to interact with others. Just as the body and soul of a person constantly interact and affect each other, the body of the law (literally, in Latin, the corpus juris) and its beliefs, values, emotions, and goals continually interact and affect one another. (Sometimes that is expressed as the intermingling of law, halakhah, and lore or theology, *aggadah,* but that way of characterizing this interaction seems to me to be too limited and imprecise.) Furthermore, just as people are very much affected by their physical, political, economic, social, and moral environments, both the body and soul of Jewish law are influenced by their ongoing interactions with God, other peoples and cultures, and various aspects of the environment in which they function.[2]

Every human being has a body, and although each of our bodies is unique in some ways (for example, its DNA), we share a great deal—so much so that a physician can treat people from widely varying genetic backgrounds. Analogously, in its bodily functions Jewish law resembles other legal systems, but even here, significant differences exist.

The same is true for the soul of Jewish law. The religious convictions at its heart make it markedly different from secular and other religious legal systems. At the same time, just as all people wrestle with some of the same emotional and psychological issues, and thus the disciplines of social work, psychology, and psychiatry can exist, Jewish law has some similarities to other legal systems in its assumptions and approaches to moral issues. In general, these similarities are a function of the bodily features of all legal systems, the aspects of law that enable it to function in the world, while the uniqueness of Jewish law is primarily a function of its soul.

Stories are a good way to get to the heart of a civilization and its laws. The first Jewish story is that of Abraham. Unlike the beliefs of all the other peoples in the ancient world, for whom the gods ruled on the basis of their power alone, where "might makes right," Abraham discovers that the ways of God are "to do what is just and right" (Gen. 18:19). So Maimonides characterizes Abraham as "the pillar of the world," for everything afterward in the Jewish tradition, including the law God gives to and through Moses, is based on that fundamental premise.[3] God is moral, even if we do not always understand how, so we must be moral too (*imitatio dei*). This fundamental conviction is graphically illustrated in Abraham's plea to God to save any righteous people in Sodom and Gomorrah, "Shall the Judge of all the earth not do justice?" (Gen 18: 25).

The other Jewish story that defines the consciousness of Jews as Jews is the Exodus from Egypt followed by the Revelation at Mount Sinai (Horeb) and the trek to the Promised Land. In that story, the model for understanding Jewish law is the Covenant between God and the People Israel. The Torah records that God had previously entered into covenants with Noah and Abraham and renewed the latter with Isaac and Jacob.[4] Only at Mount Sinai, however, is the Covenant enacted with the whole People Israel, and only there are the basic assumptions about the relationship between God and Israel and its underlying values articulated. Notably, "covenant" is not a word or concept imposed on Jewish law from external sources. Rather, it comes from the very roots of the Jewish tradition and is one of the primary ways in which the tradition expressed and understood itself. Israel's Covenantal relationship with God thus expresses the soul of Jewish law.

The way I understand the soul of Jewish law, though, goes beyond the stories and other resources within the tradition; it is also based on my own story. Indeed, because one's thoughts are inevitably connected to one's personal experiences, in understanding any theory about anything, it may help to know a bit about the experiences of the person proposing it. So, briefly, I view Jewish law as an expression of love for, and commitment to, both God and other people in part because I experienced Jewish law in immensely positive ways, growing up in a warm, supportive home and spending many summers at Camp Ramah. In both environments Jewish law was the vehicle that enabled us to celebrate Shabbat with great joy and to mourn the tragedies of the Jewish people on Tisha b'Av with real sorrow. Jewish law also demanded that we think hard about the serious issues of life and behave with others in ways that respected their inherent dignity as human beings created in the image of God, even if we did not like them or what they did, and act continuously to make human lives better. The last piece of this explains why I have done so much scholarly work in Jewish ethics and have devoted much of my time to government commissions evaluating public policy and to organizations like Jewish Family Service of Los Angeles, ultimately serving as its president, because one needs to "walk the walk" about morality.

I know that most Jews have grown up in environments that did not take Jewish law seriously, whereas others have experienced Jewish law as authoritative but also burdensome, anal, pointless, obsequious, or demeaning. Readers should know at the outset, then, that my theory grows out of a very different experience with Jewish law that has immensely enriched my life.

Readers should also understand that even though I take Jewish law seriously, and even see it as being authoritative for my life, I also think that we should apply our own *sense of judgment* to change it in the few places where the received law causes harm to people or can be altered to enhance their lives, just as people who love each other do when their relationship requires change. Moreover, unlike those who advocate legal positivism, in which the only way a law may change is to find legal sources from the past that can be interpreted or applied in a new way, my organic view of the law would allow change prompted by the entire Jewish context in which Jewish law operates, including Jewish moral values and theology and the economic, social, and political factors affecting the lives of Jews who are supposed to live by the law. All this must be taken into account in making wise judgments about how Jewish law, as it has come down to us, should be interpreted and applied today—a process I shall describe in the next chapter.

6

Applying Jewish Law to New Circumstances

For nearly forty years as a member of the Conservative movement's Committee on Jewish Law and Standards, I have witnessed the problems involved in applying an ancient tradition like Judaism to contemporary circumstances in a wise way. This problem affects some ritual areas of life, such as Sabbath observance, when so much of contemporary life involves electricity and Jews in a given community commonly live too far away to walk to the synagogue or to one another's homes for meals; and kashrut, where modern modes of food production and Jews' interactions with people of other faiths raise important questions about how to observe the dietary laws. Still, the vast majority of issues of disconnect between ancient times and our own emerge in the moral areas of life.

Originally I addressed this issue in the appendix to my 1998 book, *Matters of Life and Death: A Jewish Approach to Modern Medical Ethics*, and I returned to it in the first chapters and appendixes of my books *To Do the Right and the Good: A Jewish Approach to Modern Social Ethics* (2002) and *Love Your Neighbor and Yourself: A Jewish Approach to Modern Personal Ethics* (2003). In the text that follows, adapted and expanded from a later attempt to address this problem—a 2010 essay published in *Teferet Leyisrael: Jubilee Volume in Honor of Israel Francus*—I try to tackle the challenge by first describing ways that other thinkers have responded to it, with the strengths and weaknesses of those approaches, and then suggesting my own response, with its strengths and weaknesses.

Many moral and legal issues we face today are entirely new because of advances in technology, medicine, communications, and other fields. For example, neither Jewish law nor any other system until recent decades even contemplated, let alone provided guidance about, removing a ventilator from a dying patient or doing business on the internet. Other moral issues, such as taking care of elderly parents, have been around since the appearance of people on the planet, but how to do so honorably and effectively in the contemporary context of nuclear families with nobody home during the day requires new thought and planning. Yet other moral issues, like the place of women in society, are new because of changing moral attitudes toward those subjects and changing educational and economic conditions. Still others, like same-sex marriages, are different because of new scientific information about the development of sexual orientation and gender identity and new sociological studies about how children best flourish in different kinds of families. Classical sources in Jewish law either do not speak of these matters or do so in significantly different contexts. How, then, are we supposed to gain moral guidance from the Jewish tradition to help us decide what to do now?

No Sources Means No Guidance

One approach is to say that if nothing in the tradition explicitly deals with our situation, we should simply state that fact and look elsewhere for moral guidance. This approach has several advantages. First, it is honest. It does not pretend that the tradition says what it does not say. Second, it takes seriously the newness of modern circumstances and the need to think thoroughly about how to live nobly in very new contexts. We cannot simply rely on the past to tell us what to do. Third, it is very liberating. It allows Jews to decide the matter for themselves, with or without guidance as they want it, and without any limitations imposed by Jewish law.

Yet this approach has some serious disadvantages. Because modernity has changed our lives in so many ways, if we apply Judaism to our moral questions only when the tradition's sources are directly on point, Judaism will not be able to guide us on much of what we need its wisdom for most. This will be bad for both Jews and Judaism. Jews will be bereft of any Jewish guidance for important decisions in their lives, and Judaism will lose a major source of its attraction and significance for Jews. Given the significant disadvantages of this approach, we need to see if alternatives can serve us better.

"Everything Is in It"

The opposite end of the spectrum is typified by Ben Bag Bag's comment about the Torah, "Turn it over, and turn it over again, for everything is in it."[1] His comment is built on the theological beliefs that God is the Author of the Torah and that God built into it the answers to all questions that anybody would need to ask for all time to come. Similarly, another rabbinic statement asserts: "Even that which a distinguished student was destined to teach in the presence of his teacher was already said to Moses on Sinai."[2]

To be clear, even for Ben Bag Bag, it is not the Written Torah itself that contains the answers to everything; rather, the Torah *as interpreted anew in succeeding generations* can produce the answers to all questions. Adopters of this view believe that when people interpret the Torah, they are not inventing new meanings for it, but are *discovering* meanings that God embedded in the text and that we Jews can identify only if we are sufficiently skilled, persistent, and sensitive to see them. Thus, classical Jewish texts teach that God not only gave us the Written Torah but the Oral Torah as well.

The advantages of this methodology are apparent. If you believe that God gave the Written and Oral Torahs and you derive all your rulings on modern issues from them or later rabbinic interpretations of them, you have a much larger corpus of literature than the Written Torah alone on which to draw for guidance. You can also claim that your ruling shares in the divine authority of those texts. This methodology also provides a very strong link to the tradition, thereby preserving continuity along with authority.

On the other hand, there are significant problems with this methodology. First, the Rabbis may have been exaggerating when they said that the answers to all questions for all time are contained in the Written and Oral Torahs. Their statements may have been expressions of the love they had for the tradition and the deep meaning they found in it without really intending that everything was to be answered by interpreting it. The tradition, for example, never tells us how to bake a cake or how to fix a broken cart, and I frankly doubt that our ancestors learned those skills by consulting the Torah.

Even if the Rabbis meant such statements literally, we must recognize that they could state this because the classical Jewish texts they were creating stretched the Torah to address the issues of their world. Indeed, as Michael Fishbane has demonstrated, the later strains of the Torah are already interpreting and applying earlier strains, presumably to respond to the needs and customs of their time.[3] The ancient and medieval worlds changed far more slowly than ours does, so the likelihood that our ancestors would find answers to their problems in the texts they had inherited is much greater than it is for us.

The most significant problem with this approach, though, is that to gain guidance from ancient texts for modern dilemmas, one often must read such texts out of their own contexts. Many users of this method are doing eisegesis, reading into the tradition whatever they want to assert, rather than exegesis, deriving guidance from the tradition. This distorts the original meaning, is dishonest, and undermines the interpreters' claim to continuity and authority. Moreover, because this method applies texts to very different situations, it may lead to seriously flawed results that fit the modern issue very badly, perhaps even dangerously.

Personal Autonomy

One approach typical of, but not exclusive to, Reform thinkers is to highlight the role of the individual in deciding what to do. Reform rabbis and professors Jakob Petuchowski, Eugene Borowitz, and David Ellenson, for example, have carefully articulated such an approach.[4] Petuchowski and Borowitz especially emphasize that to be a recognizably Jewish decision, individual Jews must study the Jewish tradition and weigh the import of their decisions both for the Jewish community and themselves. Still, in the end, the individual decides what to do.

Ellenson goes even further in the direction of autonomy, saying that asking a rabbi to make a decision based on Jewish law improperly transfers responsibility for that decision to the rabbi and removes it from the person who must decide. Instead of such "halakhic formalism," he advocates a methodology in which individual Jews may consult their rabbi and, for that matter, anyone else, but ultimately, to resolve moral problems, they must assume the responsibility themselves.

This approach has the advantage of putting the responsibility for making moral decisions squarely on the shoulders of the individuals who face them, thus encouraging people to take responsibility for their actions and hopefully precluding them from thinking they can blame others for what they do (as many Nazis did when they claimed they were simply following orders). Further, it enables individuals to decide issues as they see fit. Aside from the freedom this brings, people are more likely to act on what they themselves determine to be moral.

Like its advantages, the problems with this approach are rooted in its individualism. If individuals make their own decisions, in what sense can there ever be a communal norm? Indeed, because individuals may consult their rabbi and the Jewish tradition as much or as little as they please, what makes the decisions individual Jews make identifiably Jewish? While Petuchowski and Borowitz try to answer this by having the decision-making process include knowledge of the Jewish tradition and consideration of the decision's import to the Jewish community, in truth most Jews do not know much about Judaism, especially in problematic moral areas, and they also lack the skills to apply the tradition to modern circumstances. Moreover, as Arnold Eisen and Steven M. Cohen demonstrate in their book, *The Jew Within*, most modern Jews value personal autonomy much more than their roots in the Jewish tradition, so they are unlikely to take the Jewish factors Petuchowski and Borowitz build into their approaches seriously enough to make their decisions recognizably Jewish.[5] This factor is even more problematic in Ellenson's approach, which does not explicitly require such knowledge.

Using the book of Ruth as her paradigm, Laurie Zoloth-Dorfman suggests another version of this approach: the proper way to make moral decisions is for one person to engage another and respond personally to that individual's needs.[6] Here again the accent is on individual decision-making, but specifically in the context of a decision involving another person's welfare. This situational ethics approach is less focused on individuals' own needs and views than the Reform rabbis' models, and it has the strength of encouraging empathy. Despite Zoloth-Dorfman's use of the book of Ruth, though, it shares the same problems as the other individualistic theories: lacking much justification to call this methodology Jewish.

Applying Jewish Law Wisely

I would now like to suggest a methodology for applying Jewish law and the Jewish tradition generally to new moral issues. By and large, I rely on precedent. Jewish law, however, does not exist in a vacuum. It is like the bone structure of a human being, which is influenced by every other part of the human being, including its physical, mental, and emotional components as well as its interactions with other people and its environment. Once we have grown to adulthood, our bones do not change nearly as fast as our skin cells (we lose and add thousands of skin cells daily), or even as fast as our bodies replace our blood cells (blood banks will take a donation of whole blood from a person only once every fifty-six days). Anyone who has broken a bone will remember that it took months to heal.

In a similar way, Jewish law remains quite constant relative to other features of Jewish life. Nevertheless, Jewish law is subject to change, mostly slowly but sometimes rather dramatically, just as bones change substantially in the process of growing up and during traumatic events like a skiing accident. In both the slow, evolutionary changes and the metamorphic ones, the law must be shaped through continually interacting with Jewish theology and philosophy, historical realities, economic conditions, moral sensitivities, political settings, and Jewish goals, just as it has historically done, for it to be recognizably Jewish and to express what the Torah demands: a love of God "with all your heart, with all your soul, and with all your might" (Deut. 6:5).

In practice, this means that on any given moral issue, we must first look for precedent within the corpus of Jewish law. Sometimes the precedent may be directly on point even if its applications are quite new. For example, although the internet was not available to most people until the 1990s, ample legal precedents in Jewish law (together with theological and moral concerns) exist on which to base a demand that steps be taken to secure privacy on the web. The task of modern respondents, then, is to describe what we must do to fulfill Jewish law's concerns in this new arena.[7]

On the other hand, in some areas of the law, such as removal of life-support systems or laws concerning corporations, very little, if anything, exists. Sometimes, in fact, the situation is so different that what does exist clearly does not fit. For example, Jewish sources presume that any book that is Torah should be available as readily as possible to the masses, so its view of intellectual property does not apply to anything other than books on Judaism—and, even for such books, modern authorities often maintain that authors should have some copyright privileges. How, then, can one formulate an authentically Jewish response to such new issues?[8]

I maintain that to articulate what can be recognized as an authentic Jewish response to these new issues, one must do what some call "depth theology"—that is, identify the foundational Jewish concepts and values applicable to the area in question and then apply these to the case at hand. For that matter, because I believe that Jewish law is part of the living organism that is Judaism, even when legal precedents seem to apply directly to the case at hand, one cannot simply deduce an answer from those precedents mechanically, as if one were "doing one's sums."[9] One must evaluate the precedent in terms of contemporary scientific knowledge and Judaism's long-term commitments embodied in its theology (including its concepts of God and humans), moral literature (what are the moral norms and goals for life that Jewish sacred literature lays out for us?), and customs. These factors will reenforce the precedent most of the time, but not always. For this reason, in my three JPS books on ethical issues in medicine, social interactions, and personal matters, I first delineate the fundamental concepts and values found in Jewish sources on those issues. Only with these foundational concepts and values in mind can one make authentic and genuinely Jewish moral decisions on concrete issues in any area of life.[10]

Because Judaism, more than any other religion (with the possible exception of Islam), tried to formulate its moral inquiries as much as possible in legal terms, most of the time normal legal methods will do just fine in enabling us to use previous legal materials to determine what Judaism would have us do today. Nonetheless, the law must be used with conscious attention to its foundations in Jewish theology and morality and its historical context to produce wise and appropriate, as well as genuinely Jewish, moral guidance for us now.

Furthermore, individuals, even well-schooled ones, cannot be the sole authorities to engage with the law. The law must be now, as it has always been, the product of ongoing interaction between rabbis and laypeople acting as a community. As such, although individual rabbis should and will produce responsa, for both practical and theological reasons the authority of their rulings ought to rest on their acceptance by fellow rabbis and the Jewish community as a whole. Practically, without such acceptance a ruling is simply ignored, and, to use a talmudic expression, simply "flies in the air."[11] Theologically, laypeople have to be trusted as partners with rabbis in discerning God's will for us, for "if the Children of Israel are not prophets, they are children of prophets."[12] Exactly how to balance rabbinic and lay authority in a given situation is not easily determined, but clearly the law is effective as a moral guide only if such cooperation occurs.

Ultimately, only if we pay attention to the theological and moral goals set out by the Jewish tradition can we use Jewish law appropriately to give us guidance on the moral issues of our time. At the same time, only if we also use Jewish law to its fullest, invoking not only its content but its methods, can we make decisions on most matters that carry the authority of the tradition and preserve its continuity. Both processes must be carried out by rabbis and laypeople working in consort, for only then will our efforts to gain moral guidance from the Jewish tradition bear fruit in the way Jews think, feel, and behave.

With these methodologies in mind, we can, I trust, make Jewish law for us now what it was for the Psalmist:

> The teaching of the Lord is perfect, renewing life;
> The decrees of the Lord are enduring, making the simple wise.
> The precepts of the Lord are just, rejoicing the heart;
> The instruction of the Lord is lucid, making the eyes light up.
> The fear of the Lord is pure, abiding forever;
> The judgments of the Lord are true, righteous altogether,
> more desirable than gold, than much fine gold,
> sweeter than honey, than drippings of the comb.
> Your servant pays them heed; in obeying them there is much reward.
>   (Ps. 19:8–12)

7

Applying Jewish Theology to the Moral Issue of Providing Aid in Dying

Illuminating how Jewish theology can be a potent source for making moral decisions, this chapter draws from my 2020 responsum on providing aid in dying approved by the Rabbinical Assembly's Committee on Jewish Law and Standards (CJLS).[1] First, some background: The CJLS helps determine Jewish law for the Conservative movement. Rabbis and arms of the movement pose questions of halakhic policy with broad communal implications to the CJLS, and the CJLS chair may assign a committee member to write a formal rabbinic ruling on the question. The twenty-five Conservative rabbis on the CJLS engage in considerable discussion before voting on the ruling, and if it receives six or more votes it becomes a valid option within the movement (and then appears on the CJLS website, rabbinicalassembly .org/jewish-law/committee-jewish-law-and-standards).

Notably, the responsum that follows, approved on November 16, 2020, by a vote of 9 yeses, 5 no's, and 2 abstentions, carves out exceptions to my also approved 1997 responsum on assisted dying, which had solely endorsed Jewish law's long-term stance of prohibiting suicide or helping someone die. In this case, Jewish theological convictions, foremost among them "God's compassion embraces all God's creations" (Ps. 145:9), played a prominent, even dominant, role in my reassessment of the issue twenty-three years later—a powerful example of how, in my view, law must be interpreted and even changed in light of its Jewish theological grounding and context.

On March 11, 1997, the Committee on Jewish Law and Standards approved a rabbinic ruling I wrote forbidding assisted suicide by a vote of 21 in favor, 2 opposed, and 1 abstaining.[2] Since then, however, eight American states (Oregon, Washington, Vermont, California, Colorado, Hawaii, New Jersey, and Maine) and the District of Columbia have enacted laws that permit aid in dying, and the Montana Supreme Court has ruled that nothing in its state's statutes prohibits physicians from providing medical aid in dying. According to Death With Dignity, twenty-one other states are considering aid-in-dying bills in 2019.[3] In states without such laws, courts have done everything from putting people who have helped someone die on probation without jail time to sentencing them to years or even life in prison.[4]

On June 17, 2016, Canada's Parliament passed Bill C-14 to legalize and regulate medically assisted dying throughout the country. It is also legal in Colombia (1997), the Netherlands (2002), Belgium (2002), Luxembourg (2008), and Switzerland.[5] Switzerland is the only jurisdiction listed above that allows both residents and nonresidents to receive aid in dying, which has led to a certain degree of "suicide tourism" there.[6]

These jurisdictions include areas with significant numbers of Jews, so that alone suggests that we should at least review my responsum from twenty-three years ago. More importantly, the laws adopted by these jurisdictions governing aid in dying address at least some of my concerns that led to prohibiting it, so a reassessment is in order to determine whether it should still be prohibited if the safeguards enacted by these jurisdictions make my objections moot.

The aim of this responsum is to carve out some narrow exceptions to the general prohibition on seeking or offering aid in dying, for which I argued in 1997. My stance is definitely *not* that of the euthanasia movement, which, at its most extreme, would allow people to take their lives or assist others in doing so for any reason and under any circumstance. This responsum will address only those who, according to their doctors, have fewer than six months to live because of their terminal disease, and only those whose pain cannot be controlled.

Terminology: "Assisted Suicide" vs. "Aid (or Assistance) in Dying" vs. "End of Life Option" vs. "Death with Dignity"

What has become clear to me in the years since I wrote my 1997 responsum is that those opposed to enabling people to cause their own deaths describe it as "assisted suicide," invoking the negative associations Judaism, Christianity, Islam, and Western secular, philosophical traditions have attached to suicide. (Some Asian traditions, especially Hinduism and Mahayana Buddhism in India, see self-immolation as a dignified way to end one's life or use it as a form of political protest—which has been adopted by people elsewhere as well—so in these communities suicide has positive connotations.) Those who want to discuss it without prejudice against it from the outset describe it instead as "aid in dying" or "assisted dying." California's legislation goes further in avoiding negative connotations, for its law on this is named the "End of Life Option Act," emphasizing that what is being permitted by the act is based on the patient's choice. That title also makes it clear that the moral burden for engaging in the procedure rests on the patient, who under the law is exercising an option, rather than the physician, who is assisting a suicide.[7] On the other end of the emotional spectrum, "death with dignity" attributes a positive connotation to helping someone die.

I was unaware of these distinctions when I wrote my responsum in 1997, and, in hindsight, I now realize that titling it "assisted suicide" served to substantiate my ruling that this behavior should be prohibited. The neutral terminology of "aid in dying" or "assisted dying" is much more appropriate if one is seeking to evaluate the practice fairly.

Moreover, my subsequent work on a curriculum on bioethics for the Florence Melton School of Adult Jewish Learning brought me in touch with another very cogent reason to use "aid in dying" rather than "assisted suicide." Most people seeking aid in dying have striven mightily for years to live, even with pain, and are thus not suicidal in intention. They are just facing their inevitable demise, despite multiple attempts to fight it, and they want to do that with as little pain as possible. For example:

> I'm not committing suicide, and I don't want to die. I was upset by media reports that I intend to "kill" myself. I'm not killing myself; bone cancer is taking care of that. I may take the option of shortening the agony of my final hours.—Jack Newbold

> All I am asking for is to have some choice over how I die. Portraying me as suicidal is disrespectful and hurtful to me and my loved ones. It adds insult to injury by dismissing all that I have already endured; the failed attempts for a cure, the progressive decline of my physical state and the anguish that has involved exhaustive reflection and contemplation, leading me to this very personal and intimate decision about my own life and how I would like it to end.—Louise Schaefer[8]

The Trenchant Factors in Prohibiting Aid in Dying

When people are asked in surveys whether or not they endorse aid in dying, it is always with regard to the isolated case in which the patient is actively dying due to a terminal disease and has uncontrollable pain or the prospect thereof and the desire for control over one's dying process.[9] In such cases, the ones to which this responsum will be addressed, the moral demand to relieve pain in Jewish law competes with the prohibitions against taking one's own life or aiding someone in doing so. In the vast majority of cases, though, all the following issues undermine the simple morality of relieving someone's pain:

1. Money. Money can and does complicate these situations in at least these three ways:

a. Mom is dying, and she does not want to "squander" (that is the term that is usually used) the family money on what she deems futile medical interventions to keep her alive because there is no reasonable hope for her to recover from her terminal illness.

b. Worse, from a moral point of view, are cases in which Mom's children do not want her to "squander" the family money on what they deem to be futile medical interventions to keep her alive because they want to inherit it. That said, whether it is Mom or her children who want to stop the use of family funds for Mom's medical expenses, we must recognize that dying can render individuals and families deeply in debt, and access to adequate insurance to pay for her care varies widely from family to family but usually is available, ironically, only to the more wealthy among us.

c. Much more pervasive than either of the two cases above, your insurance company, whether private or governmental, would be very happy to aid your dying process because it is much less costly to do that than to provide Mom with long-term care. So far insurance companies do not pay for medication to aid in dying, and in most jurisdictions aid in dying is illegal altogether, but one can understand why insurance companies would gladly pay for that rather than for long-term care.

2. Depression. People suffering from terminal illnesses understandably and normally feel depressed about the state of their health and its prognosis, leading to a more general dissatisfaction with every aspect of their current lives. That should lead us, though, not to assist them in dying but to take measures to counteract their depression, including the following:

   a. Medications and other therapies. Medications to counteract depression are used by people at many ages, and there is no reason to refrain from using them in terminally ill patients to relieve at least this aspect of their suffering. The same is true for cognitive-behavioral therapy and other psychological interventions.
   b. Visits. All forms of illness isolate patients from their community, but people have a deep need to interact with others. As a result, often the most effective response to patients' depression is frequent interactions with others, especially those they know and love.
   c. Alleviation of boredom. Illness often also deprives people of the activities that give meaning to their lives, so people visiting patients give them a double boost of enthusiasm for life when they not only show up but also engage the ill in discussions or activities that interest them. Topics of conversation should be the same adult topics that patients used to discuss with those who visit them. Activities that visitors may use to engage patients' interest include helping them create an ethical will or a family history to leave to their children, grandchildren, other family members, and friends. This can be done in writing or with the various recording media available to us now.

3. Psychological disorders, particularly narcissism, lead people to request aid in dying when their lives do not conform to their fantasies. Here again, treatment of those disorders is in order, not aid in dying. More prevalent and more disturbing are elderly people who are easily confused and manipulated into decisions that will benefit their heirs, doctors, medical institutions (hospitals, nursing homes, etc.), or insurance companies rather than themselves. Even if they are still mentally competent enough to use the law to ask for aid in dying, we clearly need to protect such people from this kind of exploitation.

4. A sense of being useless and a burden or other forms of existential suffering. Terminally ill people often lose the abilities that enabled them to contribute to society and gave them self-respect in the process, and they are usually indeed a burden. Pretending that those realities are not true does not help either patients or their caregivers. It is precisely here, though, when we need to remind people that their worth is not solely a function of what they can do for others (their utilitarian value), but of their inherent value as a person created in the image of God (their intrinsic value).[10] This also speaks to other forms of existential suffering, in which the patient for some other reason thinks that life is not worth living. This could include, for example, a profound sense of guilt for something they did, leading them to believe they deserve to die, or a sense that nobody cares if they live or die. Patients in these emotional states should not be immediately accommodated in their stated wishes to die. They should instead be reassured that they are well worth the effort to help them live and live meaningfully, to the extent that it is possible. This is most effectively done through family and friends who interact with the person often and express, in varying ways, how much and why they value the person who is contemplating suicide. This will clearly be the case for patients who still have their mental faculties, but even for those who do not, for the sake of our own moral standing as well as theirs, we must not let utilitarian concerns determine how we treat them.

5. **A need for control.** For many people who request aid in dying, this is the central issue: they need to feel that they can decide when and how to die. This can be rooted in a fear of death or the dying process, or simply a need to assert power over themselves when they are increasingly losing it. This is why a significant number of people who obtain the drugs to help them die never use them: they only wanted to have the power to die if they later chose to do so.

6. **Lack of sufficient pain medication.** Especially with the recent epidemic of opioid abuse, with the startling numbers of addictions, overdoses, and deaths they have caused, doctors are reluctant to use pain medications, even if they are clearly medically necessary to quell pain. American culture, with its approving attitude to those who "grin and bear it," especially for men, makes this phenomenon even worse. We clearly need to avoid addiction to pain medication, but when patients are "actively dying" and have fewer than six months to live, this concern becomes irrelevant. Moreover, in the rare cases to which this ruling applies, no amount of pain medication quells the person's pain, and the person remains conscious and screaming despite massive doses of morphine.

7. Access to health care. In the United States, probably the most trenchant objection, in practice, to offering aid in dying is the fact that some forty million Americans lack health care insurance altogether, and millions more lack adequate health care insurance to provide what they need throughout life, including the time when they are in the process of dying. This clearly is different in countries that have socialized medicine (Canada, Israel, most of Europe, etc.), but even in such nations one must determine whether what is offered is adequate to treat the physical pain and other needs of the dying. We do not live in a world of complete abundance, so all nations (or the insurers within them) will need to determine which medical interventions will be provided, which not, and to whom. Nevertheless, to the greatest extent possible, health care plans should provide people with the medical interventions needed to enable them to live and, when the time comes, to die with as little pain as possible. They should provide other supportive services as well ("palliative care"). No one should need to ask for aid in dying for lack of such medical assistance.

8. The role of doctors and their training in aid in dying. From the Hippocratic oath to the current Code of Ethics of the American Medical Association, doctors have understood helping someone die as violating the ethics of their profession, whose purpose is to prevent, cure, or at least ameliorate disease to sustain life, and, in the case of hospice and palliative care, to improve "a patient's quality of life by managing pain and other distressing symptoms of a serious illness."[11] To revise the mission of doctors to include giving people aid in dying, therefore, requires physicians to embrace a new understanding of their role and may, some doctors and physicians' associations believe, threaten patients' trust in their doctors to try to heal them, not kill them. That said, as other doctors and medical associations have asserted, aid in dying may well be within the mission of physicians, for their role is ultimately to care even if they cannot cure. This tension is evident in a statement of the American Medical Association opposed to doctors participating in aid-in-dying protocols and the fact that a number of its regions have adopted resolutions in favor of physicians participating in aid in dying.[12] Another point to note, however, is that physicians are trained in therapeutic dosing, not lethal dosing, so doctors providing aid in dying may need more training.

9. Disregard for people who are disabled. Opponents to aid in dying rightfully worry that the emphasis on youth and abilities in Western societies, which already makes it difficult for people who are disabled to function and feel valued, will get even worse if aid in dying is allowed, for then it will be all too easy for people who are healthy to think that those who need special care due to one or more disabilities should instead choose to die.

10. Theology. Jewish sources assert that our bodies, along with the rest of the world, belong to God, as articulated, for example, in these biblical verses: "Mark, the heavens to their uttermost reaches belong to the Lord your God, the earth and all that is on it!" (Deut. 10:14). "Of David. A psalm. The earth is the Lord's and all that it holds, the world and its inhabitants." (Ps. 24:1). People, then, may not have the right to destroy what is not theirs.

11. Law. Finally, and perhaps most importantly for a Jewish legal ruling such as this, Jewish law forbids taking one's own life or assisting someone else in doing so. In my 1997 responsum, "Assisted Suicide," I describe in detail the sources and nuances of this legal ban, so I will not repeat them here.

Some of these considerations (I have added to them in the list above) led me, in 1997, to write a responsum prohibiting aid in dying. That does *not* mean that we must do everything possible to keep a person alive. Exactly what we should, need not, or should not do toward that goal is governed in slightly different ways by two 1990 responsa on end-of-life issues, one by Rabbi Avram Israel Reisner and one by me.[13]

The Use of Aid-in-Dying Laws

The laws in most jurisdictions that allow aid in dying require tracking of the use of the law. California's results are typical, so they will suffice for a sense of the extent of its use, the identity of its users, and the circumstances under which it was used.

California's law went into effect on July 1, 2016. According to the California Department of Public Health, in the first eighteen months that the law was in effect (that is, through 2017), 485 Californians used it to take their lives, and an additional 283 patients received prescriptions from their physicians for the drugs but have either not filled them or not ingested the medicine.[14] Thus, as many as a third of those who request the drugs do so to enable them to determine how they will die but do not choose to end their lives.

These statistics indicate that the law is working in permitting *some, but very few* deaths through aid in dying relative to the total number of people who died in California in 2019, so there has not been a rush to die as a result of this act, as some feared. Indeed, *405 deaths through aid in dying, out of 270,492 total deaths in California in 2019, amounts to 0.15 percent of the deaths in California that year.* The data also indicates that those who took advantage of the act had terminal, irreversible illnesses, as the law requires, and 85.4 percent of them were already in hospice care, which was clearly not working to quell their pain and hence their request for aid in dying.

The California statistics do not reflect the need for aid in dying. My daughter-in-law, Dr. Tanya Dorff, is an oncologist, formerly at the University of Southern California and now at City of Hope Medical Center.[15] In an email to me, she wrote this: "The use of pain medications to relieve pain is a given. . . . We accept the sedation and potential for overdose related death and prioritize pain relief at the end of life. But there are cases (rare—to be clear; I've had 3 extreme experiences in my 15 years of caring for cancer patients) in which despite pouring morphine into a patient's veins, they are crying out or screaming in pain. They are still awake and cognizant."[16]

As she explained to me, such patients are experiencing excruciating and uncontrollable pain or other forms of physical suffering, including, for example, chronic shortness of breath. It is this reality that those of us reading this responsum, who presumably are not in such distress, must recognize, along with Hillel's dictum: "Do not be sure of yourself until the day of your death, do not judge your fellow human being until you have reached his place."[17]

Can such cases be treated with a medically induced coma? Such treatment is generally used for brain injuries and is not clinically indicated for alleviating pain. Consequently, doctors will not induce a coma to alleviate pain, and insurance companies will not pay for it.

A different procedure, terminal sedation, involves using drugs to keep a patient in a coma without administering artificial nutrition and hydration until the patient dies. In jurisdictions that allow aid in dying, terminal sedation is typically used to alleviate pain when patients are not mentally competent to decide whether to ask for aid in dying. In jurisdictions that do not permit aid in dying, some call it "euthanasia in disguise," for the ultimate intent is to help someone die.[18] As a result, whether one accepts terminal sedation morally and halakhically is as controversial as using drugs to aid a person in dying.

In addition to patients with current, uncontrollable pain, another kind of case that leads people to request aid in dying is prolonged and only partially controlled pain. On December 8, 2019, the *New York Times* published a forty-two-page special report, "The Champion Who Picked a Date to Die."[19] It describes the case of Marieke Vervoort, a Belgian who, since her teenage years, "had been battling a degenerative muscle disease that stole away the use of her legs, stripped her of her independence, and caused her agonizing, unrelenting pain."[20] In Vervoort's telling, the euthanasia papers allowed her to wrest back some control of her life. She no longer feared death because she could hold it in her hands at any time. "Because of those papers," she said, "I started to live again."[21] Indeed, she went on to win multiple competitions in sporting events for people who are disabled and lived another eleven years.

Yet another class of cases in which people have advocated aid in dying, beyond the protocols of the laws in either California or Canada, is that of people with dementia. For example, Nicholas Goldberg wrote an opinion piece in the *Los Angeles Times* in which he made an emotionally compelling case for enabling people gradually losing their minds to be offered aid in dying, using his grandmother as the case in point.[22]

These latter two kinds of cases also cry out to us for compassion, and, at some point, both civil law in many jurisdictions and our understanding of Jewish law may allow for extending aid in dying to such patients. In this responsum, however, I am arguing for a much more limited class of people to whom aid in dying should be offered—those diagnosed with a terminal disease that makes it likely that they will die within six months and who are experiencing uncontrollable pain. I am limiting my responsum to such cases for two reasons: (1) The jurisdictions that allow aid in dying in Canada and the United States have limited aid in dying to people whose death is near, which does not include prolonged pain from a disability or the prospect of becoming increasingly demented; (2) I am already stretching past Jewish law to say that we may aid people in dying when they are in great pain that cannot be controlled. To address other conditions, such as disability and dementia, would involve other considerations and should therefore be the subject of another responsum. Perhaps this will be issued years from now, when we have more experience with applying aid-in-dying laws and can ensure that these more complex cases can be handled in a way that does not lead to abuse.

Evaluating Aid in Dying through a Jewish Lens

In this responsum, I am extending the duty to alleviate pain to permit using drugs to hasten the deaths of those who are expected to die within six months and are enduring uncontrollable pain. The ultimate warrant for such an extension is theological, in accord with my theory of Jewish law that asserts that Jewish law must be interpreted and applied with Jewish theological convictions in mind.[23]

As the Psalmist (145:9) says: "The Lord is good to all, and His mercy embraces all His works." Jewish tradition has us recite this verse three times a day every day of the year, so our tradition clearly wants us to learn these attributes of God and imitate God in this way in our own lives. As the *Sifre* interprets the Torah's demand that we "walk in all God's ways" (Deut. 11:22): "Now how is it possible for a person to be called by the name of the Holy Blessed One? Just as the All Present is called 'merciful and gracious,' you, too, be merciful and gracious. . . . Just as the Holy Blessed One is called 'loving,'—you, too, be loving."[24]

God's compassion, of course, does not mean that anything goes, for both the Torah and later Jewish tradition are filled with laws that articulate what we must, may, and may not do, with penalties for violating banned acts. This responsum is arguing only that in a narrow and rare group of cases, the model of God's goodness should extend our duty to alleviate pain to permit aid in dying. Patients, of course, have no obligation to ask for such aid, and physicians and hospitals should not be forced to offer it.

It is important that we confront these cases not only pastorally, but legally, for to say that the law prohibits aid in dying but we should understand those who engage in it and comfort their families leaves the patient with tremendous guilt over asking for aid in dying and the family with shame. It is therefore critical that rabbis make it clear that, legally as well as medically, aid in dying is not a suicide but a compassionate effort to alleviate pain caused by the disease that is taking the person's life. Moreover, for Jewish doctors this clearly is a legal issue, for they will want to know that not only civil law, but also their own tradition supports what they are doing when they provide aid in dying.

Two aspects of the position I have described above are hard, however, even for me:

1. The limits of the conditions that warrant aid in dying. In her thoughtful response to an earlier draft of this responsum, Rabbi Judith Hauptman wants me to go further than this:

> I will go one step further than the author of this teshuvah. . . . I would give more leeway to the one who wishes to end his or her life. If that person faces a horrible end, for instance losing all control of bodily function, and if that person does not want to see a lifetime of savings squandered on keeping him or her alive when he or she would be little more than a physical presence without mental capacity, and if that person wants a lifetime of savings to be passed to children or grandchildren and not to a nursing home or insurance company, I would also allow that person to choose to die sooner rather than later.

A part of me agrees with her. I am worried, though, as the legislators in California clearly were, that permitting aid in dying for such cases can too easily be extended to people who should be provided other kinds of interventions. I also worry that permitting aid in dying without requiring that the person be expected to die soon would undermine our care for people who are disabled. It is much easier and much less expensive to help them die than to provide the kinds of physical, educational, social, and psychological assistance that would enable them to live lives meaningful to them and to society at large, despite the suffering involved in coping with their disabilities. I would not, however, condemn or deny normal Jewish burial rites to Jews in Canada (or in other jurisdictions) who take advantage of the civil law that allows them to seek medical aid in dying when they are subject to "a grievous and irremediable medical condition" that causes them uncontrollable pain, even though their condition does not involve a prognosis of imminent death.

2. The role of doctors in providing aid in dying. I recognize, as the Canadian law does, that some people are too feeble to administer the medication to themselves, so Canada allows "clinician-administered medical assistance in dying" in addition to permitting patients to take the drugs provided by doctors on their own. Indeed, there is a certain unfairness and maybe even cruelty in permitting aid in dying for patients who are mentally and physically competent to administer the drugs to themselves to relieve uncontrollable pain but not for patients in the same situation who cannot administer the drugs themselves and need help in doing so. These may be the very hardest cases for us emotionally. Indeed, my interpretation of Jewish law, like California law, may induce people to die earlier than they really want to for fear that if they wait too long, they will not meet the requirements of the law and will therefore be ineligible to use it.

Although I see the strength of these arguments for permitting physicians to not only provide but administer the drugs to cause a person's death under the specified conditions, as under the Canadian law, I would stop short of permitting that. First, as noted earlier, even though one could construe injecting lethal drugs into a patient suffering from uncontrollable pain to be an acceptable goal of medicine, the medical community is anything but united in seeing it that way. This is evidenced by the conflicting statements of the American Medical Association and some of its regions, noted above, on even providing the drugs, let alone administering them. Furthermore, allowing active euthanasia immediately raises the question of the motive of the person administering it. These may seem like thin lines separating active euthanasia from enabling a person to bring about his or her own death, especially to patients too feeble to take the drugs themselves, but significant moral and Jewish legal boundaries do distinguish one from the other.[25]

Consequently, as a matter of public policy, I would favor the California law on this over the Canadian one. Specifically, I would interpret Jewish law to ban euthanasia but allow physicians to provide drugs for dying to patients in uncontrollable pain who can administer the drugs to themselves and are expected to die within six months. At the same time, in jurisdictions that allow medical aid in dying to patients expected to die soon and suffering uncontrollable pain, I would stand aside without judgment of either the patient or the physician involved in the process.[26] Rabbis need to offer solace and understanding to patients and their families in all these cases.

8

The Role of Prayer in Moral Discernment and Motivation

My hometown synagogue and Camp Ramah gave me the skills to engage in traditional Jewish prayer, and a series of discussions at Ramah when I was fifteen made me interested in taking on traditional Jewish practices, including daily prayer. Yet even then I understood that it was much easier to discern the meanings of other Jewish rituals and whether I had succeeded in observing them than it was with prayer. Worse, I was anything but sure about what belief in God meant, let alone whether I shared that belief (see chapter 1). At the same time, I liked praying and did gain several forms of meaning from it, including connectedness with my Ramah community and the broader Jewish community (even though I was praying at home on my own), a reaffirmation and reminder of my deepest moral convictions, and a sense of transcendence (even though I did not yet understand the last of these forms of meaning).

All this led me to thinking—over decades—about the prayer experience itself, and about its relationship, if any, to morality. The meanings and significance of my daily prayers have continued to be influenced by my thinking about moral issues, and both my thought and prayers have been expanded and deepened by my life experiences involving moral issues.

My first published attempt to grapple philosophically with prayer was in a monograph, "Prayer for the Perplexed," published in October 1982 as part of the University of Judaism's University Papers series. It was prompted in part by my need to try to understand what I was doing every day when I was praying and why. (Professor Arthur Danto at Columbia once told us graduate students in philosophy that a philosopher is really a five-year-old child who never stopped asking "Why?") Additionally, I needed to explain to rabbinical students along with campers and staff at Camp Ramah why they should pray and what kinds of meanings they might aim to get out of it. In those educational settings, it occurred to me that I was acting very much like a coach in baseball, a sport I played and even enjoyed despite not being good at it. That led me to think that prayer was in many ways like baseball, and the 1982 monograph explored this idea. Ten years later, the chapter on prayer in my 1992 book, *Knowing God*, expanded on that monograph, and three decades thenceforth, a slightly augmented adaptation of that chapter appears below.

The English word "prayer" leads people to believe that prayer is about asking for things, as in "Do this, I pray." The implication is, if you pray for something and you do not get it, prayer is clearly worthless. A quick perusal of the traditional Jewish prayer book, though, indicates that while some petitions do appear in the daily service, the vast majority of the liturgy consists of praising and thanking God. Since God does not need our prayers, the aim of such prayers is clearly directed at us—to get us out of what philosophers call "our egocentric predicament" to see the world and our lives, as much as we can, through God's eyes. This, in turn, can help us discern the moral path and motivate us to follow it. So the moral import of prayer is part, although certainly not all, of the meaning of prayer. To see this, one needs to think more broadly about prayer.

How Prayer Is Like Baseball

In many respects, prayer is like baseball. Both require skills. Some people are naturally talented, and for them the acquisition of the necessary skills is deceptively easy. It would be a mistake, though, to conclude from watching such people function that everyone has the same ability. That would only produce embarrassment and frustration when one tried it oneself. It would also be a mistake to deduce that natural talent in and of itself is enough; even the most gifted athletes must practice. It would be an even more serious error to think that only people to whom prayer or baseball come easily can accomplish these tasks. Quite the contrary is true; for the vast majority of us, praying demands the time and effort of extended preparation—just as deft baseball playing does—but both can be effectively done by almost everyone.

Prayer is also like baseball in that even professionals attain their goals to differing degrees each time they engage in the practice. Even people who have prayed daily for years often strike out in prayer. They cannot concentrate at all on what they are doing and perhaps even resent the time they devoted to prayer that day. Such experiences are disappointing, but one should not have unrealistic expectations. Remember, even if a baseball player gets a hit—not a home run—once in three times at bat, that is a .333 average, better than the average of the vast majority of baseball players.

At other times, prayer is the rough equivalent of a walk in baseball. On such occasions, the person praying is not moved by any of the prayers but, nevertheless, is glad to have spent the time in prayer. It was, at least, a brief time spent away from the hectic schedule of the day. Even if one's mind wandered throughout the time one was saying the words of the liturgy, the exercise still carved out some time for meditation. Moreover, one might appreciate that, in more attentive moments, these prayers articulate some of the most significant aspects of one's life. Today's experience of prayer was thus worthwhile even if it was only a walk through the prayer book.

Sometimes one gets the equivalent of a base hit. A particular prayer, or sentence, or even a phrase happens to hit home. It may speak to the particular problems one has at the moment, or stimulate thought, or remind one of an important value, or add a bit of beauty to the day, or give a sense of the meaning of being a human being and a Jew. In other words, just as one can get a base hit by hitting the ball to a variety of areas within the ballpark, one can score a base hit in prayer by having a variety of different prayer experiences. Each is a base hit because that prayer has enabled the worshiper to reach one of the goals of prayer.

At other times one achieves the equivalent of a double or triple. Several of the prayers hit their mark, perhaps in very different ways, and one is left with an awareness of how important it was to pray. One's day, one's week, and perhaps even one's life has been enriched.

And then, once in a while, one hits a home run. It would not be realistic or fair to expect a home run each time one is at bat in prayer any more than it would in baseball. Those who pray very little often make that mistake. A home run in prayer, like one in baseball, requires much practice, many trials and errors, and, ultimately, consummate skill. Even that is not enough. One needs some luck too. The conditions have to be just right, and one's body, mind, and emotions have to be perfectly attuned to one another and to the task at hand. This does not happen very often.

Moreover, one should not pray only in hopes of having such an experience—any more than one plays baseball only for the times one hits a home run. Indeed, if our praying or baseball playing were to succeed on every level each time we tried, we would be very different individuals and societies from what we know, and prayer—and baseball—would have to be restructured to speak to our needs. Even though prayer (or anything else) cannot move us in all its dimensions every time, it *can* affect us on some level on many occasions. Thus it can be a valuable practice.

Gaining Spiritual Meaning from Prayer

What constitutes "success" in prayer? Even if we do not expect to hit a home run immediately, for what should we aim? We know where the outfield fence is in baseball, but what kind of experience is a home run in prayer?

Some modes of Jewish prayer place the individual praying at the center of consciousness, while others are more God-centered. This explains why people who have not developed a clear conception of God can gain meaning from many aspects of Jewish worship nonetheless.

On any given occasion, in fact, a Jew can gain spiritual meaning from prayer and even hit a home run in any or all of the following ways:

1. Expressions of one's desire, such as a desire to reconcile with a friend or family member or succeed at a task.
2. Perspective, appreciation, and meaning, for in prayer one steps back from the hustle bustle of life to reorient oneself to what is really important and to plan one's future actions accordingly.
3. Communal and historical roots of belonging to the Jewish community worldwide today and in the past, present, and hopefully the future.
4. Expanding one's knowledge of the tradition through an explanation of one of the prayers in the liturgy or a homily on the week's Torah reading prepared by you or someone else.
5. Aesthetic and emotional effectiveness by, for example, enjoying singing prayers with others, or finding that one or more of the prayers enables you to express what you are feeling that day. (A range of emotions including awe, fear, thanksgiving, remorse, and joy are all expressed in different parts of the daily liturgy.)
6. Moral effects, as described below.
7. Fulfilling the mitzvah of praying and coming into contact with God while feeling a sense of the transcendent.

The Moral Effects of Prayer

Prayer can affect the morality of our thoughts and actions. For one thing, it reminds us of the full gamut of Jewish values. Because values are not physical and concrete, we tend to forget them easily. Prayer—like ritual objects and acts of all sorts—helps us remember our commitments so that we have a better chance of making them part of our lives.

Prayer also helps us atone for the wrongs we do. Three times each weekday and more extensively and intensively on the High Holy Days, we take account of what we have done and express our regret for the sins we have committed. Morally, these prayers of confession are important in at least three ways: They can prompt us to make amends to anyone we have harmed. After we do so, they can relieve remaining guilt we feel for our past wrongs so we are not stymied by our sins. Finally, they can enable us to regain a clear vision of what we should avoid doing now and in the future.

Worship can also make us aware of moral issues and give us insights into moral problems we face. When Evangelical Christians "pray on it" to assess what to do with a moral problem, they mean more than "think about it," for praying can bring us into contact with our understandings of our moral values and ultimate reality. So, for example, thinking about whether to remove life support from Mom calls attention to our pragmatic concerns, like what Mom's current medical situation is, what will happen to her medically if we leave her on life support or suspend it, and the financial and personal costs of both alternatives. Praying on that decision includes all those factors, but also makes us aware that we should be thinking not only pragmatically, but also ethically and theologically—taking into account what the possible decisions say about us and our values, and how deciding in a particular way affects our relationship with God and what we understand God to want of us. Jews can and should learn to pray on decisions as well as think about them.

Finally, prayer can stimulate us to act as we should. The exhortative sections of the liturgy, Torah readings, and sermons can motivate us to correct the bad, and the inspirational aspects of prayer can arouse us to strive for the ideal. The regimen of prayer forces us to stop our normal activities and take a serious look at life, and that alone may enable us to strengthen our moral resolve.

9

The Roles of Autonomy and Community in Deciding How to Live as Jews

An Exchange of Open Letters between Rabbis Elliot Dorff and Eugene Borowitz

After my review of Reform rabbi Eugene Borowitz's 1991 volume, *Renewing the Covenant: A Theology for the Postmodern Jew*, appeared in the journal *Conservative Judaism*, Rabbi Borowitz responded in an open letter to me in a subsequent issue. I, in turn, replied to him in that publication.[1]

Rabbi Borowitz liked our exchange so much that he had it printed separately and distributed to every Reform rabbi in the Central Conference of American Rabbis. I, too, liked our exchange; I included it in its entirety in my book *The Unfolding Tradition: Philosophies of Jewish Law* and present excerpts from it below.[2]

This exchange is a clear example of how friends can respectfully disagree and genuinely enjoy the dialogue as part of their friendship. It also illustrates how a Reform rabbi may not be so far from a Conservative one in theory and possibly even in practice. Rabbi Borowitz, in any case, would claim that!

AUTONOMY VS. COMMUNITY

ELLIOT N. DORFF

Those who have read from the prolific writings of Rabbi Eugene Borowitz will not be at all surprised that this book is clearly written, honest and unpretentious, penetrating in its criticism of alternative approaches, and fully aware and appreciative of both the Jewish tradition and the contemporary context of Jewish life. It is also morally and theologically urgent and thought-provoking.

It is, then, very much in the spirit of Eugene Borowitz that I want to challenge him in this review. I know that he will understand—and I certainly hope that everyone else will too—that I do so with genuine love for the man and deep appreciation for his work. At the same time, we have an honest disagreement over how Jews should think about their Judaism and express their convictions in action, and my reasons must be stated clearly, rigorously, and yet respectfully. That is the model he has set for us.

This book does not present itself as distinctly Reform theology, but it certainly is. Indeed, it would be hard not to be, given that Rabbi Borowitz has been the prime Reform ideologue for a generation. Like Reform ideologies from the days of Abraham Geiger, Borowitz's approach places the ultimate source of authority on matters of belief and practice in the individual person. To believe and act responsibly as a contemporary Jew, to be sure, the individual must learn as much as possible not only about modernity but also about traditional Judaism and the various ways people have proposed to integrate the two. In the 1976 Centennial Perspective of the Reform Movement, Rabbi Borowitz writes, "Within each area of Jewish observance, Reform Jews are called upon to confront the claims of Jewish tradition, however differently perceived, and to exercise their individual autonomy, choosing and creating on the basis of commitment and knowledge."[3] This perspective is the thrust of his book.

Here, though, Borowitz has definitively spelled out how locating the locus of authority in the individual amounts to more than people doing whatever they want to do about their own Jewish identities. Borowitz does this through his concept of "the autonomous Jewish self." Individual Jews are not simply isolated people who happen to choose to affirm their Jewishness. From the moment of birth or conversion, each Jew must see himself or herself as an autonomous Jewish self. That is, we modern Jews, as an integral part of who we are as people, are Jews just as much as we are individuals. This means that we do not begin our inquiry into our own identities with a clean slate, free to choose whatever we like. We begin, instead, as Jews, and therefore as part of the Covenant between God and Israel.

This conception of our individual identities imposes upon us covenantal obligations to do God's will. We may, and will, perceive what God wants of us in our own individual ways (the autonomy of the Jewish self), but however we understand God's covenantal command, we have a duty to perform it. That is the Jewish part of our autonomous Jewish self. Like other duties, religious obligations are more than our desires. Religious duties often require us to do what we otherwise would not want to do.

My problems with this theory are, in essence, the reasons I am a Conservative Jew and not a Reform Jew. First, to be a serious Reform Jew along these lines is a *very* tall order. One must first learn both the Western and Jewish traditions thoroughly so that one's choices can be informed and intelligent. One must also learn how to recognize the voice of God, through all of this, to know how God wants one to integrate tradition and modernity. I do not doubt that Eugene Borowitz has the requisite knowledge and powers of judgment to make his theory work, but I doubt that many others do. The amount of Jewish and general education needed for such a theory to work—to say nothing of the demands of theological training and moral sensitivity—is simply too great for most Jews to master. I frankly doubt the educational systems currently in place in any of the movements could produce many people with all these qualifications, let alone a whole cadre of Jewish people with them, and I question whether even the ideal Jewish educational system—however that is defined—realistically can hope to achieve the goals of Borowitz's method of applying Jewish law.

It is precisely here where the Conservative approach, for all its difficulties, is actually easier. Like Borowitz, I want Jews (especially myself) to adopt a form of Jewish belief and practice that integrates the best of tradition and modernity. In the Conservative approach, though, I do not have to depend exclusively upon my own resources to decide how to do that. Instead, I participate in a community of people who are on the same quest, and we make those decisions as a community, as that traditionally has been done—through rabbinic decisions, individually and collectively, and through the interaction of law with custom. We may, of course, all be wrong. We are, after all, human. That is most assuredly true also for our Orthodox coreligionists, who unavoidably interpret and apply traditional Jewish texts according to their own human abilities and those of the rabbis they respect. We in the Conservative movement, in my view, are in a better position to discern God's will than the Orthodox are because we openly recognize the human component of revelation from the beginning and therefore are more keenly aware of the need to differentiate the human from the divine in those texts as we make decisions for our time. On the other hand, though, like the Orthodox and unlike Borowitz, the Conservative approach requires us constantly to check our own understanding of God's will with that of other Jews. This complicates and delays the process of making decisions, but it also relieves me of being solely responsible for the Jewish decisions I make—a Jewish and moral burden that few of us can bear intelligently and responsibly.

In addition to these practical problems with Borowitz's theory, I have some Jewish and philosophical problems with it. From the point of view of the Jewish tradition, of course, individual Jews are not vested with the right to make decisions as to what they should believe and practice. That is a communal, and ultimately a divine, matter. Borowitz, of course, would claim that modernity has irreversibly denuded Judaism and the Jewish community of that kind of authority, and that individual autonomy in matters of religion is a good thing. I have problems with both of those claims, but suffice it to say that a move to individual autonomy, at the very least, is a significant move away from traditional Judaism. That makes the "Jewish" in "the autonomous Jewish self" seriously attenuated in its meaning.

But let us look at the claims underlying virtually all of Reform thinking from Geiger to Borowitz. Is individual autonomy "all that it has been cracked up to be"? I, for one, am most grateful for the Enlightenment and its American offshoots for granting me and all others under their sway political freedoms that include freedom of religion and of speech. I not only thrive under those freedoms in a practical sense; I think that they are an important addition to what we mean by the concept of the sanctity of the individual created in God's image. Such sanctity requires mutual respect among people of all religions and denominations who honestly are seeking to discover God in their lives.

In our own time, though, we have come to see that just as communal authoritarianism can destroy the individual respect required by that divine image, so can autonomy left unchecked. Individuals should have choices in important areas of their lives. I would even go so far as to say that in political matters, the burden of proof should be on the government to show why individuals should not have a choice in a particular area. What we want from religion, though, is not simply to congratulate us for what we would have thought or done on our own anyway. We want religion to broaden our concerns, give us guidance, and challenge us to be better than we would have otherwise been. If religion is going to do those things, autonomy must be balanced not only with divinity but with community.

Borowitz spends six chapters on the issue of community and speaks eloquently about the sociality of Jewish spirituality. After all is said and done, though, that sociality does not, for Borowitz, require obeying Jewish law, "however differently perceived" (to borrow a phrase). So I frankly doubt that he has successfully protected those who follow his approach from the dangers of autonomy run amok. We need a better balance between autonomy and community, and in the area of religion, the emphasis, if there is to be one, should be on community, for only then can religion fulfill its functions. But that judgment, again, makes me Conservative and Borowitz Reform.

Finally, the very Enlightenment theory on which Borowitz's emphasis on autonomy is based is currently—and, I think, correctly—coming under attack. Contrary to the classical Enlightenment thinkers, like John Locke, we do not exist as individuals in some state of nature and then autonomously decide to enter into a social contract. Instead, as people like the French Jewish philosopher Emanuel Levinas and "communitarians" like Amitai Etzioni have pointed out, our very being is social. We come into the world with relationships already built into our existence. Those relations immediately impose duties upon us. The nature and extent of those duties, and the way Jewish law is related to this analysis of the origin of duty, are matters for lengthy discussion well beyond the scope of this review essay. I think, though, that that line of reasoning is much closer to the truth and to the grounds for a meaningful theory of Jewish obligation than is one based on autonomy—even one modified by the adjective "Jewish."

All of this is not in any way to deny the importance of this book. Here we have the premier Reform theologian articulating clearly and passionately why Jews who believe in autonomy as a cornerstone of their religious faith should nevertheless see themselves also as subject to Jewish duties. Watching him do that in the careful way he always does is a sheer delight.

THE REFORM JUDAISM OF RENEWING THE COVENANT:
AN OPEN LETTER TO ELLIOT DORFF
EUGENE B. BOROWITZ

I'm deeply grateful for your searching review of *Renewing the Covenant*. To be given serious attention is itself a considerable gift, but you are also gracious enough to say many nice things about my work over the years and that truly touched me. Many thanks indeed for your great-heartedness. Yet as you surely know, the greatest compliment of all is to have a thoughtful reader probe your ideas with great care and respond to them from the depths of his or her understanding. I was particularly happy that you devoted a significant part of your review to my effort to transform the old Enlightenment-Kantian view of the individuality of the self into something far more congenial to Judaism. As I see it, there is far more overlap in our views than your analysis indicates, though I agree that we differ in significant part.

You perceive a great divide between us because you insist that my book must be read "as a distinctly Reform theology. . . . Indeed, it would be hard not to be, given that Rabbi Borowitz has been the prime Reform ideologue for a generation." As a result, though I climax my "theology of post-liberal Jewish duty" with my notion of "the Jewish self"— intentionally not "the autonomous Jewish self" of my 1984 article— you believe I must not be saying anything much different from what Reform thinkers of prior generations said. All my talk aside, you insist that self overwhelms Jewishness with all the usual deleterious consequences for our Judaism.

Two things about this assertion particularly surprise me. The first stems from your careful emphasis on my six chapters rejecting the isolated selfhood of the Enlightenment and Kant, a notion that dominated the older Reform Judaism (and most of American Jewish non-Orthodox apologetics). Postmodern Jews, I argue, need to recontextualize selfhood for Jews as Covenantal, that is, to see the Jewish self as an individuality fundamentally grounded in God and the Jewish people's relationship to God.

I do not know how I can persuade you that I am not now and never have been a card-carrying Reform ideologue. As to my role in preparing our Centenary Perspective document, I became chair of the committee that wrote it only because a previous commission—of which I was not invited to be a regular member—failed to do so despite several years of meetings. A series of political necessities then brought the CCAR to turn to me. So though you twice credit me with inserting some specific language in it, my colleagues, vigorous exercisers of their autonomy and doughty defenders of their political diversity, never extended such deference to me. In short, I am not the Reform Robert Gordis, z"l.

Instead, I have always tried to think academically about Jewish belief and its consequences. None of my models—Cohen, Baeck, Kaplan, Buber, Rosenzweig, and Heschel—ever did their thinking as part of a movement or in the context of its ideology. They simply tried to think through the truth of Judaism in their day as best they could understand it, and I have spent my life attempting to emulate them. Only one of my books for adults and only a few of my articles deal with Reform Judaism.

If you would like some specific, if rough, examples of my view of Reform Jewish decision-making today, look at my *Reform Jewish Ethics and the Halakhah* (Behrman, 1994). That book, with all its faults (e.g., its fourteen issues were tackled by teams of students who did term papers as my kind of Reform *poskim*), will show you the distance between my functioning theory of duty and the one you have imputed to my theology. Even though the students are far more Kantian than I am, you will not find "autonomy run amok" in any of their papers.

You see three issues dividing us: practicality, Jewishness, and philosophy. The first, practicality, has two parts: the heavy burden of being a responsible (Jewish) self and the role of community in our decision-making. I agree few of us can know all we need to know to make a significant decision. When I need help in such cases, I do what most people do: consult experts and read the most responsible literature I can find. I see no reason why responsible Jewish selves will not do the same on matters where Judaism is relevant.

You say that the Jewish self will not care, as you do, about what the Jewish community says on an issue. Maybe "your" Reform Jews are supposed to believe that, but not if they took my views seriously. In addition to what you correctly said about my situating the Jewish self inextricably in the Jewish people, consider what I wrote about proper Jewish decision-making as the climax to my argument in *Renewing the Covenant* (288–295). There I explain in some detail that because of its Covenanted situation, the Jewish self should make decisions based on: (1) what it believes God wants of it as a member of the Covenanted people; (2) which means it will be concerned with what the Jewish community today is saying on this topic (more of this below); (3) but the experience of Covenant being fundamentally historical, what rabbinic tradition said on the topic must be given reverent attention; (4) as must the messianic, future-oriented thrust of the Covenant. But all those vectors finally come to rest (5) in an individual self whose individuality is not extinguished for all that it is utterly bound up with God and the Jewish people's relationship with God, historically articulated, presently lived, and projected to the End of Days. My six chapters and my second vector should make plain that I insist on community concern among Jews and know nothing of the unattached self in Judaism. If that means that I am not a Reform Jew by your standards, then so be it. It is equally clear that I am not your kind of Conservative Jew, for I do not closely identify "community" with rabbinic law-making as you do.

We disagree, however, about the possibility and desirability of law fulfilling its common function, being authoritative in our lives. You charge that my sense of "sociality does not . . . require obeying Jewish law." You are right. But has the Conservative movement, which has made law central to its ideology, yet found a way to "require obeying Jewish law"?

Your second objection to my position is that Jewish tradition knows nothing of individual Jews being given "the right to make decisions about what they should believe and practice." I agree that in sanctioning even a Covenantally limited autonomy, I, and certainly the Reform Jews who are more radical than I am, have moved away from classic Jewish faith. But by Maimonides' standards of *epikorsut*, the Conservative view (like that in Reform) that there is a significant human factor in revelation instantly puts you, too, in our situation.

I shall allow the defense to rest there. But I must point out that the authority of the self operates in contemporary Jewish law more significantly than you have acknowledged. On the simplest level, why do I know that I will find your forthcoming book on Jewish medical ethics highly persuasive, where a similar book by David Novak will be somewhat less so and the writing of J. David Bleich on the same topic will likely touch me only informationally? Surely what divides this trio is not what the legal texts objectively say, for you will all study the same ones. It is also not substantially a matter of consulting the community (though I imagine that your disparate reference groups will have some influence on you). Rather I suggest that we are dealing with the way in which the self makes itself felt even in legal decision-making. One factor in decision-making is simply who you are as a person and how you act on that individuality. Were you a different person, you would not be the *posek* (decisor) we know you to be, the author of your *shitah* (approach).

Or let me give a case more internal to the Conservative movement. Consider the situation of Conservative rabbis faced with a split decision of the Committee on Jewish Law and Standards. How do they finally reach a decision about a difficult issue? The critical texts can apparently be read in at least two ways, and they cannot ask the community to settle the matter, for it is just its leaders who are of two minds. I suggest that, in significant measure, they will follow my five-part schema: they will seek to determine what God now wants by filtering their living religiosity through Jewish history, the community's present experience, and its ongoing messianic aspiration and, finally, subject the whole to the reality of who they individually are and what they personally believe. You and they may take step three—studying Jewish law and lore—with a somewhat greater sense of obligation than I might, but we shall all be following the theology of Jewish duty explicated in *Renewing the Covenant*.

I hope you will take the length at which I have written as a token of my great personal esteem for you and your writings over the years. I have learned much from you in the past and look forward to doing so in the future. I do hope you will have the opportunity to respond to what I have written here, and I will look forward to hearing from you about it.

MATTERS OF DEGREE AND KIND: AN OPEN RESPONSE TO EUGENE BOROWITZ'S OPEN LETTER TO ME
ELLIOT N. DORFF

I love being challenged by you! Your letter, as you undoubtedly hoped, forced me to reread your book, especially the chapters to which you refer. I also pondered your letter for quite some time.

I admit that I first read your book through the prism of your earlier writings and your long association with Reform Judaism. While I recognized that there is much that is new in *Renewing the Covenant*—especially your redefined and recontextualized idea of the Jewish self—I did not appreciate the extent to which you wanted to distinguish this work from your previous writings and from Reform thought in general. For that I apologize. (Incidentally, Rabbi Robert Gordis, z"l, was no more independent in crafting *Emet Ve-Emunah: The Philosophy of Conservative Judaism* than you report that you were in editing the Reform Movement's *Centenary Perspective*. Rabbi Gordis did not write the first draft of any of the sections of *Emet Ve-Emunah*, and the commission charged with writing it debated every sentence—indeed, virtually every word. His good sense, energy, and wide respect within the movement, though, permeated our discussions and kept them on track—a role that, I would bet, you played too.)

On rereading *Renewing the Covenant*, then, I would agree that we are closer than I had previously thought. From one perspective, what separates us is, as you suggest, a matter of degree: I take studying Jewish law and lore with "a greater sense of obligation" than you do. That, though, is not only a difference in background or temperament; it is also a difference in conviction, one, I think, that ultimately amounts to a difference in kind.

As I see it now, the distinction between us centers around our conceptions of law. You draw a sharp distinction between "standards" and "duty," on the one hand, and "authoritative law," on the other. Do you mean to suggest that norms become law only when they are enforced? That is certainly a possible understanding of law, but it is an awfully narrow one, one which, I think, does not do justice to how either secular or religious law operates. Think, for example, of Prohibition. There you had nothing less than a Constitutional amendment, with the full force of the federal government behind it, yet it failed as a law and ultimately had to be repealed. Why? Because, I would suggest, the authority of any particular law or legal system is based on a whole range of factors—communal acceptance of the law or system as generally wise, moral, practical, or all three; a sense of covenantal promise to abide by the law, whether one agrees with it or not (Do you really like every American law?); love of country; fear of chaos; a desire to be part of a coherent, well-integrated community; and perhaps even an aspiration to create an ideal society. Even though the vast majority of Americans obeyed the Prohibition Amendment and the laws enacted to carry it out, federal and state police forces combined were not sufficient to enforce those laws on the small percentage of Americans who disobeyed them— precisely, I would suggest, because the other elements noted above that make a law authoritative were missing.

If Prohibition graphically demonstrates in a secular legal system the limitations of restricting law to that which is enforced, the Golden Calf incident does the same in Jewish law. Just a short forty days after the awesome thunder, lightning, and earthquakes of Sinai, the Israelites were already worshiping the Golden Calf! The Bible was thus not only philosophically sophisticated but pragmatic and wise in suggesting nine separate motivations to abide by Jewish law, and the Rabbis added several more. I discuss these at some length in my book *Mitzvah Means Commandment*.[4] Religious legal systems, like Jewish law, add motivations to obey to those inherent in secular law—motivations like the aspiration for holiness, the drive to complete a divine mission, and love of God.

This affects our discussion in two ways. First, while I, too, would distinguish between authoritative law and moral standards, I would not draw the line nearly as sharply as you do. In my view, law can be amoral or even immoral, as a dictator's dictates may be. Nazi Germany's laws obviously come to mind. But when a secular legal system, like that of the United States, strives from the very beginning to embody moral values—in America's case, to secure individuals' "unalienable rights" (the Declaration of Independence) and to "establish Justice, insure domestic Tranquility, provide for the common defence, promote the general Welfare, and to secure the Blessings of Liberty to ourselves and our Posterity" (the Preamble to the Constitution)—then the law becomes permeated with moral concerns. I am not claiming that American society was ever morally ideal or is now. I am claiming only that the law is used in America not only as a tool for social peace and defense, but also for moral goals like justice, liberty, and the general welfare.

That is even more true for a religious legal system like Jewish law, which is, according to the Torah, given by a God of justice and mercy and demands that we strive to be holy like God and to "do the right and the good in God's eyes" (Deut. 6:18). Once again, because human beings are fallible and because the conditions of life and moral sensitivities change, Jewish law as it has come down to us does not always articulate the highest moral standard, and it certainly does not guarantee that those who follow it will necessarily be moral. Nevertheless, much of Jewish law does indeed set a high standard of morality for us, for Judaism, perhaps more than any other legal system on Earth, strives to embody moral norms in legal form. Judaism cannot totally succeed in that effort, for life is too complex for any legal system to cover every possible eventuality. Moreover, life changes too much over time to be guided sensitively by the specific rules of the past. Hence there will always be a realm of moral duty and an even larger realm of moral goals beyond the limits of the law, and the law itself must be continuously subjected to moral critique. Nevertheless, a great deal of the authority of Jewish law derives from its moral base—whether or not it is enforced.[5]

Second, my understanding of the authority of Jewish law—and of its history—leads me to a different picture than you have of the role of the individual in the system. Yes, certainly, the Enlightenment gave us a new appreciation of the independence of the individual as a source of autonomous will and even moral values, and yes, certainly, I share both your gratefulness for those lessons and your commitment to individual liberty. The Enlightenment amounted to nothing short of a revolution in human thought, one that brought us many boons. Your book, more than any other I know, consciously tries to integrate that modern sense of individualism into a new approach to Jewish life and law.

In some ways, I want to strengthen your position by pointing out that even in the predominantly communitarian world of classical Jewish law, individuals always had a role in formulating it. On the other hand, though, I would claim that classical Jewish law framed the role of individuals in shaping the law in ways that are not only different from the one you propose, but, I think, ultimately healthier for individual Jews and the Jewish community.

As Louis Finkelstein, Jacob Neusner, Joel Gereboff, and others have demonstrated, the rulings of the classical rabbis were critically dependent upon their individual personalities, circumstances, and philosophies of life. Thus if you expect to warm to my treatment of Jewish medical ethics in my forthcoming book, *Matters of Life and Death,* more than you have liked David Novak's or J. David Bleich's readings of Judaism on that subject—and I deeply appreciate your support!—it may be because of the same personal factors that have affected Jewish law from time immemorial.

I would go even further. You say that the significant human element that I ascribe to Jewish law "cannot be on the basis of Jewish law and tradition, for they do not grant human beings that much power." Yes, they do! After it is all said and done, our Judaism is the religion of the Pharisees, not of the more fundamentalist Sadducees of their time or the Karaites of later generations. The Pharisees, our "Rabbis," insisted that rabbis in every generation had to determine the substance of the law. They also insisted that it was wrong to refuse to do that on the grounds that previous generations had judges like Moses and our generation's judges pale by comparison (*T. Rosh Hashanah* 1:17; *B. Rosh Hashanah* 25a–25b). The Rabbis furthermore maintained that after the destruction of the First Temple, revelation would come in the form of the Rabbis' interpretation of the Torah. They even asserted that a new, fully recog-nized revelation from God Himself could not overpower the author-ity of each generation's rabbis to determine the content of revelation in their time (*B. Bava Metzia* 59b). Some Orthodox rabbis deny this inevitable and divinely authorized human element in discerning God's will. They are misrepresenting rabbinic Judaism, however, as articulated in the texts I just cited and many others, and they are deceiving them-selves. After all, if God's will is so transparent as to be clear without any human interpretation, how can Orthodox rabbis disagree among themselves? Moreover, those rabbis who refuse to recognize the effects of their own methodology on their decisions are, I repeat, less well able to discern God's will than those who acknowledge the human element in the ongoing process of legal midrash. A striking formulation of this point was written by Rabbi Emanuel Rackman, an Orthodox rabbi himself, in his article "Challenge to Orthodoxy," reprinted in his book *One Man's Judaism*.[6]

(Incidentally, on this point we disagree as well in our interpretation of Maimonides. Maimonides takes the rabbinic idea that "the Torah was given in the language of human beings" further than the Rabbis ever did by painstakingly spelling out, in part 1 of his *Guide for the Perplexed*, the literal meanings of many of the metaphors in the Torah. Moreover, in his *Mishneh Torah* [Laws of Rebels, chapter 2], he explicitly supports the authority of rabbis in each generation to make decisions, even, at times, against the Torah. These parts of his writings indicate that he surely assumes that "there is a significant human factor in revelation" in both its process of transmission and in its legal products—although obviously not to the extent of assigning the writing of the entire text of the Torah to human beings, as modern scholarship does.)

My understanding of the place of individuals in shaping classical Jewish law thus makes your question all the stronger: If individual rabbis in all their individuality have influenced the outcome of Jewish law, why do I put so much emphasis on the community of rabbis as the ones who determine its substance? Why not think of the Jewish community much more broadly, as you do, to include each individual Jew as the one who makes that decision?

I embrace the rabbinic method for defining Jewish law because, in part, Jews have done so for generations, and I want the historical rootedness I gain in retaining this method. I also want the coherence and community that come with the rabbinic method. I fear that individualism, even in your modified form, will lead to anarchy and isolation. I also believe, as I said in my earlier statement, that individual Jews—indeed, individual rabbis, myself certainly included—do not have the expertise or wisdom to make these decisions on their own. You yourself describe the process by which individuals make decisions as consulting others when they do not know what to do. I simply want to institutionalize that process—and retain a stronger sense of community and legal coherence—by putting Jewish decisions in the hands of those who know Jewish law in addition to the realities of modern life. They, of course, may have to consult experts in other fields in formulating their decisions, just as judges in any legal system do. But the decision will then be rooted in Jewish sources and thus become recognizably Jewish to all who examine it, even to those who disagree with it. For all these reasons, we must take seriously the lessons not only of ancient times, but also of recent years, when we have increasingly come to recognize the proper limits of individualism, even of the Jewishly informed and committed self of whom you speak.

This, then, brings me to the last issue, the relationship of the rabbis to the laity. On one hand, you valorize the position of the individual—the

Jewish self—in making Jewish law. In your letter, though, your example of how your brand of Jewish individualism would work in practice is the series of essays written by your rabbinical students. That hardly argues for how lay Jews will live by your theory. Indeed, historians like Jacob Neusner assert that even at the time of the Pharisees most lay Jews did not know enough to practice Jewish law accurately, let alone make decisions in Jewish law.

What I would assert, though, is that the laity as a group do indeed have halakhic power through their communal practices, their *minhagim* (customs). Jewish law throughout the ages has been the product of an *interaction* between the spiritual leaders of the community (whether prophets or rabbis) and its members. In Jewish law, as in American law, sometimes law creates new customs, sometimes law repudiates common customs and seeks to uproot them, sometimes customs undermine laws, and sometimes customs serve as the source of new laws. In all these interactions between law and custom, the community as a whole has an immense effect on the shape of the law. That role for the laity, though, is decidedly communal, and even though the entire community may adopt a practice objectionable to the rabbis, I would much rather trust the community as a whole than individual lay members in it—just as I would rather trust the community of rabbis rather than individual rabbis, including myself.

In sum, it may be, as you say, that much of our disagreement stems from the greater sense of obligation that I assign to studying Jewish law and lore and to acting in accordance with it. I think, though, that some of the matters that divide us stem from differences in convictions about the nature of law and the respective roles of rabbis and lay people in determining its rules. With all that, we share a deep commitment to the Jewish tradition, and I love to be prodded to rethink the nature and grounding of my own commitments by your probing questions and creative ideas. May we continue to engage together in this ongoing wrestling with God and with Judaism for many years to come.

PART 3

The Real Deal

Personal and Social Ethics

10

Abortion after the Overturning of *Roe v. Wade*

My first real, nontheoretical exploration of a moral topic began in 1973, when the U.S. Supreme Court asserted a Constitutional right to abortion in its decision *Roe v. Wade*. Rabbi David Berner, then associate Hillel director at UCLA and a rabbinical school classmate of mine, had arranged a lunchtime panel at UCLA's medical school about the ruling and asked me to be the third panelist, along with a physician and a priest. At the time I had read exactly one article about Judaism and abortion, but I agreed to do David this favor. And thus began my real interest in Jewish views of medical ethics. Subsequent invitations to write about various ethical issues in academic and popular publications and to address such issues for the Committee on Jewish Law and Standards only nurtured my fascination with the subject, which I elected to explore all the more in two books, *Matters of Life and Death: A Jewish Approach to Modern Medical Ethics* (1998) and *Jews and Genes: The Genetic Future in Contemporary Jewish Thought* (2015, coedited with Laurie Zoloth).

So when the Jewish Federation Council of Los Angeles asked Los Angeles–area rabbis, including me, to respond on its website to the U.S. Supreme Court's June 2022 decision to overturn *Roe v. Wade*, it felt like coming full circle in my bioethical explorations. My response, updated for this publication, follows.

Jewish law is much more nuanced on abortion than either the Catholic position or the 1973 U.S. Supreme Court decision *Roe v. Wade*. The Catholic view classifies a fertilized embryo as a full human being, but that mistakes the potential for the actual, for we have ample evidence that somewhere between 60 to 75 percent of fertilized eggs in women's bodies miscarry, most in the first month of pregnancy, often before the woman knows that she is pregnant.[1] The Talmud, based on Exodus 21:22–25 and undoubtedly on the miscarriages that the Rabbis witnessed, classifies the developing embryo as "simply liquid" during the first forty days of pregnancy and "like the thigh of its mother" from then until birth.[2] It is only when the head or, in a breech birth, most of the fetus's body emerges from its mother's body that it becomes a full human being in Jewish law, with the attendant legal protections of that status. Consequently, in Jewish law, feticide is not the same as homicide.

At the same time, the embryo and, later, the fetus is a developing human being, and we do have a duty to procreate, an obligation that is especially important to remember in this era, when Jews are facing a major demographic crisis. So in traditional Jewish law abortion is required when the life or physical or mental health of the woman is at stake; and it is permitted, according to many but not all rabbis, when there is a risk to the woman over that of normal pregnancy or when the fetus will suffer from a lethal or devastating disease; but by and large Jewish law would prohibit abortion for other reasons. In that way, Jewish law is less permissive than *Roe v. Wade*.[3] Still, some contemporary Jewish feminist thinkers would further expand the reasons for permitting abortion in the Jewish tradition, perhaps even beyond what *Roe v. Wade* would permit.[4]

How Judaism views abortion, though, however interpreted, should not be the basis of American law, and neither should the stance of any other religion. This understanding of the necessary separation of church and state goes back to Thomas Jefferson, who asserted that when Americans overwhelmingly agree on a moral issue (e.g., prohibitions of murder, theft, and rape and positive duties to pay taxes and educate your children), the state may enforce that moral stance as law, but when Americans disagree about a moral issue, the government should leave it to each citizen to determine what is proper.[5] Abortion clearly fits into the latter category.

So the June 24, 2022, U.S. Supreme Court decision, *Dobbs v. Jackson Women's Health Organization*, which enables states to prohibit abortion altogether or substantially restrict it, violates Jefferson's wise balance of how people of multiple faiths and none can live together amicably and productively. As such, it is bad for mutual respect among Americans and for American unity. It is also a major blow to the individual liberty that is one important source of American identity and pride. It additionally violates freedom of religion, for in many states, abortion will be prohibited in cases in which Jewish law and the stances of many other religious and secular groups would require it or permit it. It effectively establishes the Catholic and Evangelical Christian view of the fetus, which categorizes a zygote as a person and therefore all abortions as murder, in violation of the Establishment clause of the First Amendment, which forbids any religion to be the source of authority for American law. For all these reasons, it is a very bad decision.

11

Sexual Orientation and Human Dignity

Growing up in the 1950s, I did not know—or, more correctly, I did not know that I knew—anyone who was anything but cisgender and heterosexual. My first widening of perspective was in college in 1961: reading Plato's *Symposium*, which asserts that the proper consummation of a teacher-student relationship between males is to have sex together. This struck me as outlandish, even funny, at the time. About a decade later, when I was teaching at the University of Judaism in Los Angeles, a rabbi in Cleveland asked me to meet with a young man who had grown up in his congregation, had become president of that United Synagogue Youth region, and had been attending the joint Columbia University–Jewish Theological Seminary program, but once he came out as a gay man, he felt shunned by the seminary community and transferred to UCLA. His rabbi wanted me to reassure him that he was still appreciated as a person and as a Jew.

This young man opened my eyes to what it was like to be a committed Conservative Jew and yet rejected by that community for who he was. I felt thoroughly embarrassed by what the Jewish tradition that we both cherished had done to him, but I did not know how to respond except to tell him what his rabbi back home had said and what I too believed: that he was a cherished member of the Conservative Jewish community, regardless of his treatment by some members.

Because of my interest in bioethics, I was a member of the Ethics Committee at UCLA Medical Center in the early 1980s, when the AIDS epidemic broke out, and then joined its special task force to determine emergency room procedures to protect doctors and nurses from contracting AIDS. Even though AIDS was primarily a heterosexual disease in Africa, where it first broke out, in the United States it largely began as a disease affecting gay men, so I met a number of gay men there. Subsequently, in 1986, I became a founding member of the Board of Nechama: Jewish AIDS Services, which, among other things, provided meals to people suffering with AIDS and their caregivers. So when the Conservative Movement's Committee on Jewish Law and Standards (CJLS) first addressed gay and lesbian identity and sexual relationships, in multiple meetings between 1989 and 1992, I was one of the few committee members who knew anyone who was openly gay.

In March 1992 the CJLS adopted three rabbinic rulings prohibiting same-sex sexual relationships for different reasons and banned gay or lesbian Jews from attending rabbinical school. I wrote a fourth rabbinic ruling suggesting that gay and lesbian Jews would rightfully ignore what we said about their sexual activity because we Conservative rabbis had never described the Jewish norms governing heterosexual couples as we interpret them for our time and that, in any case, we did not know enough about sexual orientation to rule about it; we should therefore establish a commission to write a document about Jewish norms for heterosexual couples and further research gay and lesbian identity.[1] My ruling got eight votes of the twenty-five rabbis voting, but that was enough to be an official CJLS position, and it did lead to the creation of such a commission. Moreover, the commission and the CJLS ultimately endorsed my document *"This Is My Beloved, This Is My Friend" (Song of Songs 5:16): A Rabbinic Letter on Intimate Relations*.[2] This document described Jewish values and norms for heterosexual sex within and outside marriage, noted the then-available evidence that trying to change a person's sexual orientation is both ineffective and harmful, and recorded the Rabbinical Assembly and United Synagogue of Conservative Judaism resolutions that gay and lesbian Jews should be made to feel welcome in our synagogues even though Conservative rabbis were not allowed to officiate at same-sex weddings and gay and lesbian Jews were not eligible to attend rabbinical school within the movement.

In 2003 Rabbi Reuven Hammer, president of the Rabbinical Assembly, and Judy Yudoff, president of the United Synagogue of Conservative Judaism, asked the CJLS to revisit this issue. That led to three years of discussing this issue. It included interviews of experts on sexual orientation, the heads of Episcopalian and Presbyterian commissions addressing the same issue, a gay Conservative rabbi who had been in the closet during rabbinical school, and his parents. Ultimately, on December 6, 2006, thirteen of the CJLS's twenty-five rabbis voted for Rabbi Joel Roth's responsum reaffirming the bans on Conservative rabbis officiating at same-sex weddings and on admitting gay and lesbian Jews to rabbinical school, and thirteen of the twenty-five voted for a responsum by Rabbis Daniel Nevins, Avram Reisner, and me allowing both of those.[3] (One rabbi voted for both responsa because he wanted to further pluralism within the movement.)

The Ziegler School of Rabbinic Studies in Los Angeles immediately announced that it would admit qualified gay and lesbian Jews, and after intense faculty and board discussions the Jewish Theological Seminary in New York followed suit several months later. It took more time for the Schechter Rabbinical School in Jerusalem and for the Seminario Rabbinico Latin Americano in Buenos Aires to do the same. The percentage of Conservative rabbis who have officiated at same-sex weddings has increased over time but still, to this day, some will and some will not.

Rabbis Nevins, Reisner, and I assumed that many rabbis would write ceremonies and documents for same-sex weddings and divorces, and some did, but we were increasingly asked to create at least a template for such events and documents. We did that in 2012 in an appendix to our original responsum.[4] Notably, the CJLS approved that appendix by a vote of fifteen in favor and none opposed, indicating that, in the interim, the opinion of many Conservative rabbis (along with many Jews and Christians worldwide) had shifted significantly in favor of permitting such ceremonies to honor such unions.

Today's readers of the 2006 Dorff-Nevins-Reisner responsum might find portions of it jarring.[5] Its title and content refer to "homosexuals" and "homosexuality," terms the 2012 appendix subsequently replaced. It talks about straight and gay people in a binary way rather than in today's LGBTQ+ language and does not address transgender issues. (For that, see Rabbi/Dr. Leonard Sharzer's 2017 responsum.)[6] It also suggests that bisexual people prefer the heterosexual part of their identity; a December 2022 addendum says otherwise:

> Sixteen years later it is gratifying to consider the blessings that flowed from our 2006 responsum and its 2012 companion dealing with same-sex marriage and divorce. It is now unremarkable for our clergy to officiate at weddings for same-sex couples, and for our seminaries to ordain clergy regardless of sexual orientation. In hindsight, our focus on human dignity remains cogent—it is a core principle of Jewish theology, ethics and law, and has been a powerful corrective to the negative attitudes and norms that were often expressed in prior halakhic literature. One aspect of our 2006 teshuvah has not stood up as well—our statement that Jews who identify as bisexual may not make use of the human dignity waiver from the ancient sexual norm since they, in theory, are able

to form a satisfying heterosexual relationship. The problem with this argument is that it undermines the essence of dignity—the equal ability of all people to understand their own identity and to choose their own life-partner. Rather, we now encourage Jews of all sexual orientations to establish a committed relationship and ideally a marriage with a fellow Jew who is the choice of their heart, whatever their gender identity, and to establish a faithful household among the people of Israel.

All this notwithstanding, the 2006 responsum accomplished two achievements remarkable for its time: permitting Conservative rabbis to officiate at same-sex weddings and sanctioning the movement's rabbinical schools to admit and ultimately ordain gay and lesbian Jews. Notably, underlying our responsum's arguments were two core tenets: the Jewish tradition's ascription of dignity to human beings—a dignity defined as the inherent worth each of us human beings possesses as someone created in the image of God (see chapter 3)—and the talmudic principle that human dignity overrides rabbinic rulings. Intrinsically, every human being has this dignity regardless of gender identity, sexual orientation, race, age, level of ability or disability, or even the morality of our actions, because God has implanted this worth within us.

Rabbi Nevins and I subsequently expounded on the meaning and status of human dignity in the Jewish tradition while summarizing the 2006 responsum in an article, "Dignity: A Jewish Perspective," published in *Value and Vulnerability: An Interfaith Dialogue* (2020).[7] The text below is drawn from my portions of that article.

> The stamp of God in each one of us means that we must treat everyone else with respect. This does not mean that we must like everyone else or approve of their deeds, but it does mean that we may not slander them or denigrate them. So, for example, the Torah not only allows but demands that we give constructive criticism when it is warranted— "You shall surely reprove your neighbor so that you do not hate someone in your heart"; it prohibits taking revenge or bearing a grudge against another; and it demands that we must "love your neighbor as yourself" (Lev. 19:17–18). Judaism makes moral distinctions among acts and modes of character, and it gives us guidance as to how to put those distinctions into practice; but in the end, even those who commit capital

crimes must be punished for them in ways that preserve their inherent value as creatures and reflections of God.[8]

Although in many other traditions one shows respect for others by accepting whatever they say, in the Jewish tradition the reverse is true. Showing respect means attentively listening to what other people say and taking their statements seriously enough to question them and even argue with them. This argumentative mode of the Jewish tradition is also based on a deep theological conviction that although God may be omniscient, no human being is, so the best way for us to attain truth, goodness, and wisdom is to pool our intellectual and moral resources in serious conversation. That conversation also needs to have a degree of humor in it—and Jews are also known for their sense of humor—because although we need to take life seriously and do the best we can to make it better for everyone, we also need to have a humble understanding of what we can know and do.

Conversely, rabbinic law prescribes financial penalties for shaming someone.[9] It measures that shame by any of three criteria: (1) if the person feels the shame, so sleeping people, for example, could not collect monetary damages for shame because they did not feel it, at least at the time the shaming occurred; (2) if the family feels it, so that even if the disgraced person does not feel shame, the family could collect monetary damages from those who insulted the family member; and (3) if the community considers the person to have been shamed, even if the disgraced person does not feel it.[10] Humiliating another person is considered akin to murdering them, if not in body then in social standing.[11] Furthermore, shaming a person is effectively shaming God: if you shame others, "know Who it is you despise, for 'in the image of God did God make the human.'"[12] Within the classical halakhic literature, human dignity is proclaimed to be a "great" value capable of overriding competing normative claims.[13]

Human Dignity, Sexual Orientation, and Gender Identity

In the past half century, various rights movements have asserted, more or less explicitly, that human dignity requires equal treatment—regardless of race, gender, sexual orientation, gender identity, or physical and mental ability. Jews in Western societies have advanced similar arguments for centuries (recall Shylock's soliloquy, "Hath not a Jew eyes?"), and in recent decades the Jewish community has generally, although not consistently, supported the rights agenda.[14] Classical Jewish texts about humans being created in the divine image and the obligation to love one's neighbor as oneself (Lev. 19:18) have been cited to support these newly vocalized expressions of human dignity. And yet, it is also the case that many classical Jewish norms have been experienced as obstacles, not resources, for the expansion of the realm of human dignity.

After all, Jewish classical texts are patriarchal, told from a male perspective, with females related to as "other" and frequently as subject to male demands. The Sages recognized that some people occupied intersex categories, yet their normative world was deeply binary, with men and women assigned distinct social, legal, and ritual roles. Rabbinic texts do not classify people by sexual orientation, but they do prohibit and even criminalize sexual intimacy between members of the same sex. Great sensitivity is expressed in biblical and rabbinic texts for the dignity of people who are elderly, infirm, or disabled. Yet there remains a hierarchy of Jewish obligation and thus of dignity in classical Jewish sources such that a healthy Jewish male occupies the upper echelon of the Jewish community.[15]

Rabbi Nevins and I have dedicated much of our Jewish legal writings to expanding the application of human dignity to people who have been excluded or even oppressed by our tradition. As one example, with Rabbi Avram Reisner, we wrote the 2006 responsum "Homosexuality, Human Dignity and Halakhah," making the core argument that human dignity is such a powerful value of Jewish tradition that it has the capacity to supersede all but the most explicit biblical norms that are found to undermine the dignity of gay and lesbian people. As we say there:

In this responsum, we will argue that the permanent social and sexual loneliness mandated by halakhic precedent for homosexuals undermines their human dignity. However, we reject attempts to distort this argument by claiming that, if so, every human desire deserves to be satisfied. In fact, Judaism teaches us constantly to bend individual desire to fulfill the will of God.[16] Some sexual desires must be delayed, and some must be permanently suppressed.[17] What distinguishes the situation of gay and lesbian Jews from others who experience forbidden sexual desires is that heretofore, gay and lesbian Jews have had absolutely no permitted avenue for sexual expression or for the creation of a committed romantic relationship. *It is this situation of absolute and permanent isolation that undermines their human dignity.*

We also pointed out "the strong scientific evidence . . . that current discriminatory attitudes toward gay men and lesbians do indeed undermine their dignity, evidenced by their much higher rates of suicide," as well as smoking and drug and alcohol abuse.[18] We concluded that for observant gay and lesbian Jews who would otherwise be condemned to a life of celibacy or secrecy, their human dignity requires suspension of the rabbinic level prohibitions so that they may experience intimacy and create families recognized by the Jewish community.

Tension between traditional norms and contemporary perceptions of social experience is not surprising, nor need it incapacitate responsible leaders. Our method includes both respect for and generous criticism of former generations of Jewish scholars together with curiosity and sympathy for the experiences of our contemporaries, leading us to interpretations of Jewish law that respect the wisdom of the ages and the dignity claims being expressed in our day.

12

Providing References When the
Truth May Be Harmful

Like most people, in the course of applying to schools or jobs I asked people who knew me in a relevant way to write letters of recommendation for me. Over the fifty-two years I have taught at American Jewish University (formerly University of Judaism), I must have written hundreds of such letters for my students. Additionally, as part of admissions committees for applicants to rabbinical school, I have, in turn, read hundreds of such letters written by others. So the ethics of writing and evaluating such letters has been an important part of my life.

Because many others are asked to write or read such letters, I decided to write a responsum for the Committee on Jewish Law and Standards (CJLS) on the subject. My first draft essentially concluded that writers should simply tell the truth—to which some committee members protested, "But you will be sued!"

Then I asked Marc Gary, a lawyer and lay member of the CJLS, to write a section on how to avoid being sued in writing such letters in American law, as one example of what at least one nation's laws provide to protect writers and readers of such letters from lawsuits. After all, nations have a vested interest in enabling accurate reference letters to be written to potential employers and schools so that they can function well, but civil laws also seek to protect the privacy of the subjects of those letters and ensure that they are not filled with unwarranted negative comments to the point of defamation. The responsum approved by the CJLS on April 14, 2014, (by a vote of eighteen in favor, one opposed, two abstaining) still asserted that one should tell the truth while observing the relevant rules in Jewish law that ban unnecessary negative speech about someone and included Marc Gary's instructions about how to do so with the protections available in American civil law.

Because this is a book on Jewish ethics, the text in this chapter is drawn almost exclusively from the sections of that responsum concerning Jewish law on this issue, with the exception of one paragraph in the conclusion that summarizes Gary's description of American law on this issue. Those who want to see the full responsum, which includes the relevant American legal provisions about references as well as a more extensive treatment of the Jewish values involved, can find it at https://www.rabbinicalassembly .org /sites /default /files /assets /public /halakhah /teshuvot /2011–2020 /providingreferences.pdf.

Some additional comments before we dive in. This and the next two chapters, largely focusing on forms of speech to avoid, are part of—and not the whole of—the Jewish ethics of communication. Judaism also counsels us to use our ability to communicate for beneficial purposes, including talking with others to help us think, plan, create, share ideas, bond, express love and support, and offer remorse for harm one caused others.[1] We are also to use our powers of speech to praise and thank God.

Furthermore, the Jewish tradition, like the Western liberal tradition embedded in the laws of most Western countries, values freedom of speech as an expression of the uniqueness and divine value of each one of us. The same applies to freedom of dress.[2] To protect individuals or society at large from harm, however, Jewish law imposes bounds to these freedoms—stricter ones than those in American law. As such, these three chapters describe Judaism's limits to our freedom of communication.

In many of the chapters to come, legal and moral norms interweave, such that while sometimes the discussion is either clearly legal or clearly moral in character, at other times it is more ambiguously one or the other. This reflects my own view of Jewish law, in which legal and moral norms, together with Jewish theological convictions, regularly do and should organically interact with each other.[3] That said, when appropriate, I will indicate when the norms at hand are clearly legal, or, in contrast, when they are clearly beyond the requirements of the law and therefore moral or even aspirational.

What Jewish norms govern giving oral or written references for schools or jobs? At first blush, the answer to this question seems obvious: just tell the truth. After all, the Torah demands that we "Keep far from falsehood" (Exod. 23:7). The prophet Zechariah urges, "Speak truth to one another" and "love truth and peace" (Zech. 8:16, 19). In the Talmud, R. Ḥanina declares, "The seal of the Holy Blessed One is truth"—and we, after all, are supposed to emulate God.[4] Elsewhere the Talmud asserts, "God hates the person who says one thing with his mouth and another with his mind," and Rabbi Jose ben Judah said: "Let your 'yes' be yes and your 'no' be no."[5]

So why is there any question here? There are three reasons this is a question worth considering. First, although the Jewish tradition does indeed value truth greatly, it also bids us to respect the honor of all God's creatures (*kevod ha-briyyot*), and an important way it instructs us to do that is through how we talk to and about other human beings.[6] In other words, in this area of life, as in most others, it recognizes that truth is not an absolute value but one that must be balanced with another value, in this case that of *kevod ha-briyyot*. Exactly how to do that is the topic of this responsum. Second, Jews are also governed by the laws of the nations in which they live, so with providing references they must consider not only what their religious tradition tells them to do, but also the civil laws and moral norms that govern this area of life, and hence integrate the instructions received from both legal and moral systems.

Finally, this responsum, as a responsum in Jewish law, applies directly to Jewish employees and company owners and the employees, administration, and lay leaders of Jewish nonprofit organizations. Jews, however, function in a largely non-Jewish world, so it will also address the question of Jews working for non-Jewish companies or agencies. In both contexts this responsum addresses precisely when Jews must live up to the standard of Jewish law on this issue, even at the cost of their jobs or of losing in the competitive race of business.

As we will develop below, the question at hand is both what duty does an evaluator have to tell the truth—and to whom and how much—and, conversely, what permission does an evaluator have to tell the truth—and to whom and how much—despite the real danger of undermining a person's candidacy for the school or job? Further, what are the grounds for establishing that duty and that permission? That is, what laws and values in the Jewish tradition require us to tell the truth—and to what extent—and what laws and values in the Jewish tradition permit us to do so although, because nobody is perfect, an evaluation will inevitably involve saying negative things about the person being evaluated?

The Misuse of Words

In the context of creating references for schools or jobs, the Rabbis' norms banning several forms of speech are relevant.

Lies (*Sheker*)

Telling lies—knowingly and intentionally telling someone something that you know to be false—undermines people's trust in one another. Indeed, at the extreme—that is, if everyone lied so often that one could never assume that the next person was telling the truth—social cooperation, commerce, friendships, and family relations would become impossible. We would all be living in a terrifying world. It is not surprising, then, that in several places the Torah specifically prohibits lying.[7]

The Rabbis understood the social consequences of lying: "This is the penalty for the liar: even when he tells the truth, no one believes him."[8] Moreover, they condemned lying as the worst form of theft: "There are seven types of thieves. The person who steals a person's thought (i.e., deception) is the worst of them."[9]

Why did the Rabbis think of lying as the worst form of theft? Why is it worse, say, than stealing money or property from another person? One answer is that even though people who have been robbed often feel personally violated, in the end the thief has encroached upon a person's property, and not upon that person. Often the thief does not even know the person. Deception, though, is immediately and directly personal: the liar knows you.

Of course, sometimes one tells a falsehood unintentionally, and the level of moral culpability is much less; one has simply made a mistake. Nevertheless, the Rabbis warn us against our very human desire to be seen as someone who knows everything, for that may lead us to give people false information: "Mar said: Teach your tongue to say 'I do not know,' lest you invent something and be trapped."[10]

That said, research seems to indicate that "kids who know how to deceive are smarter and better adjusted" than those who do not and that lying among adults is much more common than one might expect.[11] Still, the Jewish tradition would assert that both children and adults need to be taught not to use their abilities to lie to or deceive others. As is often the case, the fact that one can do something—in this case, deceive—does not mean that one should. On the contrary, increased ability requires increased moral sensitivity as to whether to use that power at all and, if so, under what circumstances.

Rabbinic literature does describe some exceptions to the general norm to tell the truth—lies told for the purposes of tact, peace, and providing hope:

Tact. When there is no practical purpose requiring the truth and those hearing it will only feel hurt, the Rabbis tell us to choose tact over truth, especially when the truth is a matter of judgment in the first place.[12]

Peace. The Rabbis deduce this second exception from the very words of God, who lied to Abraham to say that Sarah was worried that she was too old to have children rather than that he was; from the lie Joseph's brothers told Joseph after Jacob's death to try to attain his forgiveness and peace among the brothers; and from God's advice to Samuel to lie to Saul that he was coming to bring a sacrifice even though his real purpose was to tell him that God had decided to wrest the throne from him and give it to David.[13] The ultimate principle, then, is that "all lies are forbidden unless they are spoken for the sake of making peace."[14]

Clearly, there are some important limits to this. Lies have a way of being discovered, so lying even in the interest of making peace may not only fail to work but may make both parties angry at the peacemaker. Moreover, lies cannot cover up realities; if the parties really hate each other, false reports will not magically make things right and may well make them worse. Peace, if it is to be had, must rest on stronger foundations than lies, so one must take these biblical precedents with the proverbial grain of salt. One surely can and should omit nasty comments if one is trying to make peace; one can speak of each party's benign, broader intentions; and one can even interpret one party's remarks about the other more positively than the speaker probably meant them; but actually changing what someone said, even in the name of making peace, is asking for trouble.

Hope. Finally, rabbinic literature records some rabbis who condone or even demand that those visiting people who are very sick lie to them about the seriousness of their disease to help them retain hope for recovery. Such adherents base this on the biblical stories of Elisha's lie to the emissary of Benhadad, King of Aram (2 Kings 8:8–10, 14) and the change of fate of King Hezekiah, for both patients recovered despite predictions of their demise. The Rabbis extend this to ill patients hearing about others' deaths:[15]

Our Rabbis taught: If the close relative of a sick person dies, we do not inform the sick person lest he be emotionally overwhelmed (*tita-ref da'ato*).[16]

In modern times, however, when we often have a clearer idea of a patient's prognosis, I believe one should be truthful with patients so that they do not lose trust in what their physicians and family are telling them, and hence feel betrayed and abandoned. One *should* point out what the patient can realistically hope for and help the patient realize those hopes, if possible—hopes, for example, of reducing pain through more or different medication, reconciling with someone before death, or completing an ethical will. Pretending that the patient's physical condition is not as bad as it is, or that the prognosis is something other than what it is, ultimately serves neither the patient nor the value of truth.[17]

Tact and peace are not reasons to lie when providing references for schools or jobs, but the concern for fostering hope may be relevant. When there are reasonable grounds to believe that specific interventions will resolve particular problems in the person's candidacy, one should indicate that. This is not lying; it is providing a full picture of the candidate.

Slander (*motzi shem ra*) and Slurs (*lashon ha'ra*)

While saying false, negative things about a person (slander, *motzi shem ra*) is obviously problematic, as a form of lies intended to defame and hurt the person being described, in most situations Jewish law also prohibits negative comments that are true (slurs, *lashon ha'ra*). It even prohibits comments that are not defamatory but imply negative things about someone (*avak lashon ha-ra*, "the dust of saying bad things" or "the dust of slurs"). Maimonides defines these prohibitions this way:

> There are also words that are "the dust of slurs" (*avak lashon ha-ra*). How so? If A says to B, "Who would have ever thought that C would be as he is now?" Or A says, "Don't ask about C; I don't want to tell you what happened," and similar talk. Also, anyone who compliments a person in front of his enemies speaks the dust of slander, for that [positive talk] will cause his enemies to speak negatively of him. . . .
>
> All these are people who slur others, it is forbidden to live in their neighborhood, and even more to sit with them and listen to them.[18]

We may not defame a person, for we are required to respect each and every person as being created in the image of God. Therefore, as the following excerpt attests, to shame a person is effectively to shame God:

Ben Azai said, "This is the record of Adam's line. [When God created man, He made him in the likeness of God; male and female He created them]" (Gen. 5:1–2). This is a great principle in the Torah. Rabbi Akiba said: "Love your neighbor as yourself" (Lev. 19:18). This is a great principle of the Torah, for one should not say that because I have been shamed, let my fellow person be shamed with me, because I have been disgraced, let my fellow person be disgraced with me. Rabbi Tanḥuma said: If you did so, know whom you are shaming, for "God made him [the human being] in the likeness of God" (Gen. 5:1).[19]

One must value and protect the honor of other people, just as one values and seeks to protect one's own honor in the human community. Rabbi Eliezer said: "Cherish your fellow human's honor as your own."[20]

Furthermore, the dignity of every human being is such a strong value that it has the legal power to overrule rabbinic rulings that might diminish respect for a person or a group of people: "So great is human dignity that it supersedes a negative commandment of the Torah."[21]

The respect Jewish tradition demands for each and every human being does *not* mean that we must accept everything that anyone does. After all, the Torah is filled with laws that categorize certain forms of human behavior as prohibited and others as required, and if Jews fail to abide by those laws, the Torah demands that we reprove them (Lev. 19:17). But that reproof must be given in private, so as not to disgrace the person in public, and must be done constructively and with respect for the ultimate human dignity inherent in each of us.

When, though, may one say something negative about someone else? Indeed, when should one do so?

One may share negative information with someone else—and should do so—when ignorance of this information is likely to harm the recipient of the reference. This is in contrast to the many circumstances in which negative speech about a person serves no practical purpose for the listener but is just intended to diminish that person's honor. Rabbi Israel Meir Hakohen Kagan (Poland, 1838–1933) defines when *lashon ha'ra* is permissible and even mandatory:

One who wants to satisfy his obligations with regard to listening [to Lashon Hara] should conduct himself as follows: if someone were to approach him and should want to talk about another, and he understands that the speaker wants to speak negatively about the other person, he should ask the speaker, "Will the information that you want to tell me have future relevance to me, or will I thereby be able to rectify a situation by rebuking the offending individual, or some other positive outcome?" If the speaker replies that it does have future relevance or that he could correct a situation, it is permissible to listen to the information.[22]

Elsewhere, Rabbi Kagan lists the conditions under which one has a duty to give negative information about a person to a potential mate, business partner, or employer (and presumably the same would apply to a school considering a potential student). Although the lists are somewhat different, they both include the following conditions for revealing such information:

1. only if the problem is serious;
2. only if the person providing the reference does not exaggerate the nature or extent of the problem;
3. only if the sole motivation for revealing the information is to prevent harm to the person to whom it is supplied;
4. only if there is no way to protect the potential victim without engaging in a slur or gossip; and
5. only if there are reasonable grounds to presume that the information divulged will be a determining factor in making the decision.[23]

At the same time, another Jewish value comes into play here. We are, after all, required to help those in need, and, as Maimonides' famous ladder of *tzedakah* asserts, the highest form of doing that is by employing that person or, by extension, educating the person to be able to succeed at a job.[24] Thus, if the applicant has some negative qualities vis-à-vis the opportunity but these do not rise to the level of completely disqualifying the person or endangering the school or employer, the evaluator can and should say that this person would benefit from support in carrying out the required tasks, and specify the forms of support most likely to enable the candidate to succeed. Many schools now offer such support to students with special needs, and, in part because of the Americans with

Disabilities Act, more employers are making accommodations for some forms of disability as well.

Oppressive Speech (*ona'at devarim*)

Jewish law bans another form of speech that it calls "oppressive" based on Lev. 25:17, "Do not wrong one another." The Mishnah then defines what is included in this ban on verbal oppression:

> Just as there is wronging others in buying and selling, so too there is wronging others done by words. [So, for example,] one must not ask another, "What is the price of this article?" if he has no intention of buying. If a person repented [of his sin], one must not say to him, "Remember your former deeds." If a person is a child of converts, one must not say to him, "Remember the deeds of your ancestors," because it is written [in the Torah], "You shall neither wrong a stranger nor oppress him" (Exod. 22:20).[25]

The Mishnah's second example is relevant to our question. The Jewish tradition demands quite a lot of someone who has harmed another person. The wrongdoer must complete the process of return (*teshuvah*) described in Jewish sources, including acknowledgment of wrongdoing, remorse expressed in words to the harmed party, compensation to the victim to the extent possible, and ultimately better behavior when the same kind of situation arises again.[26] Once a person has completed the process of *teshuvah*, however, this Mishnah demands that other people not mention the person's former troubles, for doing so labels that person by the former offense, undermines the process of return, and denies the person the possibility of taking on a new, better identity—writing a new personal script, as it were. This Mishnah thus starkly contrasts with the practice in many American states, where former convicts have to list their convictions on any job application, are ineligible to apply for any government job, and, in some states, lose the right to vote.

Similar to what we saw earlier with regard to negative but true speech, however, there is an exception to this rule. If the person applies for a job that entails dealing with situations similar to the one in which the offense occurred, people who know of the person's past are not only allowed but *have a duty* to describe the offense to potential employers, to protect other people and even the applicant. The Rabbis interpret the principle of *lifnei ivair* (before those who are blind)—that is, "Do not place a stumbling block before the blind" (Lev. 19:14)—to include not only those who are physically blind, but those who are morally blind as well. So, for example, people should tell potential employers in a school, camp, or youth group setting that the applicant abused children in the past and hence would be inappropriate for the position.[27] For that matter, someone with a history of committing child abuse should not apply for such a position because the principle of *livnei ivair* applies to each individual Jew as well. Similarly, someone with a record of embezzlement should not seek, and should not be hired, to work in a company's financial office. In general, then, people should not put themselves or others in positions where they will be sorely tempted to do something wrong.

Revealing Positive or Negative Bias

Part of telling the truth about a candidate involves telling the truth about the evaluator too. For example, an evaluator who is a relative of the candidate must disclose that fact. Similarly, if the candidate owes the evaluator money, the evaluator must disclose that as well.

The Mishnah makes relatives ineligible to serve as witnesses—and, by extension, as judges—and that is later Jewish law as well.[28] In addition, any party who has a vested interest in either side of a case may not testify in court.[29] In writing an evaluation, the evaluator is indeed making a judgment about a person, and may have a positive or negative bias toward the candidate, but the evaluator's opinion is usually only one of several procured by the school or employer, so no one evaluation alone is likely to determine the outcome. Furthermore, as serious as it may be to a person's life to be denied a job or a place in a school, these are not legal penalties. So even though relatives and those with vested interests are ineligible to serve in the legal capacities of either judge or witness, they may serve as evaluators, as long as they disclose this fact to the potential employer or school.

P'sak Halakhah (Ruling)

1. The general rule: Tell the truth about the candidate. On the Jewish side of this question, because none of the exceptions to the rule to tell the truth apply to the context of providing references, we are left with the demand to tell the truth. Evaluators are cautioned to limit their remarks to what they know well about the candidate and acknowledge outright when they are not able to address select questions concerning the person's candidacy. To clarify this point, they might suggest that the inquirer contact other people who would know more about those aspects of the candidate's work than they do.

Ultimately, in accordance with the reluctance expressed in the Jewish tradition about saying negative things about people, and in recognition of the fact that past actions do not always predict future behavior, evaluators should respond to the questions asked and not volunteer negative information about a person—except if that information clearly establishes that the person would be dangerous for the school or job. Negative comments should be phrased in clear, respectful, and tactful terms, and indicate what realistic forms of support might help the candidate overcome weaknesses and thrive in the setting. Evaluators should comment on the candidate's specific actions rather than attempt to describe the person's general character, except to the extent that those character traits are relevant to the candidate's likely performance in the setting under consideration. At the other end of the spectrum, one should also avoid superlatives about the person unsubstantiated by the candidate's specific actions, for truth requires a realistic assessment of both the positive and negative aspects of a person's candidacy.

2. Telling the truth about the evaluator: Evaluators should disclose any positive or negative bias they have toward the candidate, such as the fact that the candidate is a relative of the evaluator or owes the evaluator money.

3. When to refuse to provide a reference: People asked by a candidate to provide a reference should refuse to do so if they do not know the candidate well enough to say anything substantive, or if the evaluator cannot know what facts about the candidate are relevant because the job description or the school program requiring the reference is unclear, for then the evaluation is likely to include either irrelevant or unsubstantiated negative information about the candidate. An exception to this last rule arises when the applicant is applying to a variety of different schools or jobs and requests a general letter of reference attesting to the applicant's academic or professional qualifications. If the candidate has not listed the person providing that general reference as a potential evaluator, and that person nevertheless finds out about the candidate's application for a particular opportunity, the individual does not have the right to contact the school or employer to provide such an evaluation, especially a negative one, without the candidate's consent, unless the candidate will pose a significant danger to the school or job, in which case one should inform the potential employer or school even if not asked.

4. Recipients of evaluations: Recipients of evaluations also have duties under Jewish law. They must investigate to determine whether what they are hearing about a person is indeed true. Otherwise they may be listening to outright lies or irrelevant, even if truthful, speech, thereby illegally aiding the evaluator in violating the law (*mesaye'ah l'davar aveirah*) and probably also harming the candidate. Recipients of recommendations should definitely not believe whatever they find on the internet about the person, and they should consult with several people who know the candidate to confirm what any of them says.

5. The effects of American law on this ruling: Nothing in American common law or statutory law prohibits an employer or former employer from providing truthful information regarding an employee's job performance, evaluation history, or other substantive information, whether positive or negative. In fact, the overwhelming majority of states have passed legislation designed to protect employers who—particularly in response to specific requests—provide candid job performance assessments to potential employers. To the extent that Jewish law (as described above) requires such candid references, American law does not stand as an insurmountable obstacle. Nevertheless, in our litigious society, most major companies and communal organizations have adopted what is called, based on military usage, an "NRS [name, rank, serial number] policy"—that is, one requiring employees to disclose nothing about any other employee except that the person worked at the company or studied at a school and on which dates. Saying anything more about a candidate risks facing the expense and disruption of being sued, and many institutions want to avoid that, even if they ultimately would win.

Given the compelling values underlying Jewish law on this issue, however, those are risks that Jewish employers, employees, and nonprofit organizations must accept in fulfilling their halakhic obligations. In the rare circumstances where, based on legal advice, an employee of a Jewish organization reasonably believes that a reference will subject the employer to severe financial hardship, the employee—acting with fiduciary duty to the employer—should formulate the reference in a way that best serves the underlying purposes of this responsum while protecting the employer.

6. Jews working for non-Jewish employers: Jews working for non-Jewish employers should follow this ruling when their employer has no policy about references, with the same caveat about acting consistently with one's fiduciary duty to protect the employer when the risk of severe financial hardship is present. When the non-Jewish employer has an NRS policy, Jews should generally abide by it, but see the next paragraph of this ruling.

7. A candidate who poses known risks of danger for a school or job: Regardless of whether a Jewish employee's employer is Jewish or not, and regardless of the financial risk involved, if the person asking for a reference has engaged in sexual abuse of children, committed a felony, or acted in other significantly dangerous ways relevant to the opportunity, the Jewish employee has the duty to warn the recipient of the reference of such dangers, spelling out the specific past behavior that demonstrates such danger. If the employer has an NRS policy, the Jewish employee is advised to consult with that employer before revealing the significant risk that the candidate poses, with the goal of convincing the employer either to make an exception to the NRS policy in this case or to amend the policy to permit a warning in such circumstances. Furthermore, a Jew who knows that a person will pose significant risk of harm to a school or job has a duty to inform the potential school or company even if not asked. In all such circumstances, however, one must recognize the range of certainty about the candidate's behavior and the degree of harm involved in deciding whether to violate or amend the NRS policy or inform a potential school or employer without being asked.

13

Avoiding Harmful Communication

I was very heavy in my early elementary school years. When some of the boys in my class called me "Fatty Boom Boom," I said, "Sticks and stones may hurt my bones, but names will never hurt me." The truth, though, was that the name did hurt, so much that I remember it to this day.

Years later, I was a counselor at Camp Ramah in Wisconsin, supervising a bunk of eleven-year-old boys, when about three days into the camp season, one of them began bullying another camper—but before I could intervene, another boy stopped it by saying, "No, we are not going to do that in this bunk." Bullying did not recur in my bunk that summer. The boy who intervened later became a professor and then dean of the school of social work at a major university.

In recent years, what once were episodes of harmful speech hurled at someone among a few people and unknown to others have now gone viral on the internet, leading to major harm to both the targets and the moral character of the people at fault. Some people accosted with derogatory names or remarks have developed major psychological problems and even committed suicide. Moreover, hate speech has increasingly led to hateful actions. Incidence of hateful remarks directed at Black, Jewish, Muslim, Asian, and LGBTQ+ people, individuals with disabilities, and others have dramatically risen in recent years, and the number of people harmed or killed as a result of this hate speech has also increased.[1] These personal and societal considerations prompted my responsum for the Committee on Jewish Law and Standards "Harmful Communication," from which this chapter is drawn. For the full responsum see rabbinicalassembly.org/sites/default/files/harmful_speech.final.june.pdf.

Here and in the next chapter, the concept of communication (or what I sometimes call "speech") is intended to be understood expansively to include in-person, written, behind someone's back, or posted remarks as well as what philosophers call "speech acts," such as body signals and the clothing one wears. The following text discusses forms of harmful communication that the Jewish tradition either prohibits or discourages (as distinct from chapter 12, which focused solely on forms of harmful speech that Judaism forbids: lies, slurs, slander, and oppressive speech).[2]

It is important to delineate the foundational Jewish views and values relevant to the legal topics of this responsum:

THE THEOLOGICAL CONVICTIONS AND MORAL VALUES UNDERLYING JUDAISM'S PROHIBITIONS OF HARMING OTHERS

1. **The human being is created in the image of God and thus deserves respect.** There are many ways in which this biblical concept that human beings were created in the image of God can be interpreted and applied, but surely one is that human beings deserve respect.[3] This does not mean that everything that a person does should be condoned, let alone praised, for Jewish law spells out many actions that a person should and should not do, but fundamental respect for each person is required. Conversely, disrespect of human beings amounts to disrespect of God. According to Genesis Rabbah:

Rabbi Akiba said: "Love your neighbor as yourself" (Lev. 19:18) is a fundamental principal of the Torah. You should not say that inasmuch as I am despised, let my fellow human being be despised with me, [or] inasmuch as I am cursed, let my fellow human being be cursed with me. Rabbi Tanḥuma said: If you act in this manner, know Who it is you despise, for "God made the human being in the image of God" (Gen. 1:27; 9:6).[4]

2. **As Creator of the world, God owns everything in it, including all human beings.**

Mark, the heavens to their uttermost reaches belong to the Lord your God, the earth and all that is on it. (Deut. 10:14)
The earth is the Lord's, and all that it holds, the world and its inhabitants. (Ps. 24:1)

3. **God requires us to care for others.** As Owner of everything, God insists that we use what we have to help others in need, with both their physical and emotional needs.[5]
4. **God requires that we not harm others.** Caring for others clearly also involves avoiding harming them. This includes their physical bodies, as evidenced by laws banning murder, assault, and exposing people to danger, but it also involves harming the psychological and social aspects of their beings, through words or actions that would undermine their self-respect or respect in society. Jewish laws governing some of those emotional harms are described in the previous chapter, and others are discussed in what follows in this one.

Gossip: *Rekhillut*

Gossip differs from slurs (*lashon ha-ra*) and slander (*motzi shem ra*) in that it does not necessarily involve negative information about a person. It is wrong because it divulges information about someone else that is and should remain private. Maimonides defines it in this way:

> Now what is the character of a tale bearer (*rakhil*)?—He that carries about news from one to another, and says: such and such a man said so and so; of such and such a man I have heard so and so.—Though it be true, yet it is pregnant with incalculable mischief to society [literally, destroys the world].[6]

Those perceptions and values undoubtedly motivated the Rabbis to interpret the Torah's prohibition "do not go about talebearing among your people" (Lev. 19:16), whose meaning in Hebrew is uncertain, to prohibit gossip, which violates one's privacy.[7] That said, there are some circumstances in which gossip and shaming serve important social purposes, so that the Jewish prohibition against these forms of speech needs to exclude such circumstances. In particular, gossip can reassure people that they are not the only ones with a given problem and give them information to help them solve it; it can also enforce group norms. As Benedict Carey reported in the *New York Times*:

> Long-term studies of Pacific Islanders, American middle-school children and residents of rural Newfoundland and Mexico, among others,

have confirmed that the content and frequency of gossip are universal: people devote anywhere from a fifth to two-thirds or more of their daily conversation to gossip, and men appear to be just as eager for the skinny as women.[8]

Sneaking, lying and cheating among friends or acquaintances make for the most savory material, of course, and most people pass on their best nuggets to at least two other people, surveys find.

This grapevine branches out through almost every social group, and it functions, in part, to keep people from straying too far outside the group's rules, written and unwritten, social scientists find.[9]

The discussions of gossip in Jewish sources that I have found do not talk about these socially positive uses of gossip to keep people in line, probably because the Torah also has a demand to rebuke others who do wrong, and the Rabbis then describe when and how it should be done.[10] Moreover, the Hafetz Hayyim specifically allows the communication of private and even negative information about people when it will have the practical value of protecting or aiding someone. (See chapter 11.) So although revealing private information about others is generally a violation of the Torah's commandment and prohibited as such, when that information can help someone in the same situation or when it can enable a society to identify rule-breakers and enforce communal norms, communicating it does not fall within the Torah's ban.

Purposely Misleading Others (G'naivat Da'at)

Although this type of wrongful speech could be seen as a form of telling lies, Maimonides and others treat it separately because it goes beyond a lie. It involves deliberately deceiving others in ways that can cause them harm, and thus involves fraud and its associated injuries or damages. Here is how Maimonides defines it, bringing together talmudic precedents, as he often does:

It is forbidden for a person to accustom himself/herself to flattering others (literally, "smooth talk") or seductive language; nor ought one to be otherwise in speech than one is in one's heart;[11] instead, the inner person ought to be like the outer person, so that the thoughts of one's heart are identical with the words of one's mouth.[12] Moreover it is not lawful to deceive (literally, "steal the mind of") another, not even the mind of a non-Jew. For instance, a [Jewish] person should not sell to a non-Jew the meat of a beast that died of itself as if it were the meat of a [kosher] slaughtered beast; or a shoe made of the hide of a beast that died of itself as if it were a shoe made of the hide of a [kosher] slaughtered beast.[13] Neither should a person press a friend to eat with him or her, when one well knows that the invited person will not eat with him or her;[14] nor may one try to force gifts on someone, when the giver well knows that the intended recipient will not accept them;[15] nor may one break open a barrel [of wine], which he actually needs to break open for sale, in order to persuade someone that he has opened it out of respect for him;[16] and similar matters. Even to utter one single seductive or deceptive expression is not lawful; but a person ought to have true speech (literally, "a lip of truth"), an upright soul, and a heart pure from evil designs and mischief.[17]

The biblical book of Proverbs waxes eloquent on the destructive ramifications of communicating deceitfully through words or body language, and the Tosefta maintains that "stealing a person's thought" is the worst kind of theft.[18] One particularly common and insidious example of this occurs when someone articulates an idea and does not acknowledge that the source of the idea was someone else. This happens not only in all cases of plagiarism but when someone of a higher rank in a company takes credit for an idea suggested by someone of lower status. Although this can happen in any gender combination, women often report that their male employers or bosses do this.

Purposely misleading others, however, must be distinguished from persuasive speech, in which someone is trying to convince someone else to buy something, as a salesperson does; to see a particular event in a particular way, as lawyers do for their clients before a judge or jury; or to encourage voters to elect a person to a political office. Such persuasive speech does not constitute prohibited misleading speech (*g'naivat da'at*) as long as the salesperson, lawyer, or politician does not outright lie about the product, situation, or intentions or does not hide relevant facts from the consumer, jury, or public. Such persuasive speech does not constitute prohibited misleading speech because of its context, which is critical in understanding both the meaning of words and the degree to which the hearer should trust them.

One very troubling practice that is legally acceptable in the United States allows police officers to deceive culprits in trying to extract confessions from them. Despite the U.S. Supreme Court's *Miranda* decision of 1966, many people begin talking without a lawyer present and are then subject to these deceptive techniques. Jewish law would see—and ban—such tactics as *g'naivat da'at.*

In sales situations, most countries generally abide by the Latin proverb caveat emptor, "Let the buyer beware." Jewish commercial law limits having to forewarn the buyer in cases where the communal custom is generally well known. (For example, if wine is regularly mixed with water, the buyer should expect that.) Otherwise, the Torah's ban against oppressing others (*ona'ah*) in both commerce and speech is interpreted to mean that, for example, one may not make something look better than it is by cosmetic improvements, and grain of inferior and good quality may not be mixed together and sold as if it all were of the higher quality.[19]

Similarly, deliberately spreading what one knows to be "fake news" in the media, a social platform, or anywhere else is prohibited by both the Torah's prohibition against lying and the rabbinic prohibition against deceiving others. Even sharing suspicious information must be avoided. We have the duty to tell the truth, and that requires checking to see if an assertion is in fact true if one knows, or should know, that it is likely not true.

Insulting Others: *Pi'gi'ah B'khvod Aharim*

Pi'gi'ah b'khvod aharim literally means harming the honor of others. It is different from the topic of the next subsection, *boshet*, shaming others. An insult is an attack on someone's honor in one respect but still leaves most of it intact, while shaming is a direct attempt to dishonor someone fully. This is certainly a difference in degree, but in some respects it is a difference in kind as well. The typical response to an insult, if someone is to mount one, is to attempt to correct the record on the specific issue raised. The likely response to shaming, on the other hand, is to either strike out vigorously to defend one's honor, maybe even by countershaming the perpetrator ("The best defense is a good offense"), or to go and hide.

Special care should be taken when interacting online. Insults delivered anonymously or hidden behind an account name are still insults and forbidden.

Insulting a person must be distinguished from constructive criticism of a person, which is not only permitted but required by Leviticus 19:17:

> You shall not hate your kinsfolk in your heart. Reprove your kinsman but incur no guilt because of him.

Such a rebuke must be in private and constructive. If it is done correctly, it can be understood not as an insult, but as help in becoming a better person or employee.

Why is insulting another wrong? In part, it is because the Torah says so. In the New Jewish Publication Society translation, the Torah prohibits insulting a person who is deaf:

> You shall not insult the deaf or place a stumbling block before the blind. You shall fear your God; I am the LORD. (Lev. 19:14)

Whether the Hebrew word in question, *t'kallel*, means "insult" or "curse," the result is the same: we are banned from insulting someone who is deaf. The Torah seems to be protecting the most vulnerable members of society, for presumably the person who is deaf could not hear the insult, and therefore the perpetrator could rest assured that there would be no retaliation. Beyond this, as part of one's duty to protect oneself, one should refrain from insulting those who do hear the insult and might harm us in response, for, as the Talmud makes explicit, our duty to protect ourselves takes precedence over our duty to protect others (*hayyekha kod'min*, "your life comes first").[20]

How should one respond to insults? The Rabbis advocate forgiveness rather than insulting the perpetrator back. Thus Rabbi Meir's description of the rewards for studying Torah for its own sake includes the ability of one who does so to "forgive an insult to him."[21] Maimonides later claims that such a person wins friends and sanctifies God's Name.[22]

Why would the Rabbis advocate forgiving those who insult you? Undoubtedly one of the reasons, in their minds, is that "two wrongs do not make a right." Moreover, as Maimonides suggests, forgiveness is good for the victim, for society generally, and even for God. It also fulfills the Torah's command not to take vengeance but to love our fellow humans, even when they do something unlovable:

> You shall not take vengeance nor bear a grudge against your country-men. Love your fellow as yourself: I am the LORD. (Lev. 19:18)

That said, forgiveness must be warranted. An insulted person need not and maybe should not forgive the perpetrator automatically, but should seek to repair the relationship until the person who uttered the insult makes amends (the process of *teshuvah*).[23]

Shaming Others: Prohibited *Boshet* and *Halbanat Panim* in Contrast to Acceptable and Even Desirable Political Parody and Satire

In a rightfully famous passage, the Rabbis use a Hebrew phrase for sham-ing, *halbanat panim*, literally, "turning the face white," to assert that sham-ing other people is akin to killing them because in both cases their blood drains from their faces and they turn white:

> The *tanna* taught . . : Anyone who humiliates another in public, it is as though he were spilling blood. Rav Naḥman bar Yitzḥak said to him: You have spoken well, as we see that after the humiliated person blushes, the red leaves his face and pallor comes in its place, which is tantamount to spilling his blood.[24]

As such, the penalty for shaming others is very severe. The perpetrator is not only liable for paying damages, but is among those who are perma-nently condemned to hell, however one understands that:[25]

> All who descend to Gehenna ultimately ascend, except for three [cat-egories of people] who descend and do not ascend, and these are they: A man who engages in intercourse with a married woman [other than his wife, as this transgression is a serious offense against both God and a person]; and one who shames another in public; and one who calls another a derogatory name. But the one who calls another a derogatory name is identical to one who shames him, [so why are they listed sepa-

rately?] Even if the victim grew accustomed to being called that [derogatory] name [in place of his actual name], and he is no longer humiliated by being called the derogatory name, the penalties for shaming a person apply because the perpetrator intended to insult the victim.[26]

In determining who must pay damages for shaming others, the Talmud offers nuanced discussion. One possibility is that the person must feel shamed, so shaming a sleeping person or a person who does not see the comments as shameful would not bring such penalties. Another possibility, though, is that penalties must be paid whenever the person's family would see the comments as disgraceful, and a third is when the public would see it as such, even if the person did not experience shame.[27]
Maimonides summarizes the laws against shaming others:

He who rebukes his friend should at first not use harsh expressions so as to put him to shame, for it is said: "But incur no guilt because of him" (Lev. 19:17). Thus the Sages say: lest it should be supposed that the rebuke may be carried so far as to make his face change [turn white or red out of embarrassment], Scripture warns us: "But you shall incur no guilt because of him."[28] Hence we know that it is not lawful for a person to put an Israelite to shame, and least of all in public; for although exposing a fellow person to shame is not an offense punished with the infliction of stripes, it is still a great sin. Thus the Sages say: "He who makes the face of his fellow person turn white in public forfeits his claim to the world to come."[29] A person should therefore be very careful with regard to this matter, not to put his fellow creature to shame in public, whether the victim be a person of importance or insignificant.[30] One should not call the other person by any name of which he or she may be ashamed, and one should not relate in someone else's presence anything that might cast reproach on that person.[31] This, however, applies only to relationships among people; but as regards offenses against Heaven, if the offender has turned his back to private rebuke, we may put him to shame before a multitude, make his sins public, reprove him in his presence, abuse and denounce him until he turns for the better, as all the Prophets did in denouncing Israel.[32]

Ultimately, shaming someone else is a gross violation of the Jewish tradition's demands that we respect others. It also is akin to killing them in their own eyes and in the estimation of others, as the Talmud says. In many cases, it kills the person's respect in the community, and such social excommunication is really a social death, often with terrible consequences for the person so shamed. In some cases it has led the shamed person to commit suicide.

What, though, if the person involved is a political leader or someone else in power, and the purpose of the shaming is to make the individual seem less frightful? Or what if the person in power is doing real harm to society, and shaming in public is a way to call attention to the harm, to protest it, and maybe even to stop it? Contemporary examples of this include programs on television, podcasts, Tik Tok, YouTube, and other media that mock political and other leaders through comedy, sometimes in good humor but sometimes as satire with a serious critique in mind.

Even more direct and personal than the political and social ills that political satire and serious public discussions address are the injuries of those who have been harmed and say something about it. Recent examples of many women and some men who are reporting past sexual abuse or discrimination by celebrities, companies, or religious institutions are clearly part of this story, leading to the creation of the #MeToo movement, designed to shame the perpetrators, but also—and in far greater numbers—individuals who have garnered the courage to escape from their abusers, report the abuse, and get help. This includes not only sexual abuse, but—again, in far greater numbers—those who have been harassed or bullied at home, school, or work. As explained in my responsum "Family Violence," victims of abuse of all these sorts have a hard time coming forward to report that abuse and get help, and we certainly want them to do that.[33]

In such cases, other Jewish sources come into play. In the extreme, the Torah demands that people causing public harm be executed:

If your brother, your own mother's son, or your son or daughter, or the wife of your bosom, or your closest friend entices you in secret, saying, "Come let us worship other gods," . . . Stone him to death. . . . Thus all Israel will hear and be afraid, and such evil things will not be done again in your midst. (Deut. 13:7-12)

With regard to less serious, but nevertheless serious, harms, we have the duty to protest:

> Anyone who had the capability effectively to protest [the sinful conduct] of the members of his household and did not protest, he himself is apprehended [and punished for the sins of] the members of his household. [If he is in a position to protest the sinful conduct of] the people of his town [and he fails to do so], he is apprehended [and punished] for the sins of the people of his town. [If he is in a position to protest] the sins of the whole world [and he fails to do so], he is apprehended [and punished] for the sins of the whole world.[34]

This would presumably include making the kinds of public shaming in the contemporary examples mentioned above not only permissible, but mandatory.

In short, nothing in this chapter should be read as prohibiting free speech designed to help people understand the strengths and weaknesses of the policies advanced by proposed laws or judicial decisions, or by the people in or running for office. Such speech, even if insulting and shaming, is permitted, because it is considered necessary to help citizens evaluate what they are being told in matters that concern their welfare. Such speech, however, must be truthful to meet Jewish standards of law and morality, and it must be specific in its reference to the actions, decisions, policies, or people involved rather than a blanket condemnation, which can quickly become hate speech. It also should condemn in order to construct—that is, its criticism and even shaming should be motivated by an honest attempt to oppose particular policies and those who seek to advance them in favor of other, better ways of doing things.

Bullying: *Iyyum*

Perhaps the most devastating form of shaming occurs in the form of bullying, which the U.S. government website stopbullying.gov defines as "unwanted, aggressive behavior . . . that involves a real or perceived power imbalance. The behavior is repeated, or has the potential to be repeated, over time. . . . Bullying includes actions such as making threats, spreading rumors, attacking someone physically or verbally, and excluding someone from a group on purpose."[35]

The site (focusing on schoolchildren) delineates three general types of bullying:

1. **Verbal bullying**, saying or writing mean things, which may include teasing, name-calling, inappropriate sexual comments, taunting, and threatening to cause harm.
2. **Social bullying**, or relational bullying, hurting someone's reputation or relationships, which may include leaving someone out on purpose, telling other children not to be friends with someone, spreading rumors about someone, or embarrassing someone in public.
3. **Physical bullying**, hurting a person's body or possessions, which may include hitting, kicking, or pinching; spitting, tripping or pushing; taking or breaking someone's things; and making mean or rude hand gestures.[36]

Approximately 20 percent of students between ages twelve and eighteen experience bullying, and there are demonstrated connections between bullying and family violence, sexual harassment, and dating violence, so this is a major problem in our society.[37] Jewish concepts and values described above, such as the respect we must have for each person as created in the image of God and the resulting bans on hurting anyone verbally or physically, make threatening someone with harm; doctoring photos of them or their family; doxing, outing, and all other ways of terrorizing and bullying anyone expressly forbidden. It is therefore imperative that Jews learn how to create school, work, and social and religious environments that condemn bullying and develop the skills to recognize and combat it when it occurs. The site stopbullying.gov has helpful suggestions.

Enticement, Incitement, and Rabble-Rousing: *Hasatah*

Finally, we consider the incitement to hate particular people or subgroups of the population. Even when agitators stop short of urging their listeners to harm the targeted people, the upshot of rabble-rousing is well understood by their cheering audiences, so such speech often leads to mayhem or death. In light of antisemitism, Jews are particularly sensitive to the wrongfulness and dangers of this form of harmful communication, but we need to condemn it when it is directed to other groups, such as Muslims, as well. While Jews and Muslims disagree on many things involving the State of Israel, Muslims certainly do not deserve to be the target of such provocation any more than we Jews do. The same is true of other ethnic minorities and people of varying skin colors, sexual orientations, and gender identities. Although Jews are required to rebuke people who violate legal and moral norms, to condemn any people or groups without moral or legal basis, let alone to urge other people to harm them, is a violation of justice and mutual respect. It also undermines the very basis of civil society, leading to violence and insecurity for everyone.

14

Preserving Modesty in Communication

Having taught high school, college, graduate, and continuing adult education students in both formal and informal settings for more than five decades, I have noticed a marked increase in the use of foul language, especially among the younger groups, to the point that virtually every other sentence has a swear word in it. That is one of the motivations that led me to write a responsum on what the Jewish tradition says about modesty in communication and why it should matter.

The social media setting raises modesty concerns in a completely different sense—to what extent should we talk about ourselves and our accomplishments? In light of the fact that in social media people actively seek affirmation (likes, shares, etc.) for their posts and that some jobs even require the generation of such quantifiable affirmations, how can and should Jews promote themselves professionally and socially while still observing traditional Jewish norms of modesty (*tzi'ni'ut*) in communication?

This chapter is drawn from my "Modest Communication" responsum of June 19, 2019, which addresses the ethical value of modesty in multiple senses. As we will see, many of the norms to be discussed can be understood, on the positive end of the spectrum, as either laws obligating a particular form of behavior or, in contrast, as aspirational modes of behavior (*middat hassidut*). On the negative end of the spectrum, some norms will straddle the line between legally prohibited and permitted but discouraged actions.[1] To read the full responsum: https://www.rabbinicalassembly.org /sites/default/files/modest_speech.final.june.pdf.

Two additional comments before we dive in. First, there is a distinction between how morality intersects with civil vs. religious law. Select theorists of civil law dispute the relevance of morality to legal decisions, with some ("legal positivists") asserting that only the letter of the law counts, while others claim that civil law must be interpreted with morality in mind (because the lawmaker can be assumed to be moral or because interpretations of the law must take its effects on people into account). By contrast, in my view, the religious context of Jewish law, which is given by a moral and good God, requires understanding the law as intertwined with foundational theological convictions and moral norms, far more than a secular system of law would mandate.[2]

Second, Jewish law includes norms about modesty in dress as well as in communication (defined expansively; see chapter 13). For a modern articulation of the former, see the responsum "Modesty Inside and Out: A Contemporary Guide to Tzniut."[3]

Modesty is clearly an important value in Judaism. In the Bible and rabbinic literature, it is a character trait associated with some of Judaism's most prominent representatives. Nobody was ever as humble as Moses (Num. 12:3). One should strive to be as humble as Hillel.[4] Rabbi Judah the Prince, redactor of the Mishnah, was so humble that his disciples all failed to be like him in this virtue; as the Talmud puts it, "When Rebbe died, humility disappeared."[5] Humility is also one of three things Micah demands of us in what is arguably the most famous line in prophetic literature:

> He has told you, O man, what is good,
> and what the Lord requires of you:
> Only to do justice,
> and to love goodness,
> and to walk modestly with your God.[6]

What, though, do we mean by "modesty" in the first place, and why is that important? Webster's dictionary defines the English word "modest" as follows:

> Having or showing a moderate or humble opinion of one's own value, abilities, achievements, etc.; unassuming.
> Not forward; shy or reserved, as *modest* behavior.
> Behaving according to a standard of what is proper or decorous; decent; pure; now, especially, not displaying one's body.
> Showing or caused by moderation; not extreme or excessive, as a *modest* request.
> Quiet and humble in appearance, style, etc., as in a *modest* home, apartment, etc.[7]

Maimonides defines the Hebrew equivalent, *tzini'ut*, first in dress and then, in the subsequent law, in speech:

Torah scholars conduct themselves with great modesty. They do not disgrace themselves and reveal neither their heads nor their bodies. And even at the time that he goes to the toilet, he is modest and he does not remove his clothing until he sits. . . .

The wise man should not shout and scream in his speech like a cow or wild animal; nor should he even raise his voice too high, but rather his conversation with all people should be gentle. In the gentleness of his conversation, he shall take heed not to distance himself [*yitrahek*] from the other person, or possibly quickly retreat without waiting for a response, or possibly exaggerate, using big words when simpler language will do the job so as to give the appearance of those who are coarse [or haughty]. He should also anticipate every person with his polite greetings so that all shall be pleased with him. He should judge every person favorably, speaking only of the merits of his friend and not of his faults. He should love peace and pursue peace. If he perceives that his words might prove beneficial and people will listen to him, he should speak; otherwise, he should remain silent. For instance, he should never attempt to pacify his neighbor while the latter is angry; nor should he make any effort to absolve one from his vow at the moment when it is uttered, but he should wait until the mind of the person who made the vow becomes calm and composed; nor should he comfort the mourner when his deceased relative lies before him because the mourner is too upset before the burial; and such like; nor should he watch his friend at the time of his disgrace but rather should withdraw his eyes from it; nor should he veer from his word, neither to add to it nor to diminish, except to establish peace and similar goals. The general rule is that he speaks only on matters of wisdom, or to effect benevolence, or the like.[8]

Coming directly from rabbinic literature, Maimonides's examples apply to us today as much as they did to people living in the ancient and medieval periods.[9]

The Theological Convictions and Moral Values
Underlying Judaism's Concern for Modesty

The value of modesty, like most, if not all, Jewish values, rests on broader theological convictions and values:

The human being is created in the image of God and thus deserves respect.

All human faculties were created by God and should be valued as such.

As Creator of the world, God owns everything in it, including all human beings.

Humility is appropriate. We should be humble, like some of the most important figures in Jewish tradition, because we are not God. We can be proud of what we have done; but ultimately, we must recognize that our accomplishments are small and temporary from the viewpoint of God.[10]

Gratitude is appropriate. God's ownership of the world requires us to be thankful to God for what we have. Gratitude is a core theological value in Judaism, and its opposite, ingratitude and haughtiness about one's own achievements, are the essence of a nonreligious stance as the Torah defines it:

> When you have eaten your fill, and have built fine houses to live in, and your herds and flocks have multiplied, and your silver and gold have increased, and everything you own has prospered, beware lest your heart grow haughty and you forget the Lord your God . . . and say to yourselves, "My own power and the might of my own hand have won this wealth for me." Remember that it is the Lord your God who gives you the power to get wealth, in fulfillment of the covenant that He made on oath with your fathers, as is still the case. (Deut. 8:12–14, 17–18)

God calls us to be a holy nation. Finally, the theological basis for the discussion of modesty in speech must also take note of the high standard to which Judaism asks us to aspire. None of us is perfect—morally, emotionally, socially, professionally, or in any other way—and none of us will ever be so; but the beginning of Leviticus chapter 19 instructs us, "You shall be holy, for I, the

Lord your God, am holy," and the commandments in the rest of the chapter define what holiness means, thereby teaching us that we need to aspire to be better than we would otherwise be.

Lies (*Sheker*)

One way of being immodest is to tell lies about oneself, hoping that others will think better of you than you really are. Yet intentionally telling someone something you know to be false undermines people's trust in one another, imperiling social cooperation, commerce, friendships, and family relations. (See chapter 12.) It is not surprising, then, that the Torah specifically prohibits lying. (See chapter 13.)

Lying is wrong not only in and of itself, but as a violation of proper modesty when done to get a job or simply to impress others. Job applicants, for example, ought to describe their skills and accomplishments truthfully, in proportion to the actual value and importance of their achievements.

Haughtiness and Bragging: *Ravrevanut, Hitpa'arut, Hitya'ahrut, Gassut Ru'ah*

To be clear, it is *not* a violation of Jewish rules and values of modesty to accurately and fully describe one's strengths in applying for a school or job or in any other context when there is practical necessity to do so. When, however, there is no practical reason to talk about one's accomplishments or skills, modesty would suggest that one do so only rarely and, even then, in an understated way. Haughtiness and its verbal expression, bragging, are arguably the exact opposite of humility, as Maimonides specifies in his definition of modest speech.[11] In some manifestations, particularly with regard to how many possessions one has acquired, haughtiness also violates our duty to recognize that God owns the world.

Jewish sources are united in condemning haughtiness and bragging. For example:

> For four things the property of their owners is lost to them [literally, goes to the government's treasury]: for oppressing the salary of a hired hand, or for keeping the salary of a hired hand, or for taking the yoke off their necks and putting it on their friends' backs; and haughtiness is the basis of all of these.[12]

It is certainly proper, though, for people to try to do good things in life and be proud of doing so. Therefore, Maimonides uses this human trait of degrees of self-worth (along with degrees of anger) to demonstrate the value of the Golden Mean:

And how are they to be cured? . . . If a man happens to be of a haughty mind, they direct him to accustom himself to endure the greatest contempt; to occupy the lowest position when sitting in company; to put on inferior clothes, which reflect no respect on those who wear them; or such like things, until his haughtiness of mind be uprooted from within him, and he turns to the middle course, which is the good way; and having thus turned to the middle course he ought to proceed in the same way all his days. According to this standard he ought to proceed with regard to all other dispositions; namely, if he happens to lean towards the one extreme, he ought to remove to the other extreme, and to train himself to it for a considerable time, until he returns to the good way, which is the middle course between the different dispositions.[13]

In my view, Maimonides has it right here. The desired end is a healthy sense of self-esteem—one not too haughty and not too humble but somewhere in between.

In the very next section, though, he argues that one should try to root out haughtiness in oneself altogether:

Yet there are some dispositions, in regard to which it would not be commendable for a man to remain in the middle cause only, but rather to remove from one extreme to the other. Now this is the case with *haughtiness of mind*; for it is by no means the good way for a man to be *meek* only, but he ought really to be of a *humble* mind, and an exceedingly low spirit; and, therefore, it is said with regard to Moses our Teacher, that he was not only meek, but very meek. Our sages have therefore strictly enjoined us: *Be of an exceedingly humble mind.* Again they say: that he who has a haughty mind denies the radical religious principle; for it is said: *Then your heart will be lifted up, and you will forget the Lord your God* (Deut. 8:14); and again they say: He ought to be held in contempt who is in the least disposed to an overbearing spirit.

I think Maimonides has gone overboard here. It is certainly a proper recognition of one's frailty and God's governance to be humble, but people do need a sense of self-worth. In fact, one major factor characterizing people in prison for violent behaviors is a lack of a sense of self-esteem.[14] Of course, Maimonides is condemning haughtiness and not self-worth, but in my view, in advocating being as humble as he describes it here, he is understating the importance of having a sense of self-esteem.

This, in fact, is a dispute in the Talmud itself: after a number of passages condemning arrogance, Rava asserts that Jewish scholars who have either too much or too little self-worth are to be held in contempt (the term can also mean "should be excommunicated"), while Rav Nahman bar Yitzhak argues that Jewish scholars should have no pride at all.[15] I am with Rava on this, and I think the following Hasidic saying had it right:

> Rabbi Bunam said: Everyone must have two pockets, so that he can reach into the one or the other, according to his needs. In his right pocket are to be the words: "For my sake was the world created" and in his left, "I am earth and ashes."[16]

In any case, whatever the proper *degree* of self-worth, the prophet Jeremiah succinctly delineates the *reasons* for one's self-esteem, what one should be proud of:

> Thus said the LORD:
> Let not the wise man glory in his wisdom;
> Let not the strong man glory in his strength;
> Let not the rich man glory in his riches.
> But only in this should one glory:
> In his earnest devotion to Me.
> For I, the LORD, act with kindness, justice, and equity in the world;
> For in these I delight—declares the LORD. (Jer. 9:22–23)

Incivility (*Gassut, Boorut, Hoser Nimus*)

As quoted more fully above, lack of civility in speech is part of the core of what Maimonides defines as lack of modesty:

Torah scholars conduct themselves with great modesty. . . . The wise man should not shout and scream in his speech like a cow or wild animal; nor should he even raise his voice too high, but rather his conversation with all people should be gentle.[17]

Incivility in language violates the respect we need to have for others, including those with whom we disagree, as well as our own self-respect. As such, crude speech besmirches and diminishes the image of God embedded in all human beings.

One form of incivility is calling people derogatory names, such as "pathetic," "crazy," "disgraceful," or "a loser." In some cases, such discourse can harm the person and is wrong on that account. But beyond this, even if the speaker's reputation suffers more than that of the intended victim, the belittling of others comes at the expense of society as a whole. It devalues the level of social discourse, undermines the respect we should have for each other, and unravels our ability to plan cooperatively for the future.

Rudeness, it turns out, is bad for business. Employees who are treated badly take out their frustration on customers. Creativity also suffers, performance and team spirit deteriorate, and customers turn away.[18]

The requirement to be civil in one's interactions with other people straddles the border between law and morality. It is part of Maimonides' code of Jewish law *and* part of *Pirkei Avot*, the section of the Mishnah devoted to moral instruction and character formation. So, for example, Shimon ben Shetah and Avtalyon teach us there that we need to be careful with our words, for ill-chosen words can lead to lies, exile, and death.[19] Further, as Hillel instructs, "A boor cannot fear sin. . . . Where there are no worthy persons, strive to be a worthy person."[20] Shammai says, "Receive every person with a pleasant countenance."[21] Hillel says, "Be of the disciples of Aaron, loving peace and pursuing peace, loving people and bringing them closer to Torah."[22]

Foul Language: *Nivvul Peh*

Incivility and immodesty in speech are augmented by using expletives, which violates the third part of Webster's definition of modesty, "Behaving according to a standard of what is proper or decorous." The Rabbis clearly thought that those who utter obscenities (*divrei nevailah*), along with those who are haughty or speak ill of other people, are in line for a bad ending:

A haughty person, those who tell slurs (*lashon ha-ra*, true but defamatory things about people), those who speak obscenities, and those who are wise in their own eyes are described in this verse: "For lo! That day is at hand, burning like an oven. [All the arrogant and all the doers of evil shall be straw, and the day that is coming—said the Lord of Hosts— shall burn them to ashes and leave of them neither stock nor boughs.]"[23]

Nowadays, vulgar language seems to be ubiquitous. Writing in the *Los Angeles Times* on August 1, 2017, Jonah Goldberg noted:

Among the rank and file on Twitter and Facebook, etc., there's a competition to be as vulgar as possible or to be as vigorous as possible in defending presidential vulgarity.

Of course, the president [Trump] is not only changing standards— he's the product of them. Over the last decade or so, a whole cottage industry of young anti-left sensationalists has embraced the romantic slogan, *Epater la Bourgeisie!* Their crudeness isn't a bug, it's a feature. . . .

And the competition to seem verbally authentic has spilled over the ideological retaining wall. The Democratic National Committee sells a T-shirt that reads "Democrats Give a S*** About People." Several leading Democrats have started dropping F-bombs and other phrases to prove their populist street cred.[24]

At the same time, Benjamin Bergen, a professor of cognitive science and director of the Language and Cognition Laboratory at the University of California, San Diego, cited several studies pointing to the lack of correlation between profanity use and honesty: "When you dig into the details . . . it becomes clear that swearing does not reliably signal honesty. Even the best evidence is not particularly convincing. . . . So here's the rub. Profanity may leave a good impression in certain ways, but our impressions are not reality. The potty-mouthed among us . . . may or may not be speaking honestly and may or may not be passionate, regardless of how much their word choices make them seem that way."[25]

Ultimately, there is no good rationale for using foul language. Even if the aim is to stress how intensely one feels about a given subject, people can express strong feelings without using foul language. Additionally, swearing often leads to verbal inflation, at which point the swear words lose their power. Furthermore, people living in Western countries swear using words that reveal their discomfort with their sexual and excretory functioning. Jewish tradition, however, teaches that God has made our bodies, including our sexual and excretory parts, no less than our minds, our emotions, our wills, and all other parts of our inner being (our "souls"). In fact, in the Rabbis' interpretation of the Torah, God commands sex within marriage for both procreation and the mutual bonding and enjoyment of the couple.[26] Also, we are supposed to recite a blessing after every act of excretion, thanking God that our bodies excrete properly, for without that ability, "It would be impossible to exist and to stand before You."[27] Consequently, to use sexual or excretory terms to curse or denigrate others is not only to insult other people, but also to slur God.[28]

Finally, obscenities befoul the social atmosphere, making it rough and uncouth rather than respectful and polite. It is, as this source suggests, a form of pollution:

> Rabbi Elazar ben Jacob said: A pleasant and praised person who utters something unseemly (coarse) with his mouth is like a big, beautiful parlor room in which there is a pipe [spewing foul odors] from a tannery planted in the middle of it; so is a pleasant and praised person who utters something unseemly (coarse) from his mouth.[29]

The Rabbis undoubtedly had some of these factors in mind when they ascribed many maladies to using foul language:

> Because of the sin of using foul language (*nivlut peh*), problems increase and harsh decrees are instituted, and the youth of Israel die,[30] orphans and widows shout out and there is nobody to answer them, as it says (Isa. 9:16–17), "That is why my Lord will not spare their youths, nor show compassion to their orphans and widows; for they are ungodly and wicked, and every mouth speaks impiety." . . . Rabbah bar Sheilah said in the name of Rabbi Hisda: Anyone who uses foul language falls deeper into hell, as it says, "The mouth that speaks perversity is a deep pit" (Prov. 22:14). Rabbi Nahman bar Isaac said, "Also for one who hears and is silent [does not protest], for it is said [in the next part of the same verse], He who is doomed by the Lord [for not protesting] falls into it." (Prov. 22:14).[31]

Salacious Talk: *Z'nut ha-peh v'ha-ozen*

Closely related to foul language, and often including it, is salacious talk, where the point is to articulate lust and presumed power over someone else's body and person. Sometimes known as "locker-room talk," salacious talk often involves descriptions of another person's body as sexually alluring. Sexual attraction is one of God's great gifts in creating our bodies as they are, and there is nothing wrong—and, indeed, everything right—with having feelings of sexual attraction and acting on them in appropriate contexts. Salacious talk, however, objectifies other people, making them solely the objects of one's desires, and thus disempowers and dehumanizes them.

Moses Hayyim Luzzato (1707–1746, Italy) describes speaking and listening to such talk as prostituting the mouth and ear. He cites the Jerusalem Talmud, which, based on a play on words between *davar* (thing) and *debbur* (words), makes swearing nothing less than a violation of the Torah itself:

> With regard to prostitution of the mouth and the ear, that is, speaking words of prostitution (*z'nut*) or listening to them, our Sages "screamed like cranes" (J. *Terumot* 1:4 [6b], that is, emphatically denounced such actions) in saying, "'Let God not find any unseemly thing among you' (Deut. 23:15), that is, unseemly words," which is befouling one's mouth (*nivvul peh*). . . . If one would gain your ear and tell you that the Sages said what they did about obscene speech only to frighten you and to draw you far from sin, and that their words apply only to hot-blooded individuals who, by speaking obscenities, would be aroused to lust, but not to those who air them only in jest, who have nothing whatever to fear—tell him that his words are those of the evil inclination; for the Sages have adduced an explicit verse in support of their statements (Isa. 9:16): "That is why my Lord will not spare their youths, nor show compassion to their orphans and widows; for they are all flatterers and speakers of evil, and every mouth speaks impiety . . ." This verse mentions neither idol worship, nor illicit relations, nor murder, but flattery and slander and obscene utterance, all sins of the mouth in its capacity of speech; and it is because of these sins that the decree went forth. . . . The truth, then, is as our Rabbis of blessed memory have stated, that uttering obscenities constitutes the very "nakedness" of the faculty of

speech and was prohibited as an aspect of fornication along with all other such forms of it. Although outside the realm of illicit relations themselves (as indicated by the fact that [the penalty for] obscene speech is not as harsh as it is for illicit sexual relations, [which is] being cut off from the Jewish People [*karet*] or the death penalty), obscene speech is nonetheless prohibited in itself, apart from its leading to immoral sexual acts.[32]

In Sum

Like Jewish law generally, the norms of modest speech described above are not intended for saints or for some ethereal realm. They are intended to govern real people living in the contemporary world. Nobody is perfect, of course, so even people who generally abide by these norms may slip from time to time, but we Jews should endeavor to uphold these norms habitually to foster a civil, cooperative, and productive society. Abiding by these norms will also help us achieve the aspirational goal that the Torah sets for us (in Exod. 19:6): to be "a kingdom of priests and a holy nation."

15

The Ethics of Playing Violent and Defamatory Video Games

The video game industry accounts for an enormous percentage of the entertainment industry. According to a 2018 Pew Research Center report, 43 percent of all adults, 97 percent of teenage boys, and 83 percent of teenage girls play video games.[1] Their ethical status varies widely. Some stimulate the minds of the elderly, others raise preparedness scores of those about to enter the Israeli army, others help youngsters learn everything from music to mathematics, and still others are violent or defamatory.

Violent games involve *gratuitous* brute force intended to harm someone else, in contrast to the physical or military actions that are sometimes necessary to defend oneself or take part in a justified war. Characters in these games attack, maim, and murder other people for the adrenaline rush it gives the players.

The defamatory character of the games addressed in this chapter involves defaming and degrading specific groups of people. Most often these are women, police officers, or minority groups, including people different from the majority in ethnicity, race, religion, or sexual orientation. Usually, the defamation is accompanied by violence against them.

In addition to the *content* of all such games, the *context* in which violent or defamatory video games are played is relevant. Who, for example, is responsible for the minors who play these games and the effects the games may have on their behavior? Their parents? The shops that sell them? The companies that produce them? Many adults, too, play games that involve immoral acts; is that acceptable when playing only in cyberspace for fun? One can imagine arguments on both sides of that question. How should we draw the line between what is simply bad taste and what is morally unacceptable? And how is what is morally unacceptable related to Jewish law?

Finally, some introductory words about the *scope* of this chapter are in order. Jewish law clearly prohibits many of the actions depicted in these videos—murder, assault, theft, rape, etc.—when they take place in reality.

At the other end of the spectrum is passively reading a magazine or book or watching a television show or movie that depicts these actions. This chapter *offers no direction on how we should treat violence or defamation in media where the observer is passive.* It focuses solely on the middle of that spectrum, where players are actively involved in these actions, acting out their fantasies (rather than more passively imagining what it might be like to act in such a way) without paying the legal price this behavior would entail in real life.

In the early years of video games, their content posed few, if any, moral problems. The games consisted of a few colors and shapes, with very simple objectives. While some games involved shooting at alien invaders or asteroids, the shooting was very unrealistic and abstract. Few, if any, asked whether it is good to create games in which the objective is to shoot something, presumably because archery, bowling, and other long-established games do the same thing.

Shooting today in video games, however, is quite different. The targets are very realistic depictions of people in the everyday world; in fact, the images are often effectively photographs of real people and things. The player can choose weapons and methods of injuring other people and is rewarded for the killing. Quite often the player is placed in a "kill or be killed" situation, with the latter translating into losing the game.

This chapter was prompted by a course paper written by my rabbinical student Joshua Hearshen in the early 2000s. He went to a neighborhood Blockbuster and requested popular games that are controversial and have questionable content. The clerk produced a number of games that carried an "M" (Mature) rating, intended for audiences seventeen years of age or older.[2] Here is Hearshen's description of one of the most popular ones:

> "Grand Theft Auto: San Andreas" is . . . the latest release in the Grand Theft Auto series, and the video stores have trouble keeping them in stock because the demand is so great. In this game the main character is a member of . . . a street gang. He must complete a large number of tasks that include stealing cars, killing people, robbing, dealing with drugs, and much more. The majority of the women in the game are scantily clad prostitutes. Having sex with a prostitute is the method for regaining health points. There is also a well-known way to cheat, which is built into the game. The player needs to pay for the prostitute to increase

health points, so the player is able to pay the prostitute, have sex, and then kill her to take back the money. The game uses many racial and ethnic slurs in addition to offensively foul language. Finally, the police are portrayed in a very negative fashion, as corrupt and evil, and for all intents and purposes they are the bad guys.

After Hearshen's paper (which included the aforementioned statistics) opened my eyes to the popularity and realities of such games, I suggested to him that we coauthor a responsum for the Committee on Jewish Law and Standards. What follows is drawn from my portion of this CJLS responsum, passed on February 4, 2010, from the dual perspectives of Western ethical theories and Jewish law. To read the full responsum: https://www.rabbinicalassembly.org/sites/default/files/assets/public/halakhah/teshuvot/20052010/videogames%20dorff%20hearshen%20final.pdf

Western theories of ethics divide into three general approaches—consequentialist, deontological, and virtue (or character) ethics. This will help us identify the relevant factors and concerns in Jewish law, for they also are partially consequentialist and partially principled, but primarily a matter of character.

Consequentialist Issues

The consequentialist approach holds that one needs to measure the *consequences* of an action or set of actions to determine its moral quality. In any fair consequentialist analysis, one must state the potential positive effects as well as the negative ones. The potential advantages of video games, even violent or defamatory ones, include improved problem-solving skills for both life situations and text study, increased dexterity, comfort with technology, ability to combat loneliness by connecting with others (including parents, grandparents, and friends a long distance away) to play the game together, and pleasure.

What are the negative consequences? Even though a high percentage of older people believe that violent video games are one of the causes of the epidemic of gun violence in American society, the vast majority of people who play these games do not engage in criminal or defamatory acts.[3] Indeed, the American Psychological Association has affirmed, based on multiple studies, that in general, "There is insufficient scientific evidence to support a causal link between violent video games and violent behavior."[4]

The National Institutes of Health, however, conducted a review of 1800 studies over thirty years about the effects of media consumption on children, selecting 173 that met stringent research standards. The results of their review were this: "In a clear majority of those studies, more time with television, films, video games, magazines, music, and the Internet was linked to rises in childhood obesity, tobacco use, and sexual behavior. A majority also showed strong correlations—what the researchers deemed 'statistically significant associations'–with drug and alcohol use and low academic achievement."[5] Harvard Health also points out that "gaming has also been associated with sleep deprivation, insomnia and circadian rhythm disorders, depression, aggression, and anxiety, though more studies are needed to establish the validity and the strength of these connections."[6] Between 0.3 percent and 1 percent of the people who play video games become addicted to them.[7]

How are we to evaluate these facts through a Jewish lens? Jewish law insists that we not put ourselves in danger.[8] So, for example, the Torah requires that "when you build a new house, you shall make a parapet for your roof, so that you do not bring bloodguilt on your house if anyone should fall from it" (Deut. 22:8), and the Rabbis say, *sakkanta hamira mei'issura*, "[avoiding] danger is more strongly required of us than [avoiding the transgression of] a prohibition."[9] Furthermore, on the basis of the Torah's verse prohibiting us from putting a stumbling block in front of a person who is blind (Lev. 19:14), the Rabbis determined that we may not put moral stumbling blocks like temptations in people's way either.[10] So if there are good chances that these games will lead boys and young men, in particular, to binge on them and thereby endanger themselves or others, such dangers would argue against using them.

The normal activities of life, though, involve multiple dangers, so Jewish law had to determine the level of risk that is prohibited. Individuals, then, may engage in activities that most people do without injury (e.g., driving), and the Talmud invokes the verse from Psalms, "the Lord preserves the simple" (Ps. 116:6), to ignore merely possible risks if they are generally accepted within the community.[11]

Jewish law also insists that we take reasonable steps to preserve our life and health, including our mental health, for we are God's property and thus have a fiduciary duty to God to take care of ourselves.[12] The question, then, is how to evaluate the potential benefits and dangers of playing video games, especially violent or defamatory ones, for our health.

Like many areas of life, the health risks of playing video games, including violent or defamatory ones, occur only when one does it too much, especially for a prolonged period of time. Even at their best, video games should not take over the whole of one's life or even a significant part of it. Playing video games to that extent risks the possibility of their becoming nothing short of an idol, making them the focus of one's life to the exclusion of all other things that are good for the body, soul, family, and community. Short of that, though, there is no credible evidence that playing these games has deleterious effects on either the vast majority of players or anyone else, so our objections to them, if any, cannot be consequentialist.

Deontological Concerns

Deontology determines the moral quality of an act by the degree to which it accords with moral principles embedded in some aspect of existence, whether it is the human mind (e.g., Kant), intuition (e.g., W. D. Ross), nature (e.g., Aristotle, Aquinas), or God (e.g., classical Judaism). For this school of thought, the intentions of the actor, not the consequences of the act, determine its moral status. As Kant, for example, put it, "Nothing can possibly be conceived in the world, or even out of it, which can be called good without qualification, except a Good Will."[13] Furthermore, in contrast to consequentialists, who seek the greatest good for the greatest number, for deontologists like Kant, one must treat each and every human being as an end in oneself and never as merely a means to an end (the second version of his categorical imperative).[14] So communal concerns cannot ride roughshod over concern for the individual.

As applied to our question, deontology raises a number of contradictory considerations. On one hand, the Kantian demand not to treat another person merely as a means would argue that games that do precisely that for one's own entertainment are immoral. Kant, however, was talking about actual people, not depictions of them, and it is not clear that he himself would argue that we have the same principled moral duties to representations of people as we have to actual people. Furthermore, deontology asserts the importance of intention, and few, if any, of the players of video games intend to carry out in practice the actions depicted in the games.

They simply intend to live out their fantasies in a way that does not harm anyone in the real world. Furthermore, deontology valorizes individual freedom, including free speech—and the Eighth Circuit Court of Appeals in the United States has specifically affirmed that playing these games is covered by constitutional guarantees of free speech.[15]

Jewish law thrives on vigorous debate, but it also includes far stricter limitations than American law on what constitutes appropriate speech (see chapters 12–14). This is part of a larger picture. Although Western cultures certainly value groups like families, communities, and nations, they emphasize individual rights.[16] In contrast, classical Judaism focuses on group ethics.[17]

Even so, deontological concerns applicable to our topic are not absent from Jewish thought and law. For example, consider the following selections from *Pirkei Avot*:

> Rabbi Joshua said: the evil eye, the impulse to evil, and hatred of God's creatures put a man out of the world.[18]
> Rabbi Eleazar ha-Kappar said: Envy, lust, and ambition put a man out of the world.[19]
> Rabbi Dossa ben Horkinas said: sleep into the morning, wine at midday, childish chatter, and sitting in at gatherings of the ignorant put a man out of the world.[20]

Rabbi Joshua speaks of the "impulse" to do evil (*yetzer ha-ra*), and these games certainly express that impulse. Indeed, some people have defended these games as a necessary release of violent and sexual inclinations, contending that without these games, players would be doing these things in real life. However one evaluates this argument, players surely intend to, and succeed at, expressing their inclinations to berate and harm people.

Rabbi Eleazar says that envy, lust, and ambition are the culprits that drive a man out of the world, and the plots of these games glory in all three of these. Many of the games are built on stealing money and other things. They also push sexual lust to the extreme.

Rabbi Dosa's observation about the lazy person closely describes people playing these games for hours on end. If he knew about video games, he surely would have said that excessive video game playing takes people out of the world and makes them lazier. As noted earlier, studies have demonstrated a link between the rise in obesity in younger people and the rise in the popularity of video games.[21]

People playing violent and defamatory video games are, of course, not actually engaged in those acts in real life. If they did, obviously, they would be liable under multiple Jewish laws.[22] The question, though, is the status of one's fantasy life in Jewish law. Does it violate Jewish law to fantasize about murder or rape? If so, does one violate Jewish law when one intentionally plays video games to stimulate such fantasies?

The evidence here is mixed. On one hand, Jewish laws do prohibit fantasizing about committing illegal acts. So, for example, Rabbi Pinchas ben Ya'ir is quoted in the Talmud as banning thoughts of sexual infractions for fear of arousing a man to seminal emission: "Do not think [illicit thoughts] in the day and come to nocturnal emission of seed."[23] Maimonides links the larger category—the ban against thinking about violating any of the commandments (*hirhur davar ha-asur*)—to the biblical ban "Do not follow your heart and eyes in your lustful urge" (Num. 15:39). He then uses this verse to prohibit not only experiencing such fantasies but also doing anything that is likely to cause them.[24] Here Maimonides is claiming that if someone actively pursued fantasies of doing something illegal, that would violate Numbers 15:39, which in ancient times would have required bringing a guilt offering to the Temple to show remorse to God for having done something wrong. In other words, engaging in the fantasy life of something akin to violent and defamatory video games should make one feel guilty enough to take action to seek God's forgiveness.

On the other hand, another strain in rabbinic tradition makes a sharp distinction between one's liability for thoughts and for actions. So, for example, the Talmud (B. *Kiddushin* 40a) says that God rewards us for our good intentions even if we have not been able to carry them out, but God does not link our evil intentions to action to punish us as if we had committed the actions. Also, the Rabbis transformed the coveting prohibited in the last of the Ten Commandments to action:

> You might think that [one is liable for violating the tenth of the Ten Commandments] even if one covets through words [he *says* that he wants X. That, however, is not the case for] the Torah says, "You shall not covet the silver and gold on them [the images of their gods]" (Deuteronomy 7:25). Just as there [in the case of idolatry, the person is not

liable] until he engages in an act, so too here [he is not liable] until he engages in an act.[25]

On the positive side, in Jewish law fulfilling one's duty to pray does not require the proper intention (*kavvanah*) except for praying the first line of the *Shema* and the first blessing of the *Amidah*.[26] Jewish law thus distinguishes between intention and action in judging only our actions during the rest of the service.

David Brodsky has demonstrated that the sources in our tradition that equate intention with action are predominantly Babylonian (so it is Rav, Rav Nahman, Rava, and Ravina who assert this).[27] This, he claims, is the result of influence from Zoroastrian sources, which also equate intention with action.[28] In contrast, Tannaitic sources, written by rabbis in the Roman province of Palestine (in earlier centuries and now called Israel) in the first two centuries CE, require action for legal culpability.[29] The Palestinian Amora'im, rabbis living there in the fourth and fifth centuries CE, manifest a mix of these positions, probably because of some influence from their Babylonian confreres.[30]

In addition, because one can control one's thoughts and feelings much less than one's actions, both secular and Jewish law generally deal only with actions, not thoughts. In sum, playing violent or defamatory video games cannot be banned altogether on deontological grounds, for the dominant stream of Jewish legal thought prohibits or requires actions, not thoughts or feelings.

Concerns of Character

This leaves us with the virtue ethics strain of Jewish law. What does it say about playing violent and defamatory video games?

Jewish law most commonly uses deontological terms—*assur* (forbidden), *muttar* (permitted), and *hayyav* (required). It is *not*, however, limited to such black-and-white categories. A rich strain of Jewish law speaks the language of virtue ethics, where actions are not clearly forbidden or permitted but are encouraged or discouraged. This is not the morality or the law of rules, but the morality and law of aspiration. This is the ethic portrayed by the biblical prophets and the books of Psalms and Proverbs, perhaps most famously in Isaiah's call for us to be "a light of nations."[31]

Moreover, it is the ethic inherent in the Torah's overarching demand, "You shall be holy for I, the Lord your God, am holy" (Lev. 19:2).

In line with this, the Rabbis discourage us from certain kinds of conduct. Most relevant to our case is the disparaging remark *ru'ah hakhamim 'aina nohah haymenu*, "the spirit of the Sages is not pleased with him," which they apply to all the following: those who do not fulfill their verbal agreements; those who leave their children no inheritance, assigning it by will to others; and those who accept money from a thief or a lender on interest who repented, lest people who commit these crimes in the future be discouraged from repenting.[32] Other such derogatory categories include *minhag rama'ut*, the behavior of a cheat, and *yesh bahem mishum mehusarai emunah* (they are untrustworthy, dishonest).[33] Later, Nahmanides introduces the category of *naval b'reshut ha-Torah*, a scoundrel within the bounds (or, possibly, with the permission) of the Torah.[34]

On the other hand, rabbinic concepts that express pleasure at exemplary behavior include *ru'ah hakhamim nohah heimenu*, the spirit of the Sages is pleased with him; *kiddush ha-Shem*, a sanctification of the Divine Name and, by extension, of the Jewish people associated with worshiping God; *middat hassidut*, (the person is exemplifying) the virtue of loyalty (or, possibly, loving kindness); *lifnim m'shurat ha-din*, going beyond the requirements of the law; and *derekh eretz*, a term sometimes used to mean a job, but sometimes it refers to decency and right living.[35] Finally, "Rav said: The commandments were given to Israel only in order that people should be purified through them."[36]

But purified toward what end? The Jewish tradition does not synthesize the picture of the ideal person, and, in fact, different strands of Judaism paint somewhat different pictures. So, for example, the ideal person in Deuteronomy is one who obeys Jewish law. The ideal person in the view of Micah and many of the other prophets is the one who goes beyond the demands of the law to reach the moral ideal: "He has told you, O man, what is good, and what the Lord requires of you: Only to do justice, and to love goodness, and to walk modestly with your God" (Mic. 6:8). The ideal man, according to Kohelet (Ecclesiastes), is the one who is neither too righteous nor too wicked but follows a moderate path in life and enjoys it with his wife.[37] The ideal person in rabbinic literature is much more studious than any of the above depictions. There is yet more variation in the depiction of the ideal Jew in the works of later Jewish writers, such as Maimonides' *Mishneh Torah* (especially *Hilkhot De'ot*) and the writings of Bahya ibn Pakuda, Moshe Hayyim Luzzato, Israel Salanter, and others.

Still, even with all this variation, it is possible to locate reasonably centrist depictions of the ideal person in biblical and rabbinic literature in a variety of texts, including Psalms 1, 15, and 112; the book of Proverbs, including the ode to the ideal woman that we use on Friday nights (31:10–31); and the Mishnah's tractate *Avot (Ethics of the Fathers)*. Another place to locate what classical Judaism ultimately wants of us is in the Talmud's description of what God asks of us when we die:

> Rava said: At the time that they bring a person before the [Heavenly] court, they say to him: Did you transact your business honestly? Did you fix times for the study of the Torah? Did you fulfill your duty to procreate? Did you hope for the salvation [of the Messiah]? Did you search for wisdom? Did you try to derive one law from another [in study]? Even should all these questions be answered affirmatively, only if "the fear of the Lord is his treasure" (Isaiah 33:6) will it avail; otherwise, it will not.[38]

Nobody in real life lives up to the full picture of any of these Jewish depictions of the ideal person, of course, but the virtue ethics stream in Jewish law would ask how a particular action or set of actions contributes to a person's ability to get further along the path toward becoming the ideal. Or, conversely, it would ask the degree to which the action or set of actions moves a person further away from that ideal.

How, then, do violent and defamatory video games fare in such an evaluation? Not well. First, although sometimes killing someone is the right thing to do (as, for example, in self-defense, where no alternative for saving your own life exists), it is decidedly not virtuous to kill someone over and over again in a plethora of ways. Similarly, it is decidedly not virtuous for a man to have sex, even virtual sex, with multiple women. The Jewish tradition explicitly outlaws rape and other forms of physical and sexual assault. It is also decidedly not virtuous to run over multiple pedestrians or rob people of their cars or other possessions.

Thus, the virtue ethics strand of Jewish law, using the requirements and prohibitions of Jewish law as well as Jewish visions of the ideal as the basis for evaluating actions, would find problems in both the lack of choices presented to the player in violent and defamatory video games and the encouragement they provide to make immoral choices. Finally, the virtue ethics category begs people to ask themselves: Would this be something that someone I hold up as being virtuous would do? More directly, is this how I want to see myself and how I want others to see me?

There is no way we could imagine publicizing that such games would be played at a youth or adult event at a synagogue or convention. These games simply fail the newspaper test: they are not what you would want published about yourself on the front page of the newspaper. And if that is the case, they are not worthy of someone who is trying to live by Jewish standards—to be, indeed, a part of "a kingdom of priests and a holy nation" (Exod. 19:6).

This, of course, is using Jewish law to express aspirations, and some understand Jewish law to be more limited in its scope, articulating only what is minimally required. My philosophy, however, along with many sources in the Bible and rabbinic literature, is that Jewish law can and should speak to the divine spark within each one of us. It includes ideal standards as well as minimal norms, as I have argued elsewhere.[39] This follows the lead in moral theory of J. O. Urmson, who pointed out in 1958 that morality is concerned not only with minimal standards but with shaping "saints and heroes."[40]

In line with this, Jews should avoid violent and defamatory video games because they violate some deep Jewish commitments. Playing violent video games veers from the standards of virtue our tradition challenges us to uphold. Moreover, to carry out the parental duty of education, which includes character education, parents and Jewish educational institutions must ban the use of violent or defamatory video games to properly educate the children in their charge.

16

A Modern Jewish Approach to War

Professor Asa Kasher of Tel Aviv University created the first version of the State of Israel's code of ethics for its defense forces, titled "Israel Defense Forces: Ru'ah Tza'hal-Code of Ethics," in 1994.[1] I had written about the ethics of war and international intervention.[2] This may have been the reason he invited me in 2010 to join a number of other scholars for a conference in Israel, to think together afresh about what a code of ethics for Israel's Defense Forces (IDF) should look like. He had updated the code in 2001.[3] Thus he was clearly convinced that the Israel Defense Forces needed to reconsider its code of ethics periodically, as it unfortunately had to confront new military challenges.

Another attendee was Professor Michael Walzer, a permanent faculty member in the School of Social Science at the Institute for Advanced Study in Princeton and author of *Just and Unjust Wars* (1977), among many other books. It turned out that, in our presentations at the conference, he and I had both begun with the same historical outlook: Jews had governed what wars they were fighting and how only in ancient times or since the State of Israel's founding in 1948, so Jewish sources on war were either very old or very young. Professor Walzer concluded that we should therefore borrow from the just war theory created by non-Jewish thinkers over many centuries. I suggested that we instead delve deeply into Jewish concepts and values to create a Jewish ethic of war for our time. Professor Kasher, who was also serving as editor of the journal *Philosophia*, liked the juxtaposition so much that he published both essays in *Philosophia*'s September 2012 edition.[4] What follows is drawn from my essay.

The only times before 1948 when Jews ruled themselves and made their own decisions as a nation as to when to go to war and how to wage it were between ca. 1250 BCE and 586 BCE (the conquest of Canaan and the First Temple period) and between 165 BCE and 63 BCE (the Maccabean period). Jewish sources on war are therefore either very old or only theoretical, without a basis in the actual experience of deciding to go to war and the strategies to use. Jews participated in the armed forces of their nations of residence over the centuries, but the Jewish tradition never governed those wars, either in the grounds for going to war or in its rules of conduct. Now, however, with the modern State of Israel's establishment and its unfortunate surfeit of experience with war, Jews are very much occupied with such decisions. To what extent, and in what way, can the Jewish tradition apply to those decisions?

This is parallel to the problem Jews have in gaining guidance from their tradition on any issue where the science, technology, or social or political conditions have changed radically. Any reasonable Jewish treatment of addressing such issues must take relevant classical sources into account but also go beyond them to locate the underlying Jewish concepts and values that can guide our contemporary decisions.

Professor Walzer, responding to the dearth of Jewish sources that come from actual experience in making decisions about war, suggests that Jews do what we have often done—learn from the non-Jewish world, in this case from Christian just war theory. Precedents for borrowing from other cultures abound in Jewish law and thought, so in suggesting a different approach, I am not denying the Jewish authenticity of doing what he suggests. The problem with that, though, is that at some point one wants to know what makes the borrowed material Jewish, especially if it presumes concepts or values significantly different from those of the classical Jewish tradition. In this case, Professor Walzer would undoubtedly argue that the values underlying Christian just war theory are Jewish values too, and in my view by and large he would be right about that. So I too would want to learn from what Christian thinkers have produced on this issue—but, in my case, only after spelling out the Jewish concepts and values relevant to war and peace, so that in borrowing from Christian just war theory, we are aware of the Jewish lens through which we evaluate what and what not to borrow from it.

My thesis, then, is that to articulate an authentic Jewish ethic of war for modern times, one must do "depth theology," considering the ultimate Jewish understandings of God and humans, including the degree, on one hand, to which they are understood to be prone to war in their character and activities, and, on the other, their penchant and hope for peace. One must also consider how peace is construed in the first place. In this process, one must look at modern as well as ancient Jewish sources—taking seriously, for example, what the State of Israel has drawn from the Jewish tradition in defending itself as manifested in documents like the IDF code of ethics as well as Israel's policies and practices in waging war.

War and Peace in the Nature of God

Many Jews do not like to confront this fact, but God is depicted in the Bible as a God of war. A check of the biblical concordance indicates that the phrase "*Adonai tz'va'ot*" ("Lord of armies") appears 244 times in the Hebrew Bible, and together with similar phrases such as "*Adonai elohei tz'va'ot*" ("the Lord, God of armies") the description of God as a God of war appears 286 times in the Hebrew Bible. God, in fact, not only does battle; God commands the Israelites to go to battle to conquer the Canaanite nations.[5] With regard to Amalek, God tells Moses: "Inscribe this in a document as a reminder, and read it aloud to Joshua: 'I will utterly blot out the memory of Amalek from under heaven!' . . . The Lord will be at war with Amalek throughout the generations" (Exod. 19:14–16.). King Saul later loses his throne for not killing all the animals of Amalek as well as the people (I Sam. 15). Furthermore, messianic visions of future times in the Bible regularly include God waging war with Israel's enemies and even with the parts of nature that served them to actualize a promised state in which the Israelites will rule themselves and peace and justice will suffuse the world.[6]

At the same time, other sources in the Bible serve as the basis for the belief in a God of compassion and peace. For example, a biblical passage used often in the liturgy quotes God describing the Divine self as follows:

> The Lord passed before him [Moses] and proclaimed: "The Lord! The Lord! A God compassionate and gracious, slow to anger, abounding in kindness and faithfulness, extending kindness to the thousandth generation, forgiving iniquity, transgression, and sin; yet He does not remit all punishment, but visits the iniquity of parents upon children and children's children, upon the third and fourth generation."[7]

The Rabbis cite this passage to assert that God desires peace:

> The Lord says to Gideon: "'You will have peace; have no fear, you shall not die.' So Gideon built there an altar to the Lord and called it 'Adonai Shalom' ('The Lord of Peace')." (Judg. 6:23–24)

Based on this verse the Rabbis say: "Great is peace, for all blessings are contained in it. . . . Great is peace, for God's name is peace."[8] Furthermore, God's blessings of the people Israel repeatedly include a blessing of peace, perhaps most notably when God instructs Aaron and his descendants to bless the Israelites by saying: "May the Lord bless you and protect you! May the Lord deal kindly and graciously with you! May the Lord bestow His favor upon you and grant you peace."[9] Thus, any formulation of a Jewish approach to war and peace must take into account that God is depicted in the traditional sources as the author of both war and peace.

The Nature of Human Beings

If God as described in Jewish sources has conflicting tendencies toward both war and peace, human beings do likewise. This begins with the tradition's insistence, as articulated in the Garden of Eden story, that human beings know the difference between good and evil and have the free will—and therefore the responsibility—to choose between them.[10]

The Rabbis understand the human moral situation as an eternal battle between our *yetzer ha-tov* and our *yetzer ha-ra*, our altruistic instincts and our self-serving ones. (See chapter 3.) This even includes, according to Ecclesiastes, learning when to wage war and when to seek peace:

A season is set for everything, a time for every experience under heaven:
A time for being born and a time for dying,
A time for planting and a time for uprooting the planted;
A time for slaying and a time for healing,
A time for tearing down and a time for building up . . .
A time for ripping and a time for sewing,
A time for silence and a time for speaking;
A time for loving and a time for hating,
A time for war and a time for peace. (Eccles. 3:1–3, 7–8)

Self-Defense for Individuals

The legal foundation for Jews going to war begins with the right to defend oneself from attack, a duty first announced in Exodus 22:1–2: "If a thief is seized while tunneling [under a wall for housebreaking], and he is beaten to death, there is no bloodguilt in his case. If the sun has risen on him, there is bloodguilt in that case." The Talmud concludes that "the Torah [thereby] says: If someone comes to kill you, kill him first."[11] The Torah probably means "the sun" literally, ruling that at night there is no liability for killing the intruder because one cannot discern whether the intruder's intent is to kill you or only to rob you, but during the daytime there is liability if one overreacts to a robber who has no clear intention to kill. Later Jewish law, however, understood "if the sun has risen upon him" metaphorically to mean "if it is as clear to you as the sun that the intruder does not intend to act peacefully with you [and intends to injure or kill you], kill him, but if not, do not kill him," so that the issue is not the time of day but the perceived intention of the intruder, even if the robbery is at night.[12] This puts a greater burden on the homeowner to make sure one's life is really at stake before killing the intruder. In the theater of war, one might presume that enemy soldiers want to kill you, but when policing occupied populations, one cannot automatically presume that. This, of course, makes it very hard for Israeli soldiers in our time to know what to do when stationed in the West Bank.

Jewish tradition also teaches that when unfortunate circumstances require that you choose between saving someone else's life or your own, you must choose your own:

Two people are traveling on a journey [far from civilization], and one has a pitcher of water. If both drink, they will both die; but if only one drinks, s/he can reach civilization. Ben Petura taught: It is better that both should drink and die rather than that one should witness his/her companion's death. Rabbi Akiba came and taught: "that your brother may live *with you*" (Leviticus 25:35) [implies] your life takes precedence over his/her life.[13]

The Ritba, a Spanish commentator of the thirteenth century, suggests that Ben Petura based his decision on Leviticus 19:18, "Love your neighbor as yourself," meaning that each person must make every other person a full equal, even in access to life. Most commentators maintain that Rabbi Akiba would have agreed with Ben Petura if both or neither of the travelers owned the jug, but Rabbi Akiba ruled this way because he assumed that only one of them did. That person, Rabbi Akiba maintained, may not give up his or her own life by sharing the water because suicide is just as prohibited as murder. In this morally impossible situation, he was claiming, let the circumstances determine who drinks the water, even if it is just who happens to own the jug of water, and then let nature take its course so that the people involved do not have the moral burden of making a decision to commit either suicide or murder.

Another famous and controversial source, which I discuss fully elsewhere, affirms that one may not save one's own life and the lives of other innocent people by sacrificing the life of another person.[14] The exception is if the person to be sacrificed has been found guilty of a capital offense—and even then it is not clear that one should give up that person's life to save others. The difficulty of this decision is evidenced by the differing opinions recorded in the sources, which are open to divergent interpretations, and by the fact that the story appears in two different forms:

> Caravans of men are walking down a road, and they are accosted by non-Jews who say to them: "Give us one from among you that we may kill him; otherwise we shall kill you all." Though all may be killed, they may not hand over a single soul of Israel. However, if the demand is for a specified individual like Sheva, son of Bikhri, they should surrender him rather than all be killed.
>
> Rabbi Judah said: When do these words apply [that they may hand over to the enemy only someone who is named and also liable for the death penalty like Sheva ben Bikhri]? When he [the individual in question] is inside [the city walls] and they [the enemy] are outside. But if he is inside and they [the enemy] are inside, because he would be slain and they [the other city dwellers] would be slain, let them surrender him [that is, even someone named by the enemy but not liable for the death penalty] so that not all of them will be slain.[15]

The Jerusalem Talmud, however, adds two sections that complicate matters further:

> Resh Lakish stated: [He may be surrendered] only if he is deserving of death as Sheva, son of Bikhri. Rabbi Yohanon said: Even if he is not deserving of death as Sheva, son of Bikhri.

Ulla, son of Qoseb, was wanted by the [non-Jewish] government. He arose and fled to Rabbi Joshua ben Levi at Lydda. They [troops] came, surrounded the city, and said: "If you do not hand him over to us, we will destroy the city." Rabbi Joshua ben Levi went up to him, persuaded him to submit, and gave him up [to them]. Now Elijah [the prophet], of blessed memory, had been in the habit of visiting him [Rabbi Joshua], but he [now] ceased visiting him. He [Rabbi Joshua] fasted several fasts and Elijah appeared and said to him: "Shall I reveal myself to informers [betrayers]?" He [Rabbi Joshua] said: "Have I not carried out a mishnah [a rabbinic ruling]?" Said he [Elijah]: "Is this a ruling for the pious (*mishnat Hasidim*)?" [Another version: "This should have been done through others and not by you."][16]

As diverse as the various responses to these two situations are in these two sources, they clearly affirm that one has both a right and a duty to defend oneself, but not at all costs. Ben Petera would limit self-defense to those situations where you are not taking other innocent lives in defending your own, and Rabbi Akiba, according to many commentators, would agree with him if neither traveler nor both owned the jug of water. The various positions on responding to an enemy demanding one of your own on pain of killing all of you exquisitely articulate the moral dilemma of saving yourself at the expense of other people, even those condemned to death by law. Rabbi Akiba rules that "your life comes first," but the story of the caravan severely limits that.

Unfortunately, Jews responding to morally excruciating situations in the Holocaust, such as whether to suffocate their own babies to prevent their hiding places from being discovered, or whether to commit suicide so as not to reveal the hiding place of other Jews under torture, provide concrete examples of the limits of the right and duty of self-defense. Similarly, in the modern State of Israel, not only police and soldiers, but ordinary citizens regularly confront situations in which Arab civilians might kill them. Under those circumstances, which security measures are and are not legitimate as a matter of self-defense?

War and Peace in Jewish Law

When we look at the few sources in the Jewish tradition that specifically deal with war, we find, first, a passage in the Torah that may well reflect its ethic of war during the First Temple period, when Jewish rulers had the responsibility and power to decide whether to go to war and how to conduct it. The relevant passage is Deuteronomy 20–21. In it, the Torah demands that Israelites make an offer of peace before waging war, but this is not what one might think—a negotiated peace in which both parties live and let live. It is an offer of bloodless conquest and forced labor, which any army would prefer over the risk of losing their lives in battle if they thought that they would lose. Furthermore, the Torah allows for such bloodless conquest only for distant wars; the Israelites are commanded to kill every person in the Canaanite nations they are to occupy as their homeland.

The Rabbis later add limitations on how Jews should conduct war. So, for example, they interpret one verse of this biblical passage to say this: "['When you approach a town] to attack it'-—and not to make it suffer starvation or thirst and not to make it die the death of sicknesses."[17] As gruesome as war is, the Rabbis here are saying that outright killing is better than torturing people to death.

Furthermore, because the beginning of this biblical passage is discussing wars against distant cities, beyond the conquest of Canaan, the Rabbis maintain that the exemptions from service at the very beginning of this passage apply only to such discretionary wars:

> To what does this [the exemptions from service] apply? To discretionary wars [*milhamot reshut*], but in wars commanded by the Torah [*milhamot mitzvah*] all go forth, even a bridegroom from his chamber and a bride from her canopy. Rabbi Judah says: To what extent do these verses apply? To wars commanded by the Torah [*milhamot mitzvah*], but in obligatory wars [*milhamot hovah*] all go forth, even a bridegroom from his chamber and a bride from her canopy.[18]

Because this Mishnah introduces categories of war, the Talmud seeks to define them:

> Rava said: All [i.e., the Rabbis of the majority opinion and Rabbi Judah] agree that the wars waged by Joshua to conquer Canaan [and the war against Amalek] were commanded; they also agree that the wars waged by the House of David for territorial expansion were voluntary; they

differ with regard to wars [Israelites undertake] against heathens so that they shall not march against them. One [Rabbi Judah] calls them obligatory and the other [the majority opinion] voluntary, the practical issue being that one who is engaged in the performance of a commandment is exempt from the performance of another commandment.[19]

The Talmud thus describes three kinds of wars: those directly commanded by God (*milhamot mitzvah*), discretionary wars to expand Israelite territory (*milhamot reshut*), and preemptive wars to defend against future attacks (*milhamot hovah*, obligatory wars). In other places the Talmud allows discretionary wars only with the concurrence of the Sanhedrin and an oracle issuing from the High Priest's breastplate.[20] Thus when neither of those existed anymore, the only type of war allowed was a war not explicitly listed here but presumably assumed—namely, a war carried out in self-defense. The debate as to which wars are legitimate then narrows to the legitimacy of preemptive wars taken in the name of self-defense but before the Israelites are actually attacked:

> Rav Judah stated in the name of Rav: If foreigners besieged Israelite towns, it is not permitted to sally forth against them or to desecrate the Sabbath in any other way on their account. . . . This, however, applies only where they came for the sake of monetary gain, but if they came with the intention of taking lives, the people are permitted to sally forth against them with their weapons and to desecrate the Sabbath on their account. Where the attack, however, was made on a town that was close to the frontier [the loss of which would constitute a strategic danger to the other parts of the country], even though they did not come with any intention of taking lives but merely to plunder straw and hay, the people are permitted to sally forth against them with their weapons and to desecrate the Sabbath on their account.[21]

Furthermore, rabbinic law requiring the approval of the Sanhedrin and, especially, the oracle of the High Priest's breastplate has been interpreted as requiring that Jews engage only in those battles that they have a good chance of winning. To do otherwise would violate the prominent Jewish norm of protecting and saving life. At the same time, Jewish laws forbidding idolatry as well as precedents in the Bible, the Maccabean period (the Hanukkah story as told in the books of Maccabees), and Jews in the Middle Ages going to war or dying the death of martyrs to avoid idolatry would argue that some wars are necessary for that purpose even if the alternative exists to worship the idol and stay alive.

If Jewish sources give us some guidance in determining when to go to war, they provide precious little guidance as to the conduct of war. Sometimes the instructions one finds in the tradition are downright self-contradictory. So, for example, Deuteronomy 20 requires Israelites to slay all the enemy's men and permits Israelites to take as booty all the enemy's women, children, and property. One story during Joshua's conquest, however, records a dramatic confrontation of those Israelites who took booty, and that story was used during the Six-Day War, in 1967, to publicly embarrass those few Israeli troops who did so.[22] King Saul is told to kill all the inhabitants of Amalek, women and children included, and to destroy all its property, and he loses his throne because he follows the rule in Deuteronomy (1 Sam. 15). According to biblical scholars, however, Deuteronomy was written some four centuries after King Saul, so this may be evidence of an evolving ethic of war rather than a self-contradiction in the sources. Deuteronomy 21 bans the destruction of fruit trees, and it also establishes rules about what Israelites must do if they wish to marry a woman taken captive.

Finally, and most importantly, the Jewish tradition does not valorize war. It sees self-defense and the avoidance of idolatry as making war necessary sometimes, and it honors Jewish warriors who prevent or fend off enemy attacks. That is the context of seeing the ancient Maccabees and modern Israeli soldiers as heroes. War, though, is not to be desired, and it certainly is not to be honored as the way that a man shows he is a man. On the contrary, the rabbinic tradition, on which Judaism is based, honored the scholar and saw military might and even physical prowess as demonstrated in sports as a pagan, Roman value at odds with what Jews should prize. That, of course, may be because Jewish Zealots had tried to revolt against Rome several times and failed, so the voices we are hearing in the rabbinic tradition are those who objected to war in the first place. Even if that historical explanation is true, however, the fact is that the Jewish tradition, while not completely pacifist, much prefers peace. Thus the Rabbis, citing the verse in Psalms that says "Seek peace and pursue it," say this:

The Law does not order you to run after or pursue the other commandments, but only to fulfill them on the appropriate occasion. But peace you must seek in your own place and pursue it even to another place as well.[23]

In addition, peace is a major element in Jewish prayers; in fact, many of the major sections of the liturgy (e.g., the *Amidah*, Grace After Meals) end with a prayer for peace. Peace is also a major component of Jewish visions of the pinnacle of Jewish hopes, the Messianic Era, perhaps most famously articulated in this passage from Isaiah:

> In the days to come,
> The Mount of the Lord's House
> Shall stand firm above the mountains
> And tower above the hills;
> And all the nations
> Shall gaze on it with joy.
> And the many peoples shall go and say:
> "Come, let us go up to the Mount of the Lord,
> To the House of the God of Jacob;
> That He may instruct us in His ways,
> And that we may walk in His paths."
> For instruction shall come forth from Zion,
> The word of the Lord from Jerusalem.
> Thus He will judge among the nations
> And arbitrate for the many peoples,
> And they shall beat their swords into plowshares
> And their spears into pruning hooks:
> Nation shall not take up sword against nation;
> They shall never again know war.[24]

Implications for a Modern Jewish Theory of War

Now, having examined Judaism's larger conceptions of God, the human being, and the goals of human life, along with the Jewish tradition's sources on war, what emerges as at least some of the elements of a contemporary Jewish approach to war and peace? I would suggest the following pieces of such a theory:

Jus Ad Bellum: Justifications for Going to War

1. **War sometimes must be fought.** The Jewish concepts of both God and people understand them as sometimes making war.

2. **Although conquest of territory justified war in the past, now only self-defense and avoidance of idolatry are acceptable reasons to go to war.** Some wars will be clearly defensive in nature, but nowadays, with the rise of terrorism, guerrilla warfare, and hidden nuclear bombs and other weapons of mass destruction, sometimes the claimed need to go to war for self-defense purposes is much harder to prove.

3. **Self-defense may include preemptive strikes when the bellicose intention of the enemy is clear.** This was certainly the case when Egypt's Nasser blocked the Straits of Tiran and publicly engaged in extensive saber-rattling in the days before the Six-Day War, in 1967. It proved not to be the case in President George W. Bush's invasion of Iraq, in 2003, to destroy the weapons of mass destruction that were supposed to be there but were not.

4. **Jews as a nation should fight only in those wars that they are likely to win.** This is a clear derivation of the demand to preserve our life and health as the property of God.

5. **War should be avoided if at all possible; peace must be actively sought.** This is articulated not only in rabbinic sources that say this explicitly, but also in all the prayers and hopes of the Jewish tradition for a world without war. The Jewish culture accepts war when necessary to defend oneself and honors those who succeed in that task but does not glorify war as the way to prove a man's masculinity and a nation's power.

Jus in Bello: Proper Conduct of War

1. **Kill as few people as possible.** Judaism's strong emphasis on protecting and saving life demands that even in a defensive war one must seek to kill as few people as possible. Even though Ben Gurion was a secular Jew, this element of the Jewish religious tradition undoubtedly influenced him in formulating his doctrine of *tohar ha-neshek* ("purity of arms"), according to which soldiers may shoot only those who have attacked them first. This was clearly not the norm in the

conquest of Canaan, when the Israelites were commanded to kill all the inhabitants, but that series of wars occurred some three thousand years ago and, most importantly, the rules governing those wars do not constitute precedents for any wars thereafter.

2. **Preserve your own life and that of your comrades in arms.** One has primary responsibility to protect and defend one's own life and those of one's comrades in arms and community. Therefore, even though one should seek to win while killing as few of the enemy as possible, one must kill as many as necessary to protect one's own life and those of one's army and community.

3. **Damage the environment as little as possible.** Hence the remarkable requirement in Deuteronomy to preserve the fruit trees, a mandate that can easily be applied to modern environmental concerns in war, such as the use of Napalm in the Vietnam War.

4. **War does not justify rape or other forms of torture, humiliation, or injury of the enemy not required to defend oneself and one's community.** This stems directly from the respect we must have for all human beings as creatures of God, created in the Divine Image. It leaves open the possibility, recognized by the Israeli Supreme Court, of some forms of physical pressure to reveal the whereabouts of terrorists about to kill many people (the "ticking bomb" case), but only if such procedures can be demonstrated to prevent such terrorism.

5. **The norms with regard to booty and other forms of enemy property are unclear.** This emerges from the conflicting norms found, on one hand, in the Joshua and Saul stories, both of which see the taking of booty as unacceptable, and the law permitting the taking of booty in Deuteronomy, on the other.

These rules do not constitute a full-blown Jewish theory of just war, but they illustrate that such a theory can be built on the basis of Jewish precedents, concepts, and values. This does not preclude borrowing from other traditions, as Professor Walzer suggests, to supplement what we can learn from the Jewish tradition, but it does demonstrate that we need not satisfy ourselves with that. We can build the foundation for a Jewish theory of war and peace—and judge which elements from outside the Jewish tradition we want to borrow—on the basis of what we find in Jewish sources.

17

Addressing Donations from Ill-Gotten Gain

In 2003 the director of one of the Conservative movement's Ramah camps asked me what the Jewish tradition would have Ramah do in a situation where a grand jury had indicted a major donor to the camp for money laundering and stock fraud. My response to him evolved into a formal responsum on the broader issue of donations from ill-gotten gain for the movement's Committee on Jewish Law and Standards, and the CJLS unanimously approved it on June 4, 2009.[1] In a subsequent article that CJLS member and lawyer Marc Gary and I wrote together, he added an explanation of how American law would respond to these questions. Notably, the underlying ideologies of the two legal systems—Jewish and American law—lead them to approach the same issues differently and to ask different questions altogether when responding to the case.[2] What follows is drawn from sections of my CJLS responsum on a Jewish moral and legal response to this case and others like it.

Because this case arose at a Ramah camp, Ramah was the example used throughout the responsum. Its reasoning and conclusions, however, apply equally to all Jewish communal institutions—synagogues, schools, federations, social service agencies, national and international religious and educational organizations, etc. To read the full responsum: http://www.rabbinicalassembly.org/sites/default/files/public/halakhah/teshuvot/20052010/Dorff_Donations%20of%20ill-Gotten%20gain.final.062909.pdf.

Mr. and Mrs. Jones (not their real family name) send their children to one of the Ramah camps (summer camps for youth of the Conservative/Masorti movement), and they have become very friendly with that particular Ramah community, to the extent that Mrs. Jones is on its board of directors. Several years ago they donated money to that Ramah. It was used primarily to build a facility at camp that bears their family name, though some funds remain for Ramah to use for other purposes. A grand jury just indicted Mr. Jones for money laundering and stock fraud, and the cover story in the local Jewish newspaper described the indictment in great detail. The Jones family belongs to an Orthodox synagogue, whose rabbi gave a sermon on the Shabbat following the indictment denouncing Mr. Jones and announcing that the facility the family had donated to the synagogue would no longer bear their name.

Questions

1. May or should Camp Ramah treat Mr. Jones as if he were already convicted of the crime of which he is accused after he is indicted but before he is convicted?
2. If Mr. Jones is convicted of the crime of which he is accused, may or should Camp Ramah remove the Jones family name from the facility they donated? What if the facility was named for Mr. Jones alone?
3. Must Camp Ramah use funds it has raised from other sources to return this money to the Jones family if it has already been used to construct the building in their name?
4. Must Camp Ramah return the money the Jones family donated that has not yet been used?
5. May Camp Ramah accept any further donations from Mr. Jones?
6. May Camp Ramah accept any further donations from the Jones family?

Between Indictment and Conviction

At the moment the question was asked, Mr. Jones had been indicted but not convicted. Jewish law presumes even more strongly than American law that a person is innocent until proven guilty, for in American law, one may confess to both civil and criminal liability, while in Jewish law, one may confess to civil liability ("a litigant's admission is like one hundred witnesses") but not to culpability for a crime, for "one may not make oneself a wicked person."[3] Thus, during the time between the indictment and the court verdict, rabbis need to inform anyone who asks about this case that the strong presumption of innocence in Jewish law requires everyone to think and act accordingly; failure to do so is a violation of the prohibition to slander others (*motzi shem ra*).[4]

After Conviction: Removing the Jones Family Name from the Building

May—or should—Ramah remove the Jones family name from the building if the donor is convicted of a felony? Even though a pervasive principle in the Talmud is that we should not reward a sinner (*shelo yeheh hoteh niskar*), even more important is the pervasive talmudic principle that we must uphold people's honor and, conversely, avoid embarrassing them.[5] The Talmud compares one who embarrasses people in public to a murderer, and it denies a place in the World to Come to someone who embarrasses another in public.[6] In fact, Jewish law requires that one who embarrasses another pay damages for the shame (*boshet*) involved. (See chapter 11.)[7]

For these reasons, even if Mr. Jones is convicted, Ramah should not on its own initiative remove the family name, for fear of causing further embarrassment to him and his family. Indeed, the Mishnah specifically allows a community to honor someone with a moral cloud over his head:

> Similarly, if an [accidental] killer was exiled to a city of refuge and the people of the city wanted to honor him, he should say to them, "I am a killer." If they say to him, "Even so [we want to honor you,]" he may accept [the honor] from them, as the Torah says (Deuteronomy 19:4), "This is the word of the killer" [where "word" is in the singular, suggesting that the killer need only tell them once and need not repeat his announcement of his tainted moral status].[8]

The Jones family name may and should be removed from the facility if the family requests this.

Different considerations apply if the building is named solely for the donor of ill-gotten gains, as distinct from its bearing the family name, where, as discussed, other family members are presumed to be innocent of involvement in ill-gotten gains and might be embarrassed by the removal. If only the donor's name appears, an organization might ask itself, would it remove the names of donors who did not pay their pledges for this building? If so, the level of malfeasance that triggers this action is apparently lower than that for actual crimes, so removing the name may not be as shameful as it would be in other contexts. That is, *community standards* play a role in this decision, especially if they are built into contracts with major donors.

The decision also depends critically on *the level of the crime*. A violent crime or fraud committed to the extent that Bernard Madoff did might well justify removal of the name.

Where, though, is the line for triggering this response? This is a *very* slippery slope, and if all forms of malfeasance disqualified donations, most, if not all, charities would cease to exist. Exactly how pure must donated money be, and how would a charity know this?

In the end, then, Ramah and all other charities should attempt to specify in their contracts with major donors the conditions under which they are accepting money and offering honors. Because of the difficulty of specifying such conditions in legal contracts—apart from failing to pay one's full pledge—discussion with the donor(s) about removing a name from a facility is the best way to proceed when faced with this question.

After Conviction: Returning Donated Money that Had Already Been Used

The prophets warn us repeatedly against complicity in illegal actions and their financial earnings. Amos, chronologically the first of the literary prophets, already sets the tone:

> Listen to this, you who devour the needy, annihilating the poor of the land, saying, "If only the new moon were over so that we could sell grain, the sabbath, so that we could offer wheat for sale, using an ephah [a dry measure] that is too small and a shekel that is too big, tilting a dishonest scale and selling grain refuse as grain! We will buy the poor for silver, the needy for a pair of sandals." The Lord swears by the Pride of Jacob: "I will never forget any of their doings." Shall not the earth shake for this and all that dwell on it mourn?[9]

Furthermore, Deuteronomy 23:19 specifically forbids us from accepting for the Temple any donation whose source is ill-gotten—in its specific case, the wages of a prostitute:

> You shall not bring the fee of a whore or the pay of a dog [a male prostitute] into the house of the Lord your God in fulfillment of any vow, for both are abhorrent to the Lord your God.

The Talmud and the codes then make it clear that it is forbidden—"a great sin"—to acquire stolen property from a thief:

It is forbidden to acquire from a burglar the object that he stole, and it is a great sin [to do so], for that strengthens the hands of one who violates the law and causes him to steal other things, for if he would find no buyer, he would not steal, and on this Scripture says, "He who shares with a thief is his own enemy" (Proverbs 29:24).[10]

It is forbidden to acquire anything robbed from the robber, and it is forbidden to help him change it so that he may legally acquire it, for anyone who does these things or anything similar strengthens the hands of transgressors and violates [the Torah's law], "Before a blind person do not put a stumbling block" (Leviticus 19:14).[11]

Some might then plausibly argue that Ramah should take the high moral road of returning the Jones family money, so that Ramah is not tainted in any way by Mr. Jones's illegal actions. Ramah may choose to do this, but Jewish law does not require that response. Ramah accepted the Jones money without knowing it was ill-gotten gain; it therefore has the protection of *takkanat ha-shuk*, and they need not return anything to either Mr. Jones or the people from whom he stole, if they could be identified. The Rabbis instituted *takkanat ha-shuk*, the enactment of the market, according to which a person who acquired something not knowing that it was stolen need not give the original owner either the property or its value unless the seller was a known thief, "because otherwise no person would purchase anything, for fear that it had been stolen."[12] Indeed, as Rabbi Ben Zion Bergman, z"l, pointed out to the CJLS in discussing this responsum, the same logic that moved the Rabbis to institute *takkanat ha-shuk* to enable people to trust that they will not have to part with what they buy innocently in the market applies to charities just as well and perhaps even more. To rule otherwise "would put an onerous burden on every communal institution to question whether any major gift was pure as the driven snow, lest they have to return it later. . . . Therefore, considering that it is in society's best interest to encourage charitable institutions and to facilitate their efficient operation, requiring the return of a charitable contribution of questionable provenance would be highly detrimental to the public interest."[13]

Moreover, Ramah has already used the money to finance the building bearing the Jones name. There has thus been a change in the nature of the gift from money to a building, and a *shinnuy ma'aseh* (an irretrievable change in form) confers ownership on the thief.[14] According to Maimonides, the reason that change of form confers ownership is to encourage thieves to repent for their thievery.[15] It is consequently called *takkanat ha-shavim*, "the enactment for those who repent."

If a permanent change confers ownership on a thief, it presumably has even greater power to transfer ownership to an innocent recipient of the stolen assets who permanently changes the form of what was stolen—in this case, Ramah, which changed Mr. Jones's money into a building. Thus, Ramah owns the building, and, contrary to the thief, Ramah has no obligations to the people Mr. Jones defrauded to pay them back. Mr. Jones has the duty to restore to his victims the money he stole from them, as described by Maimonides in the source cited above, but Ramah, as an innocent recipient of his money, does not have that duty.

In fact, in this specific case, Mr. Jones defrauded the government and therefore cannot really identify the specific individuals hurt by his actions. In such cases, the specific way that Jewish law provides for him to compensate his unknown victims is to contribute to a public charity like Ramah:

> The form of return (repentance, *teshuvah*) for shepherds, charity collectors, and tax collectors is difficult because they stole from the public, and they do not know to whom to return [what they stole]. Therefore, they should do with it [what they stole] public works, like wells, ditches, and caves.[16]

In light of this, some might rightfully object to Ramah using other money to reimburse the Jones family on the grounds that Ramah should not waste any money it collects and desperately needs for its sacred purposes on something like this, particularly when Jewish law specifically provides that Ramah has no duty to return it and may actually undermine Mr. Jones's ability to repent if it does so. In other words, what appears to be the high moral road—returning the money to the Jones family—is not that after all, but an irresponsible use of money donated by others.

After Conviction: Returning Unused Donated Money

Unlike the money already used to construct the Jones family building, a smaller portion of the donated funds has not undergone a change in form;

it is still money. Thus, the laws cited in the previous section invoking a change in form do not apply to them.

Of the three parties in the case—the original owners, the thief, and the buyer (or the receiver of a gift)—thieves are the ones with presumably the least money and therefore are the least likely to be able to pay a judgment against them. Thus, in the laws described below, the party that has to claim against the thief is at a real disadvantage, for thieves may not be able to pay what they owe.

Mr. Jones was not a "known thief" (*ganav me'fursam*) before the recent accusations. If he were, the enactment of the market would not apply. Ramah would have to give the money back to its original owners (in this case, the government) and seek to force Mr. Jones to make good on his pledge.[17]

In our case, however, Mr. Jones was not a known thief, so the enactment of the market applies. Even without a change in form, if a thief sold or gave a stolen object or money to a third party who did not have reason to suspect that it was stolen, the exchange of the property (*shinnuy reshut*)—that is, the change of possession, together with the original owners' despair of getting it back—is sufficient to confer ownership on the buyer or recipient.[18] If, on the other hand, the original owner has not yet despaired of getting it back, the duty to return it to the owner still applies, because ownership has not transferred to anyone else.

One contemporary case in which the purchaser would not acquire ownership under Jewish law is that of artwork stolen by the Nazis and then acquired from them, sometimes in a series of purchases after World War II. Increasingly, international law agrees with Jewish law on this: because the original owners—or their descendants—may not have even known about their ancestors' possessions and certainly did not despair of recovering them, purchasers must return the artwork to the original owners or their heirs.

Ramah did not buy anything from Mr. Jones; it received money from him as a gift. Nevertheless, as the *Shulhah Arukh* specifies, the same law applies, for both selling and gifting confer ownership on the receiver, assuming that the original owners despaired of getting their money or object back.[19]

The question here, then, is whether the owners despaired of getting their money back. If the government were the only aggrieved party, Ramah would not need to return any money it received from Mr. Jones once the government settled its civil case with him. In cases such as this, though, prosecution by the Securities and Exchange Commission is often followed by civil suits filed by individual stockholders or other aggrieved parties, such as employees and those with whom the accused party contracted for goods or services. This would have the practical effect of preventing Ramah from benefiting from any of the unused funds that Mr. Jones donated until a substantial period of time had passed.[20] The difficulty of demonstrating that the original owners despaired of recouping their losses may give charities incentive to spend donated money rather than keep it in the bank, where it is essentially held conditionally, subject to disgorgement if found to be tainted.[21]

After Conviction: Accepting Further Donations from the Jones Family

What if Mr. Jones has paid the compensation and fines or served the prison sentence imposed by the court and now wants to donate further money to Ramah? May Ramah accept such donations?

As noted, according to Jewish law, people may not buy from known thieves or accept any further gifts from them.[22] The Rabbis instituted this prohibition lest buyers from thieves or recipients of gifts from them thereby induce thieves to steal more, thus violating Leviticus 19:14, "Do not put a stumbling block before a blind man," which the Rabbis understood to mean not only physically blind, but morally blind as well.[23] So assuming that Mr. Jones is convicted, any future gifts by him must be declined.[24]

There is one exception to this rule, however. If Mr. Jones specifically and publicly indicates that, in addition to the compensation, fines, or prison sentence the court imposed, he wants to donate more money to Ramah as a form of *teshuvah*, of return to proper conduct and the good graces of God and the Jewish community, Ramah may accept such a donation if it has good reason to believe that Mr. Jones legally earned the money it is now getting and is genuinely engaged in the process of *teshuvah*. His intentions, of course, are difficult, if not impossible, to determine. As a result, people might presume that Mr. Jones is just trying to buy back respectability, and they might say that Ramah should not be the vehicle to enable him to do that. Still, Jewish law requires us to judge one's fellow's intentions favorably, especially when they are accompanied by good deeds, so if Ramah can be assured that the new money was legitimately earned, it may accept additional donations from him as part of his *teshuvah*.[25] Further, as noted above, it may definitely take the money if the victims of Mr. Jones's thievery are not known, for then the way that Jewish law would have him compensate his unknown victims is by contributing to a public charity.[26] The Jewish tradition believes strongly in the need for, and the power of, return (*teshuvah*).[27]

Rulings

1. **General rule about economic transactions.** In general, charities may accept donations from donors without investigating the sources of the money as a result of *takkanat ha-shuk*, the enactment of the market, the Rabbinic rule that in all monetary transactions, including charitable ones, the recipient can assume that the money used has been legitimately obtained. The one exception is if the person using or giving the money is a known thief (a *ganav mefursam*), in which case the recipient of the money bears the legal burden of assuring that it has been legitimately obtained for use in this transaction.

2. **Indictment vs. conviction.** Until and unless Mr. Jones is convicted, Jews individually and collectively must think and act toward him on the strong presumption in American law and the even stronger presumption in Jewish law that he is innocent. To do otherwise would violate the ban on slander (*motzi shem ra*).

3. **Names on facilities.** If Mr. Jones is convicted, Ramah should *not* remove the family name from the facility unless his family specifically requests this. To otherwise do so would violate Jewish laws prohibiting public embarrassment of innocent family members.

   If the building is named solely for Mr. Jones, whether to remove his name depends in part on community standards. What, besides crimes, would lead the nonprofit to remove the names of donors? And what is the level of his crime? If Mr. Jones violated the law in a less serious way, then the question of shaming him by removing his name from the facility should not even arise. If, on the other hand, Mr. Jones committed a violent crime, multiple crimes involving the oppression of individuals and society in general, or much more extensive fraud than he is alleged to have committed in this specific case, then Ramah or any other nonprofit organization should remove his name from the facility so that people do not think that the nonprofit honors the kinds of acts Mr. Jones committed.

In any case, the community has a duty to give emotional and other forms of support to the innocent members of Mr. Jones's family and even to Mr. Jones himself as they go through this painful period in their lives, for they are, after all, members of our community—indeed active and contributing members—who should be thought of not solely for the crime that Mr. Jones committed but also for the good that he and his family have done.

4. **Money already used.** If Mr. Jones is convicted of the crimes, Ramah need not return the money already used to erect the building that bears the family's name because a permanent change of form (*shinnui ma'aseh*) and despair of the original owners (*ya'ush ha-ba'alim*) have occurred.

5. **Money not yet used.** If Mr. Jones is convicted of the crimes, Ramah need not return the unused money if both the government and all aggrieved parties have settled their cases with him or the statute of limitations has run out for any aggrieved parties to file further civil suits. In other cases, the nonprofit institution must determine whether both a transfer of possession (*shinnui reshut*) and the owners' despair of retrieving their property (*ya'ush ha-ba-alim*) have occurred to decide whether it is legally entitled to keep the donation. If both transfer of possession and the owner's despair have occurred, they may keep it; if not, they must return it.

6. **Accepting further donations from Mr. Jones.** If Mr. Jones is convicted, Ramah may not accept any more money from him unless (a) Mr. Jones has publicly specified that, in addition to the compensation, fines, or prison time the court imposed, he wants to make this further donation as part of his process of *teshuvah* and (b) Ramah can determine that he earned the new money legitimately.

7. **Accepting further donations from the Jones family.** If the Jones family offers to donate more money to Ramah, the camp may accept it if either (a) the assets were transferred, before Mr. Jones's conviction, to his family members, who received them

with no knowledge that they were the fruit of illegal activities (i.e., there had been a change of ownership, a *shinnuy reshut*, to innocent parties before the indictment) and the original owners had despaired of retrieving their property (*ya'ush*), along the lines defined in ruling (4) above; or (b) the assets of Mr. Jones himself are a minority of what the Jones family is contributing and it is not known whether his portion was stolen or not.

8. **Protecting the reputation of the nonprofit agency.** Even though it is legally permissible to act in the ways described above, if Mr. Jones is convicted, the Ramah Board may decide that it is in the camp's best interests to return the money received from the Jones family or to refuse to accept any more money from them, just as it may decide to accept or reject any other proposed gift from anyone else. Likely considerations in this judgment—although not the only possible ones—are the level of Mr. Jones's crime; the extent to which keeping the Jones's gifts will undermine the mission, values, or reputation of the nonprofit; and the likelihood that keeping their gifts will deter future donations from others.

18

Final Thoughts

The title of this book is *Ethics at the Center* because I believe the core mission of the Jewish tradition is ethical. Hence, the previous chapters have discussed both the theory and some areas of practice of the Jewish tradition that advance its ethical goals.

A center, though, exists only in the middle of a circle that surrounds and interacts with it. Likewise, ethics is far from the sum total of the Jewish tradition. Other elements of Jewish identity definitely, but more indirectly, affect the moral guidance and motivation that Judaism provides:

Family and Community. My service, on over a hundred rabbinic courts, interviewing people converting to Judaism has brought this reality home to me: the two reasons people almost always give for wanting to convert to Judaism are the ability to ask any question and the strong ties of family and community that they see among Jews. Not only a sociological feature of the Jewish community, shaped in part by the need to bond together to respond to antisemitism in its various forms, this abiding sense of community is also grounded in a strong moral commitment embedded in the Jewish tradition's demand that "all Israelites are responsible for one another" and our sense of belonging to a people in Covenant with God with a mission to be "a light to the nations" (Isa. 42:6; 49:6; 60:3; see also chapters 3 and 4). Jews gain a strong sense of belonging to the Jewish community all over the world and past, present, and future, and that sense, whether motivated by religious tenets or not, means a lot to most Jews. The existence of the modern State of Israel, since 1948, is another important source of communal meaning, even though Jews living in Israel and in the Diaspora strongly disagree among themselves about its policies. Ultimately, though, we are all members of "the Tribe."

Even though family and community are important to us for many reasons apart from their ethical import, they do affect our moral understanding and motivation. We learn, after all, what is and what is not appropriate behavior first from our parents and then from the community in which we live. Our desire to continue to be accepted and even respected within our family and community is an ongoing motivation for us to act morally. Especially when it is hard to act morally, the Jewish concepts of *kiddush ha-Shem* (sanctifying God's name) and its opposite, *ḥillul ha-shem* (desecrating God's name), apply. We need to do that which will honor and not desecrate God and the Jewish People in covenantal relationship with God. We are thus proud of our fellow Jews who do good things and embarrassed by those who do bad things, even though we personally had nothing to do with either. For the first time in over two thousand years, the State of Israel is a Jewish self-governing nation, and that poses new and difficult moral issues, some of which were addressed in chapter 16.

Holidays and Rituals. Some Jews incorporate Jewish rituals and holiday celebrations in their lives because they believe that God commanded them to do so, either directly in the Torah or through rabbinic expansions of the Torah's laws and through custom. Other Jews are motivated by the power of ritual to identify community. Eating exclusively kosher foods, for example, identifies them as Jewish. Still others appreciate the power of rituals to mark moments in time. When certain moments are marked as different from others, the days of our lives become different as well—and, for that matter, the morning of one day is different from that day's afternoon and evening. And still others find meaning in rituals because they enhance family relationships—as, for example, parents bless their children around the Sabbath table—and help make an art of life, giving life character and flavor.

Rituals, though, can also have moral import. For example, the Jewish tradition honors work to enable people to earn a living and to gain self-respect and the respect of others: "Great is work, for it honors the worker."[1] Work is, in fact, a commandment: "Six days shall you labor and do all your work" (Exod. 20:9; 23:12, etc.). That we are also commanded to desist from work on the Sabbath, however, ensures that, each week, we do not make work an idol, allowing it to consume every waking moment and all our attention, concern, and resources. Instead, at least weekly, we remember and nurture other important values, such as our relationships with family, community, God, and tradition. It also returns us to a Garden of Eden–like state, where we live in nature rather than try to change it.[2] The Sabbath is even important for our work, as it enables us to step back to see it in perspective, reevaluate it, and regain insight and strength to continue it.[3]

Similarly, in as much as the holidays and fasts of the Jewish year mark the seasons of the year or remind us of historical events, many also have ethical import. Passover and Hanukkah, for example, emphasize the importance of both physical and religious freedom, and the High Holy Days require us to examine how we are striving to improve the ways we relate to both God and people.

The Jewish dietary laws restrict the animals we are allowed to eat to approximately 4 percent of the animal kingdom, and they must be slaughtered so as to cause minimal pain to them, thus ensuring that we respect animal life, even if we are killing animals to eat. In recent decades, an increasing number of Jews have taken this concern further by becoming pescetarian, vegetarian, or vegan, while others continue to eat meat but only if produced under strict moral standards about how the people and animals involved are treated.[4] Blood, the sign of life (Gen. 9:4; Lev. 17:14; Deut. 12:23), must be removed from the animal to make its eaters distance themselves from eating life itself, thereby reenforcing respect for the lives of animals and building moral character in the humans who eat them. Meat and dairy foods and utensils must not be mixed to distinguish meals in which we are taking an animal's life from those in which we are eating milk, the paradigmatic life-giving substance for mammals—another way kashrut rituals call attention to the value of life itself.[5]

Theology. For some Jews, our individual and communal relationships to God in prayer and responding to God's commandments in action are deeply meaningful. Experiences of God in our lives can motivate gratitude, humility, and compassion for other human beings, and in those and other ways influence our moral character. As discussed on a theoretical level in chapters 4–6 and illustrated in chapter 7, theology can and should also influence how Jewish law on moral issues is interpreted and applied, for we are to aspire to be holy like God (Lev. 19:2).

Study. Many Jews are attracted to the intellectual part of the Jewish tradition—whether studying traditional texts (e.g., Bible, Mishnah, Talmud, Midrash, and the commentaries on all of those classic texts) or later materials (e.g., Jewish philosophy, history, and literature). The typical Jewish approach of probing materials by asking questions about them and challenging what they say makes Jewish study especially engaging.

Additionally, study contributes to our moral character. Traditional Jewish study in groups (_ḥavruta_) does that by forming ties of friendship and common work as well as honing moral character traits such as responsibility, care, self-control, punctuality, exactitude, and wise judgment.[6]

Music, Dance, and Art. Shelomo Bardin, z"l, a very thoughtful educator in his role as director of the Brandeis Camp Institute (two yearly summer programs of a month each for college and graduate students), insisted that on weekdays the institute include two hours of daily Israeli singing and dancing (each one for an hour) beyond the two hours of daily study. When I asked him why, he said, "Because Judaism is caught, not taught."

I frankly believe that Judaism is both caught and taught, but he certainly was right in pointing out the critical ways in which Jewish music, dance, and the other arts attract many Jews to their Jewish identity and reenforce it. Moreover, these elements of Jewish identity have moral import as well. They reenforce the lessons of the opening chapters of Genesis that creativity is a characteristic we share with God. We should therefore continually reevaluate what we are doing in all areas of life and seek to improve on it. Because the arts involve creativity, they encourage us to demonstrate and appreciate the individuality of each person and thus the inherent respect we need to have for everyone. At the same time, they bring us together as a community to learn from each other and share activities of joy and meaning, reenforcing Judaism's insistence that we acknowledge and value our communal ties—and lead ultimately to Judaism's claim that we are responsible for each other.

Jewish Law. Most Jews living in nations governed by Enlightenment principles see themselves as individuals with rights, limited only by what the civil law forbids or demands. (See chapter 3.) The Jewish tradition, though, sees all Jews as part of a community governed by Jewish law, and Jewish law serves, in part, to delineate and motivate our moral behavior (in ways described in chapters 5 and 6). Even though most contemporary Jews live in lands that guarantee many individual rights, they may want to see their Jewish practices not as things they do simply because they like specific rituals or moral norms, but because they view themselves as being obligated under Jewish law to do them. That may be because law gives structure and therefore a sense of security in what we can reasonably expect of each other morally. It does this in part by spelling out minimal standards of behavior, both negatively and positively—that we may not, for example, harm other people's persons or property and that we must take measures to preserve our own health and care for other people. At least as importantly, it tells us the limits of our responsibilities. In this, law is very different from moral principles that obligate us without limit and thus may be idealistic but unrealistic in practice. So, as discussed in chapter 10, even though saving human lives is of paramount importance, that does not apply to fetuses in the same way that it does to born human beings.

At the same time, while law delineates our minimal responsibilities, Jewish law, unlike civil law, requires us "to go beyond the limits of the law" (*lifnim me'shurat ha-din*) in trying to imitate God (Lev. 19:2) and to become "a kingdom of priests and a holy nation" (Exod. 19:6). As such, Jewish law is not an excuse to do as little as possible to act within moral bounds. One may not, as Naḥmanides said in his commentary to Leviticus 19:2, be a *naval b'reshut ha-torah*, "a scoundrel within the limits of (or the permission of) the law."

Law also enables us to balance conflicting moral norms—telling us, for example, as discussed in chapter 7, that even though saving lives is of paramount importance, there are even limits to this duty when someone has a terminal illness and is in great pain. Additionally, through the rules and tools of legal argumentation, law provides the grounds and a forum for discussing—and, yes, arguing about—hard moral issues, as, for example, how we communicate with one another. Thus, as discussed in chapters 12, 13, and 14, we need to tell the truth about someone else, even if that is negative, if that person is applying for a school or job and the admissions officer or potential employer needs to know whether the person can be expected to succeed in that position. Without a practical need to know, however, we may not spread negative information or feelings about someone else (*lashon ha-ra*, "language about the bad"), even by implication (*avak lashon ha-ra*, "the dust of negative speech"), let alone communicate in ways intended to bully or otherwise harm someone else. Even gossip is prohibited as an invasion of a person's right to privacy.[7]

In sum, ethics is central to Judaism not only in the parts of Judaism where one might expect it to be the focus. It underlies or provides necessary guidance even to those aspects of Judaism that ostensibly address other parts of our being.

Source Acknowledgments

Chapter 1, "A Philosopher Describes What Faith in God Means." *Masorti* (December 2022). Reprinted by permission of Rabbinical Assembly.

Chapter 2, "How Judaism Understands God." Excerpted from "Jewish Images of God," in *Personal Theology: Essays in Honor of Neil Gillman*, edited by William Plevan, 18–41. Boston: Academic Studies Press, 2013. Reprinted by permission of the publisher.

Chapter 3, "How Judaism Understands Human Beings." In Elliot N. Dorff, *To Do the Right and the Good: A Jewish Approach to Modern Social Ethics*, 5–12. Philadelphia: Jewish Publication Society, 2002. Reprinted by permission of The Jewish Publication Society.

Chapter 4, "The Multiple Sources of Judaism that Define, Motivate, and Educate a Moral Person and Society." In Elliot N. Dorff, *Love Your Neighbor and Yourself: A Jewish Approach to Modern Personal Ethics*, 311–44. Philadelphia: Jewish Publication Society, 2003. Reprinted by permission of The Jewish Publication Society.

Chapter 5, "A Statement of My Own Theory of Jewish Law." In Elliot N. Dorff, *For the Love of God and People: A Philosophy of Jewish Law*, 45–48. Philadelphia: Jewish Publication Society, 2007. Reprinted by permission of The Jewish Publication Society.

Chapter 6, "Applying Jewish Law to New Circumstances." Excerpted from "Applying Jewish Law to New Circumstances." In *Teferet Leyisrael: Jubilee Volume in Honor of Israel Francus*, edited by Joel Roth, Menahem Schmelzer, and Yaacob Francus, 189–99. New York: Jewish Theological Seminary, 2010. Reprinted by permission of Jewish Theological Seminary.

Chapter 7, "Applying Jewish Theology to Moral Issues." *Assisted Suicide/Aid in Dying* (Rabbinical Assembly). Based on Elliot N. Dorff, "Assisted Suicide/Aid in Dying Reconsidered," a responsum for the Committee on Jewish Law and Standards, adopted on November 16, 2020, and posted to its website, https://www.rabbinicalassembly.org/sites/default/files/2021-04/Assisted%20Suicide%20Revisited%20final.pdf. Reprinted by permission of Rabbinical Assembly.

Chapter 8. "The Role of Prayer in Moral Discernment and Motivation." In Elliot N. Dorff, *Knowing God: Jewish Journeys to the Unknowable*, 154–58, 171–72. Northvale NJ: Jason Aronson, 1992. Reprinted by permission of Rowman and Littlefield.

Chapter 9, "Autonomy vs. Community." *Conservative Judaism* (Rabbinical Assembly) 48, no. 2 (Winter 1996): 64–68; 50, no. 1 (Fall 1997): 61–65; and 50, no. 1 (Fall 1997): 66–71. Reprinted by permission of Rabbinical Assembly.

Chapter 10, "Abortion after the Overturning of Roe v. Wade." Originally posted on the website of the Jewish Federation Council of Los Angeles in July 2022, along with the reactions of other Los Angeles rabbis, to the U.S. Supreme Court's *Hobbs* decision overturning *Roe v. Wade*. Reprinted by permission of Jewish Federation Council of Los Angeles.

Chapter 11, "Dignity: A Jewish Perspective." Excerpts from *Value and Vulnerablity: An Interfaith Dialogue on Human Dignity*, edited by Matthew R. Petrusek and Jonathan Rotchild, 92, 101, and 117–18. South Bend IN: University of Notre Dame Press, 2020. Reprinted by permission of Rabbinical Assembly and University of Notre Dame Press.

Chapter 12, "Providing References for Schools and Jobs." Excerpted from Elliot N. Dorff and Marc Gary, "Providing References for Schools and Jobs," a responsum for the Committee on Jewish Law and Standards, adopted and posted to its website on April 30, 2014, https://www.rabbinicalassembly.org/sites/default/files /assets/public/halakhah/teshuvot/2011-2020/providingreferences.pdf. Reprinted by permission of Rabbinical Assembly.

Chapter 13, "Harmful Communication." Excerpted from Elliot N. Dorff, "Harmful Communication," a responsum for the Committee on Jewish Law and Standards, adopted and posted to its website on June 19, 2019, https://www .rabbinicalassembly.org/sites/default/files/harmful_speech.final.june.pdf. Reprinted by permission of Rabbinical Assembly.

Chapter 14, "Modest Communication." Excerpted from Elliot N. Dorff, "Modest Communication," a responsum for the Committee on Jewish Law and Standards, adopted and posted to its website on June 19, 2019, https://www .rabbinicalassembly.org/sites/default/files/modest_speech.final.june.pdf. Reprinted by permission of Rabbinical Assembly.

Chapter 15, "Violent and Defamatory Video Games." Excerpted from Elliot N. Dorff and Joshua Hearshen, "Violent and Defamatory Video Games," a responsum for the Committee on Jewish Law and Standards, adopted and posted to its website on February 4, 2010, https://www.rabbinicalassembly.org/sites/default/files /assets/public/halakhah/teshuvot/20052010/videogames%20Dorff%20Hearshen %20Final.pdf. Reprinted by permission of Rabbinical Assembly.

Chapter 16, "War and Peace: A Methodology to Formulate a Contemporary Jewish Approach." *Philosophia* 40 (2012): 643–61. Reprinted by permission of Springer.

Chapter 17, "Donations of Ill-Gotten Gain." Excerpted from Elliot N. Dorff, "Donations of Ill-Gotten Gain," a responsum for the Committee on Jewish Law and Standards, adopted and posted on its website on June 4, 2009, https://www .rabbinicalassembly.org/sites/default/files/assets/public/halakhah/teshuvot /20052010/Dorff_Donations%20of%20Ill-Gotten%20Gain.FINAL.062909.pdf. Reprinted by permission of Rabbinical Assembly.

Notes

INTRODUCTION

1. Elliot N. Dorff, *Matters of Life and Death: A Jewish Approach to Modern Medical Ethics* (Philadelphia: JPS, 1998), 411–12.
2. Pew Research Center, "Jewish Americans in 2020," Section 2, "Jewish Identity and Belief," pewresearch.org/religion/2021/05/11/jewish-identity-and-belief/.
3. "Max Muller," *Britannica*, britannica.com/biography/Max-Muller.
4. Diana L. Eck, "What Is Pluralism?" The Pluralism Project, Harvard University, http://www.pluralism.org/pluralism/what_is_pluralism.
5. I would like to thank Rabbi Ari Lucas for pointing out the significance of the order of the modeh ani prayer, as described in what follows this endnote in the text. B. *Menaḥot* 43b; S.A. Oraḥ Ḥayyim 46:3.
6. B. *Menaḥot* 43b; S.A. Oraḥ Ḥayyim 46:3.
7. Erika Andersen, "23 Quotes from Warren Buffett on Life and Generosity," *Forbes*, December 2, 2013, forbes.com/sites/erikaandersen/2013/12/02/23-quotes-from-warren-buffett-on-life-and-generosity/?sh=123545ef891b.

1. WHAT BELIEF IN GOD MEANS

1. Louis Jacobs, *Principles of Jewish Faith: An Analytical Study* (New York: Basic, 1964).
2. Joseph Albo, *Sefer Ha-Ikkarim: Book of Principles*, trans. Isaac Husik (Philadelphia: JPS, 1946).
3. Joseph Albo, *Sefer Ha-Ikkarim: Book of Principles*, trans. Isaac Husik (Philadelphia: Jewish Publication Society, 1946).
4. Hasdai Crescas, *The Light of the Lord*, bk. 2, pt. 6, chap. 1, trans. Warren Zev Harvey, in *Physics and Metaphysics in Hasdai Crescas* (Amsterdam: J. C. Gieben, 1998).
5. Here, for example, in chronological order of publication, are some recent collections of what some Jewish thinkers have written about God: Elliot N. Dorff and Louis E. Newman, eds., *Contemporary Jewish Theology: A Reader* (New York: Oxford University Press, 1999); Daniel H. Frank, Oliver Leaman, and Charles H. Manekin, eds., *The Jewish Philosophy Reader* (London: Routledge, 2000); Elliot Cosgrove, ed., *Jewish Theology in Our Time: A New Generation Explores the Foundations and Future of Jewish Belief* (Woodstock VT: Jewish Lights, 2010); Kari Tuling, ed., *Thinking about God: Jewish Views* (Philadelphia: JPS, 2020); Richard Agler and Rifat Sonsino, eds., *A God We Can Believe In* (Eugene OR: Wipf and Stock, 2022).

6. A. J. Ayer, *Language, Truth, and Logic* (London: Gallanz, 1936) and republished several times since. Alfred ("Freddie") Jules Ayer (1910–1989) was Jewish, and Rabbi Louis Jacobs told this author that they were good friends.

7. J. L. Austin, *Sense and Sensibilia* (Oxford: Clarendon Press, 1962) and also his *How to Do Things with Words* (Oxford: Clarendon, 1962). For a short description of this theory and its later philosophical developments, including examples of performative utterances in life, see "Performative Utterances," encyclopedia .com/humanities/encyclopedias-almanacs-transcripts-and-maps/performative -utterances. The same distinction is used by anthropologists. See, for example, D. S. Gardner, "Performativity in Ritual: The Mianmin Case," *Man* 18, no. 2 (June 1983): 346–60, jstor.org/stable/2801439?seq=1. For an example of how the way that one categorizes a sentence as performative or descriptive can make an important legal difference, see Elliot Dorff, "A Second Wedding Ceremony," rabbinicalassembly.org/sites/default/files/2021–07/A%20second%20wedding %20ceremony.pdf.

8. Martin Buber, *Two Types of Faith* (New York: Macmillan, 1951).

2. GOD AS THE SOURCE

1. See Elliot Dorff, *Knowing God: Jewish Journeys to the Unknowable* (Northvale NJ: Jason Aronson, 1992), 209–48, an earlier formulation of this chapter's content, for additional discussion of the differences between images, creeds, and symbols.

2. Paul Tillich, *Systematic Theology* (Chicago: University of Chicago Press, 1957), 2:9; see also vol. 1, 237–86.

3. Wilbur M. Urban, *Humanity and Deity* (London: George Allen and Unwin, 1951), 238.

4. In one critic's words, "Tillich's *via symbolica* becomes a *via negativa*." See Lewis S. Ford, "Tillich and Thomas: The Analogy of Being," *Journal of Religion* 46, no. 2 (April 1966): 244. See also John Y. Fenton, "Being-Itself and Religious Symbolism," *Journal of Religion* 55, no. 2 (April 1965): 79; Paul Edwards in Norbert O. Shedler, ed., *Philosophy of Religion, Contemporary Perspectives* (New York: Macmillan, 1974), 186–205.

5. For example, Earl R. MacCormac, *Metaphor and Myth in Science and Religion* (Durham NC: Duke University Press, 1976), 93; Lyman T. Lundeen, *Risk and Rhetoric in Religion* (Philadelphia: Fortress, 1972), 192–93.

6. Emotive: A. J. Ayer, *Language, Truth, and Logic* (London: Dover, 1936), 102–19. Ethical: R. B. Braithwaite, *An Empiricist's View of the Nature of Religious Belief* (Cambridge: Cambridge University Press, 1955).

7. Dorothy M. Emmett, *The Nature of Metaphysical Thinking* (New York: MacMillan, 1957), 4.

8. B. *Berakhot* 61a.

9. See also James William McClendon Jr. and James M. Smith, *Understanding Religious Convictions* (Notre Dame IN: University of Notre Dame Press, 1975), esp. 2–16.

10. Deut. 6:5. This is part of the *Shema*, one of the core prayers of Jewish liturgy.

11. See Clyde A. Holbrook, *The Iconoclastic Deity: Biblical Images of God* (Lewisburg PA: Bucknell University Press, 1984), 202–11; see also 61 and 192–98.

12. Numbers Rabbah 14:4.

13. Even Richard Rubenstein, who denies a God who acts in history, has trouble with the imagery of God as dead because it is, in his eyes and those of other Jewish writers, much too Christian; see his book *After Auschwitz* (Indianapolis: Bobbs-Merrill, 1966), 243–66, with further references to this point in 227–42.

14. God studies Torah: B. *Avodah Zarah* 3b; teaches Torah: B. *Bava Metzi'a* 85b–86a.

3. INDIVIDUALS AND COMMUNITIES

1. See Gen. 1:26–27; 3:1–7, 22–24.

2. See Gen. 2:18–24; Num. 12:1–16; Deut. 22:13–19. Note also that *ha-middaber,* "the speaker," is a synonym for the human being (in comparison to animals) in medieval Jewish philosophy.

3. Maimonides, *Guide for the Perplexed*, pt. 1, chap. 1.

4. See Deut. 6:5; Lev. 19:18, 33–4. In the traditional prayer book, the paragraph just before the *Shema* in both the morning and evening services speaks of God's love for us; then the first paragraph of the *Shema* commands us to love God.

5. Consider the prayer in the traditional early morning weekday service: "*Elohai neshamah she-natata bi,*" "My God, the soul (or life-breath) that you have given me is pure. You created it, You formed it, You breathed it into me; You guard it within me." Jules Harlow, *Siddur Sim Shalom* (New York: Rabbinical Assembly, 1985), 8–11. Similarly, the Rabbis describe the human being as part divine and part animal, with the latter consisting of the material aspects of the human being and the former consisting of that which we share with God; see *Sifre Deuteronomy*, para. 306; 132a.

6. M. *Sanhedrin* 4:5.

7. M. *Sanhedrin* 4:5.

8. Rabbi Bunam, cited by Martin Buber, *Tales of the Hasidim*, vol. 2 (New York: Schocken, 1948), 249–50.

9. Genesis Rabbah 24:7.

10. J. *Eruvin* 5:1. Along the same lines, Shammai, who was not known for his friendliness and who in the immediately previous phrase warns us to "say little and

do much," nevertheless admonishes, "Greet every person with a cheerful face" (*Avot* 1:15), undoubtedly in recognition of the divine image in each of us.

11. For a thorough discussion of this blessing and concept in Jewish tradition, see Carl Astor, ". . . *Who Makes People Different": Jewish Perspectives on the Disabled* (New York: United Synagogue of America, 1985).

12. J. *Terumot* 7:20; Genesis Rabbah 94:9. Maybe not even then: J. *Terumot* 47a. For a full discussion of these positions, see Elliot N. Dorff, *Matters of Life and Death: A Jewish Approach to Modern Medical Ethics* (Philadelphia: JPS, 1998), 291–99. See also Elijah J. Schochet, *A Responsum of Surrender* (Los Angeles: University of Judaism, 1973). For one specific example of the difficulty of applying this and other precedents regarding triage, see the responsa by Rabbi Daniel Nevins and me on removing a ventilator from one person in order to save another when ventilators were scarce in 2020, during the early months of the COVID-19 pandemic. We ultimately decided to come to the same conclusion, but he focused on the ethics that emerges from the clinical setting, and I instead used the perspective of public health. His responsum, "Triage and Sanctity of Life," https://www.rabbinicalassembly.org /sites/default/files/2020-05/Triage%20and%20the%20sanctity%20of%20life %20with%20consensus%20psak%20-%20final.pdf. My responsum, "Triage in the Time of a Pandemic: The Sanctity of Saving as Many Lives as Possible," https://www.rabbinicalassembly.org/sites/default/files/2021-03 /TriageinTimePandemicDorff.pdf.

13. B. *Berakhot* 61a.

14. *Avot d'Rabbi Natan* 16; see also B. *Sanhedrin* 91b.

15. B. *Berakhot* 61b.

16. *Avot d'Rabbi Natan* 16.

17. *Genesis Rabbah* 9:7.

18. B. *Avodah Zarah* 5a.

19. B. *Ta'anit* 24a.

20. *Sifre Deuteronomy*, par. 32.

21. For example, B. *Sukkah* 52a.

22. B. *Kiddushin* 30b. For other recipes, see B. *Berakhot* 5a, B. *Avodah Zarah* 5b, and, most remarkably, B. *Ḥaggigah* 16a: "If a man sees that his evil impulse is gaining mastery over him, let him go to a place where he is unknown, put on black clothes [as a sign of mourning to sober him, or as a way of hiding his identity], and do what his heart desires; but let him not profane God's Name publicly."

23. The classical statement of the Jewish conception of *teshuvah* is M.T. *Laws of Return*, esp. chaps. 1 and 2. For a contemporary restatement of that concept, see Elliot N. Dorff, *Love Your Neighbor and Yourself: A Jewish Approach to Modern Personal Ethics* (Philadelphia: JPS, 2003), 207–30.

24. B. *Bava Metzi'a* 62a.

25. For the statements and pastoral letters of the USCCB, see usccb.org/resources/library.

26. See, for example, Walter Rauschenbusch, *A Theology for the Social Gospel* (Nashville TN: Abingdon, 1978); Charles Howard Hopkins, *The Rise of the Social Gospel in American Protestantism, 1865–1915* (New York: AMS, 1982).

27. See, for example, J. David Turner, *An Introduction to Liberation Theology* (Lanham MD: University Press of America, 1994); Gustavo Gutierrez, *A Theology of Liberation: History, Politics, and Salvation*, trans. and ed. by Sister Caridad Inda and John Eagleson (Maryknoll NY: Orbis, 1973); Dennis McCann, *Christian Realism and Liberation Theology: Practical Theologies in Conflict* (Maryknoll NY: Orbis, 1981).

28. On responsibilities stated in the Torah, see B. *Makkot* 23b.

29. For a general description of Jewish law and practice with regard to serving the poor, see Elliot N. Dorff, *To Do the Right and the Good: A Jewish Approach to Modern Social Ethics* (Philadelphia: JPS, 2002), 126–60.

30. The Preamble to the Constitution of the United States, https://constitution .congress.gov/constitution/preamble/.

31. For a fuller delineation of the various rationales the Bible provides for abiding by its laws, see Elliot N. Dorff, *For the Love of God and People: A Philosophy of Jewish Law* (Philadelphia: JPS, 2007), 131–88.

32. M.T. Laws of Kings and their Wars 12:5.

33. See Lev. 19:16–18. The Rabbis interpret the duty not to stand idly by the blood of your neighbor (Lev. 19:16) as the duty to rescue; see B. *Sanhedrin* 73a.

34. Christians have made a sharp dichotomy between the City of God and the City of Man, as Augustine put it, reserving individualistic thinking about salvation for the City of God and understanding earthly societies in accordance with the corporate theories prevalent before the Enlightenment.

35. Used in the sense that we share in communal sins: B. *Shevu'ot* 39a; B. *Sanhedrin* 27b. Used in the sense that we share in communal virtues: *Midrash Tanḥuma*, Nitzavim 2:1; *Midrash Tanḥuma Buber* 5:2; and *Tanḥuma Buber* on Deut. 29:9. Our interconnectedness with one another as a Jewish People means that we are all responsible to each other to learn, teach, and fulfill the Torah of our God; see *Pesikta Zutarta (Lekaḥ Tov)* 12a. Maimonides asserts this sense of mutual responsibility forcefully in M.T. *Laws of Repentance* 3:4.

36. B. *Shabbat* 54b. Along with Jeremiah (31:29–30) and Ezekiel (18:20–32), this punishment of later generations for the sins of earlier ones offends most Jews' sense of justice for each individual, but the familial and communal ways in which each of us affects everyone else is a fact of our existence, so the prophets prophesized that God will assess each individual individually only in the future.

37. Milton R. Konvitz, *Judaism and the American Idea* (New York: Schocken, 1980), 143, 150; and see also chap. 5 generally. Hillel's words are in B. *Sukkah* 53a.

38. See also T. *Avodah Zarah* 8:4; B. *Sanhedrin* 56a; *Seder Olam*, ch. 5; *Genesis Rabbah* 16:6, 34:8; *Canticles Rabbah* 1:16; M.T. *Laws of Kings* 9:1. For a thorough description and discussion of this doctrine, see also David Novak, *The Image of the Non-Jew in Judaism* (New York: Edwin Mellen, 1983).

39. Num. 15:15–16; see also Exod. 12:49, 22:20; Lev. 24:22; Num. 9:14, 15:29; Deut. 24:14–15; etc. According to the Talmud's count (B. *Bava Metzia* 59b), the demand to treat the stranger on a par with the citizen appears thirty-six times in the Torah. A stranger had recourse to Israelite courts: Exod. 22:21, 23:9; Deut. 24:17, 27:19. One must even "love" the stranger and treat him as a citizen: Lev. 19:33–34; Deut. 10:18.

40. M. *Gittin* 5:8–9; *Mekhilta*, "Pisha," 15; B. *Gittin* 61a; B. *Bava Metzia* 70b; B. *Bava Batra* 113a; Maimonides, *Commentary to the Mishnah, Kelim* 12:7; M.T. *Laws of Sale* 18:1. See "Gentile," *Jewish Encyclopedia* 5: 615–26; "Gentile," *Encyclopaedia Judaica* 7: 410–14.

41. On not missionizing: B. *Yevamot* 47a–47b; J. *Kiddushin* 4:1 (65b); M.T. *Laws of Forbidden Intercourse* 13: 14–15; S.A. *Yoreh De'ah* 268:2. See "Proselytes," *Encyclopedia Judaica* 13: 1182–94.

42. T. *Sanhedrin* 13:2; B. *Bava Batra* 10b; M.T. *Laws of Repentance* 3:5. According to Samuel, on the Day of Judgment there is no distinction between Jew and Gentile: J. *Rosh Hashanah* 1:3 (57a).

43. T. *Gittin* 3:18; B. *Gittin* 61a.

44. M.T. Laws of Gifts to the Poor 9:3.

45. Lancelot Addison, *The Present State of the Jews* (London, 1675), chap. 25, quoted in Israel Abrahams, *Jewish Life in the Middle Ages* (New York: Atheneum, 1969), 307. For a general description of Jewish law and practice with regard to serving the poor, see Dorff, *To Do the Right and the Good*, 126–60.

46. Lev. 19:14. See Astor, ". . . *Who Makes People Different*."

47. B. *Eruvin* 13b. But see its correlative in B. *Sotah* 47b.

48. Milton R. Konvitz has emphasized this point; see also his *Judaism and the American Idea* (New York: Schocken, 1980), chap. 1, esp. 33–41.

49. Deut. 17:18–20; 2 Samuel 11–12; I Kings 21. See also the talmudic story of the confrontation between Simeon ben Shetaḥ and King Alexander Yannai: B. *Sanhedrin* 19a–19b.

50. M. *Avot (Ethics of the Fathers)* 4:10.

51. For rabbinic sources and further discussion on these points, see Dorff, *For the Love of God and People*, 189–276.

4. INCULCATING MORALITY

1. Lawrence Kohlberg, *Essays on Moral Development* (San Francisco: Harper and Row, 1981).

2. B. *Avodah Zarah* 20b.

3. See Elliot Dorff and Arthur Rosett, *A Living Tree: The Roots and Growth of Jewish Law* (Albany NY: State University of New York Press, 1988), 110–23, 249–57; also see Elliot Dorff, *For the Love of God and People: A Philosophy of Jewish Law* (Philadelphia: JPS, 2007), 211–44.

4. B. *Sotah* 14a.

5. God is depicted as Israel's marital partner a number of times in the Bible, whether fondly, as in Jeremiah 2:2, or angrily, when Israel proves to be an unfaithful lover, as in Hosea, chap. 2. The phrase requiring us to go beyond the requirements of the law in our actions appears many times in the Talmud, perhaps especially B. *Bava Kamma* 100a. See also *Bava Metzi'a* 24b and 30b. God serves as a model for us in this, for in the talmudic imagination God prays that God too will treat people beyond the requirements of the law (B. *Berakhot* 7a) and in some cases actually does (B. *Avodah Zarah* 4b).

6. See, for example, Boaz Cohen, *Jewish and Roman Law: A Comparative Study* (New York: Jewish Theological Seminary of America, 1966).

7. B. *Avodah Zarah* 18b.

8. See, for example, George J. Annas and Michael A. Grodin, eds., *The Nazi Doctors and the Nuremberg Code: Human Rights in Human Experimentation* (New York: Oxford University Press, 1992).

9. B. *Pesaḥim* 50b, and in parallel passages elsewhere.

5. THEORY OF JEWISH LAW

1. Dorff, *Knowing God: Jewish Journeys to the Unknowable* (Northvale NJ: Jason Aronson, 1992), 43–90.

2. Western philosophy, beginning with Plato, makes a sharp distinction between the body and the mind—so much so that the way that the two are connected is a stock issue in Western thought (the mind-body problem). Similarly, Christianity, influenced heavily by Gnosticism, makes a sharp distinction between the body and the soul, with the ideal person (the priest, nun, or monk) denying the body as much as possible to cultivate the soul. Judaism acknowledges the distinction between functions of our body and soul, but, in sharp contrast to both Western thought and Christianity, it asserts the integration of body and soul. See, for example, B. *Sanhedrin* 91a–91b. This interaction asserts personal responsibility for our actions and is also at the heart of the Rabbis' recipe for a good life: "An excellent thing is the study of Torah combined with a worldly occupation, for the labor demanded by both of them causes sinful inclinations to be forgotten. All study of the Torah without work must, in the end, be futile and become the cause of sin" (M. *Avot [Ethics of the Fathers]* 2:1). For more on this, see Elliot N. Dorff, *Matters of Life and Death: A Jewish Approach to Modern Medical Ethics* (Philadelphia: JPS, 1998), 20–26; and Elliot N. Dorff, *Love Your Neighbor and Yourself: A Jewish Approach to Modern Personal Ethics* (Philadelphia: JPS, 2003), 19–26.

3. On Abraham as the "pillar of the world": M.T. Laws of Idolatry 1:2 (end). Maimonides uses the same term for Abraham in his *Guide for the Perplexed*, pt. 3, chap. 29.

4. For the covenant with Noah: Gen. 9. For the covenant with Abraham: Gen. 15, 17. For the covenant with Isaac: Gen. 26:2–5. For the covenant with Jacob: Gen. 28:13–15.

6. NEW CIRCUMSTANCES

1. M. *Avot* 5:22.
2. J. *Pe'ah* 17a.
3. Michael Fishbane, *Biblical Interpretation in Ancient Israel* (New York: Oxford University Press, 1985).
4. Jakob J. Petuchowski, "Some Criteria for Modern Jewish Observance," in *Tradition and Contemporary Experience*, ed. Alfred Jospe (New York: Schocken/B'nai Brith, 1970), 99–128; Eugene B. Borowitz, "The Jewish Self," in his *Renewing the Covenant* (Philadelphia: JPS, 1991), 284–299; David H. Ellenson, "How to Draw Guidance from a Heritage: Jewish Approaches to Mortal Choices," in *A Time to Be Born and a Time to Die: The Ethics of Choice*, ed. Barry Kogan (New York: Aldine de Gruyter, 1990), 219–32.
5. Stephen M. Cohen and Arnold M. Eisen, *The Jew Within: Self, Family, and Community in America* (Bloomington: Indiana University Press, 2000).
6. Laurie Zoloth-Dorfman, "An Ethics of Encounter: Public Choices and Private Acts," in *Contemporary Jewish Ethics and Morality*, eds. Elliot N. Dorff and Louis E. Newman (New York: Oxford University Press, 1995), 219–45.
7. See Elliot N. Dorff and Elie Kaplan Spitz, "Computer Privacy and the Modern Workplace," https://www.rabbinicalassembly.org/sites/default/files/assets/public/halakhah/teshuvot/19912000/dorffspitz_privacy.pdf.
8. See two very different Jewish applications of Jewish law: Barry Leff, "Intellectual Property: Can You Steal If You Can't Touch It?," https://www.rabbinicalassembly.org/sites/default/files/assets/public/halakhah/teshuvot/20052010/leff_ip.pdf; Neil Weinstock Netanel, *From Maimonides to Microsoft: The Jewish Law of Copyright Since the Birth of Print* (New York: Oxford, 2016).
9. Oliver Wendell Holmes uses this phrase to describe lawyers and judges who mistakenly think the law can be determined deductively without regard to the lawyers' or judges' values and concepts; see Oliver Wendell Holmes, "The Path of the Law," *Harvard Law Review* 10 (1897): 457.
10. See Elliot Dorff, *Matters of Life and Death* (Philadelphia: JPS, 1998), 14–34; Elliot Dorff, *To Do the Right and the Good* (Philadelphia: JPS, 2002), 1–35; and Elliot Dorff, *Love Your Neighbor and Yourself* (Philadelphia: JPS, 2003), 1–32, esp. 19–32.
11. B. *Shavu'ot* 29a; J. *Nedarim* 9a; J. *Shavu'ot* 17a; *Exodus Rabbah* 21:5; *Numbers Rabbah* 12:3; *Deuteronomy Rabbah* 1:22.
12. B. *Pesaḥim* 66a, 66b.

1. The full responsum is here: https://www.rabbinicalassembly.org/sites/default /files/2021-04/Assisted%20suicide%20revisited%20final.pdf. The responsa text appearing in this chapter includes stylistic updates to the original 2020 document but no changes in essential content.

2. Elliot N. Dorff, "Assisted Suicide," https://www.rabbinicalassembly.org/sites /default/files/assets/public/halakhah/teshuvot/19912000/dorff_suicide.pdf.

3. "While before 2015, only two or three states at the time considered physician-assisted dying bills, in the 2015 legislative session no fewer than 25 states considered such bills. In 2016, 20 jurisdictions, in 2017, 30 jurisdictions, in 2018, 25 jurisdictions, and in 2019, 21 jurisdictions considered such bills." https://www .deathwithdignity.org/faqs/#laws.

4. A sentence of probation for mercy killing: Brian Skoloff, "Arizona Man, 86, Gets Probation in Mercy Killing Case," *Christian Science Monitor*, March 30, 2013, https://www.csmonitor.com/usa/Latest-News-Wires/2013/0330/Arizona-man -86-gets-probation-in-mercy-killing-case. A sentence of four years in prison for involuntary manslaughter, followed by the suicide of the convicted person before going to prison: George Houde, "Woman Who Killed Disabled Daughter Found Dead 2 Days Before Prison Sentence Was to Begin," *Chicago Tribune*, November 27, 2017, https://www.chicagotribune.com/news/breaking/ct-met -bonnie-liltz-dead-killed-disabled-daughter-20171126-story.html. A sentence of six years for aggravated murder with a firearm, but fewer than the minimum of twenty-three years the law requires for that crime: Crimesider Staff, "John Wise, Ohio Man, Gets 6 Years in Wife's 'Mercy Killing,'" cbs *News*, December 13, 2013, https://www.cbsnews.com/news/john-wise-ohio-man-gets-6-years-in -wifes-mercy-killing/; Gavin Drake, "Churchgoer Is Given a Life Sentence for 'Mercy Killing,'" *Church Times*, June 12, 2015, https://www.churchtimes.co.uk /articles/2015/12-june/news/uk/churchgoer-is-given-a-life-sentence-for-mercy -killing; Michael Miller, "'I Hope I Can Be Forgiven': Man Gets 100 Years for 'Mercy Killings' of Wife, Sister," *Washington Post*, August 11, 2016, https://www .washingtonpost.com/news/morning-mix/wp/2016/08/11/i-hope-i-can-be -forgiven-man-gets-100-years-for-mercy-killings-of-wife-sister/?noredirect=on &utm_term=.2bfd46dd5ce3. See also Brooke Baitinger, "Caregivers Who Kill Their Spouses Share Traits, Experts Say," *Sun Sentinel*, April 21, 2017, https:// www.sun-sentinel.com/local/palm-beach/fl-pn-family-caregiver-homicide -20170418-story.html.

5. Although Wikipedia is not an academically reliable source, its summary of the law in Switzerland will do for our purposes: https://en.wikipedia.org/wiki /Euthanasia_in_Switzerland.

6. "Suicide Tourism," https://en.wikipedia.org/wiki/Suicide_tourism.

7. Rabbi Stuart Kelman pointed out this ramification of the differing terminology.

8. Death with Dignity National Center, "Terminology of Assisted Dying," https://www.deathwithdignity.org/terminology.

9. Death with Dignity National Center, "Terminology of Assisted Dying."

10. This is clearly also relevant to how the people whom members of the disabled community call "the temporarily abled" treat those who are disabled. For more on this as understood and practiced in the Conservative movement, see the United Synagogue sourcebook by Carl Astor, ". . . *Who Makes People Different": Jewish Perspectives on the Disabled* (New York: United Synagogue of America, 1985) and the following responsa of the Committee on Jewish Law and Standards: James Rosen, "Mental Retardation, Group Homes, and the Rabbi," https://www.rabbinicalassembly.org/sites/default/files/assets/public/halakhah/teshuvot/19912000/rosen_grouphomes.pdf; Daniel S. Nevins, "The Participation of Those Who Are Blind in the Torah Service," https://www.rabbinicalassembly.org/sites/default/files/assets/public/halakhah/teshuvot/20052010/nevins_blind.pdf; and Pamela Barmash, "Status of the Heresh and of Sign Language," https://www.rabbinicalassembly.org/sites/default/files/assets/public/halakhah/teshuvot/2011-2020/Status%20of%20the%20heresh6.2011.pdf, with its appendix on reading Torah in sign language and the varying concurring opinions by Rabbis Daniel Nevins and Avram Reisner, each with others.

11. The Hippocratic oath: https://www.nlm.nih.gov/hmd/greek/greek_oath.html. American Medical Association, Code of Medical Ethics, Opinion 5.7, https://www.ama-assn.org/delivering-care/ethics/physician-assisted-suicide. American Academy of Hospice and Palliative Medicine, "AAHPM and the Specialty of Hospice and Palliative Medicine," https://aahpm.org/about/about.

12. The AMA statement on physician-assisted suicide: American Medical Association, "Physician-Assisted Suicide," https://www.ama-assn.org/delivering-care/ethics/physician-assisted-suicide. Dr. Toby Schonfeld pointed out the level of debate among doctors about this and the fact that most physicians are not trained in how to administer lethal doses of drugs appropriately. On AMA statements in favor of physicians aiding patients in dying: Compassion and Choices, "Medical Associations and Medical Aid in Dying," https://compassionandchoices.org/resource/medical-associations-medical-aid-dying/.

13. Avram Israel Reisner, "A Halakhic Ethic of Care for the Terminally Ill," https://www.rabbinicalassembly.org/sites/default/files/assets/public/halakhah/teshuvot/19861990/reisner_care.pdf; Elliot N. Dorff, "A Jewish Approach to End-Stage Medical Care," https://www.rabbinicalassembly.org/sites/default/files/assets/public/halakhah/teshuvot/19861990/dorff_care.pdf; and Avram Israel Reisner, "Mai Beinaiyhu?" https://www.rabbinicalassembly.org/sites/default/files/assets/public/halakhah/teshuvot/19861990/maibeinaihu.pdf.

14. The text in this paragraph combines the website data for the six months of 2016 that the law was in effect and 2017. California Department of Public Health, End of Life Options Act, https://www.cdph.ca.gov/Programs/chsi/Pages/End-of-Life-Option-Act-.aspx.

15. City of Hope, Tanya Hope MD, https://www.cityofhope.org/tanya-dorff.

16. An email from Dr. Tanya Dorff to this author on April 7, 2020, in response to his question of how, in practice, pain relief medication is used while there are still patients who need aid in dying.

17. M. *Avot* 2:4 (2:5 in some editions).

18. A good, if somewhat dated, article that distinguishes the two practices and records the disparate reasons for and extent of their usages in the Netherlands in 2001 is Judith A.C. Rietjens, et. al., "Terminal Sedation and Euthanasia: A Comparison of Clinical Practices," *Archive of Internal Medicine* 166, no. 7 (2006): 749–53, https://jamanetwork.com/journals/jamainternalmedicine/fullarticle/410108 .

19. Andrew Keh, "The Champion Who Picked a Date to Die," *New York Times*, December 5, 2019, https://www.nytimes.com/interactive/2019/12/05/sports/euthanasia-athlete.html.

20. Belgium allowed aid in dying beginning in 2002.

21. Keh, "The Champion Who Picked a Date to Die."

22. Nicholas Goldberg, "Dementia Patients Deserve Access to Aid-In-Dying Laws," *Los Angeles Times*, July 15, 2020, https://www.latimes.com/opinion/story/2020-07-15/california-aid-in-dying-law-assisted-suicide-alzheimers-dementia.

23. See Elliot Dorff, *For the Love of God and People: A Philosophy of Jewish Law* (Philadelphia: JPS, 2007), especially chaps. 3 (87–128) and 6 (211–43).

24. *Sifre*, Ekev, on Deut. 11:22.

25. This distinction between aid in dying, where the patient administers the drugs, and active euthanasia, where someone else administers the drugs, is different from, and, in my view, stronger than the distinction between active and passive euthanasia, which many in the bioethics world see as a distinction without a difference, for in both active and passive euthanasia people other than the patient are making the decision about the patient's treatment. For an early and oft-cited challenge to distinctions between active and passive euthanasia, see James Rachels, "Active and Passive Euthanasia," *New England Journal of Medicine* 292, no. 2 (January 9, 1975): 79–80, reprinted in many books on bioethics and ethics generally.

26. This author has not included "at the hands of a close family member" here because that raises the question of motive even more deeply.

1. Eugene Borowitz, *Renewing the Covenant: A Theology for the Postmodern Jew.* (Philadelphia: JPS, 1991); Elliot N. Dorff, "Autonomy vs. Community," *Conserva-*

tive Judaism 48, no. 2 (Winter 1996): 64–68; Eugene B. Borowitz, "The Reform Judaism of *Renewing the Covenant*: An Open Letter to Elliot Dorff," *Conservative Judaism* 50, no. 1 (Fall 1997): 61–65; Elliot N. Dorff, "Matters of Degree and Kind: An Open Response to Eugene Borowitz's Open Letter to Me," *Conservative Judaism* 50, no. 1 (Fall 1997): 66–71.

2. Elliot N. Dorff, *The Unfolding Tradition: Philosophies of Jewish Law* (New York: Rabbinical Assembly, 2011), 506–22.

3. "Reform Judaism: A Centenary Perspective" (1976), para. 4, "Our Religious Obligations: Religious Practice," https://www.ccarnet.org/rabbinic-voice /platforms/article-reform-judaism-centenary-perspective/.

4. *Mitzvah Means Commandment* (New York: United Synagogue of Conservative Judaism, 1989). This book is now out of print, but a later articulation of the same list of biblical and rabbinic motivations to obey Jewish law can be found in Elliot Dorff, *Love Your Neighbor and Yourself: A Philosophy of Jewish Law* (Philadelphia: JPS, 2007), 131–88.

5. For a discussion of the ways in which Jewish law is similar to or different from a legal system see Elliot Dorff, "Judaism as a Religious Legal System," *Hastings Law Journal* 29, no. 6 (July 1978): 1331–60.

6. Emanuel Rackman, *One Man's Judaism* (New York: Philosophical Library, 1970), 262–83.

10. OVERTURNING OF *ROE V. WADE*

1. "Miscarriage," Medline Plus, National Library of Medicine, https://medlineplus .gov/ency/article/001488.htm.

2. "Simply liquid" during the first forty days of pregnancy: B. *Yevamot* 69b; "like the thigh of its mother": B. *Ḥullin* 58a and elsewhere. B. *Niddah* 17a distinguishes the first trimester from the remainder of gestation.

3. For more on a Jewish view of abortion and related issues, see Elliot Dorff, *Matters of Life and Death: A Jewish Approach to Modern Medical Ethics* (Philadelphia: JPS, 1998), 128–33.

4. For example, Sandra Lubarsky, "Judaism and the Justification of Abortion for Nonmedical Reasons," *Journal of Reform Judaism* 31 (1984): 1–13; Rebecca Alpert, "'Sometimes the Law is Cruel': The Construction of a Jewish Anti-Abortion Position in the Writings of Immanuel Jakobovits," *Journal of Feminist Studies in Religion* (Fall 1995): 27–38; Alana Suskin, "A Feminist Theory of Halakhah," in Elliot N. Dorff, *The Unfolding Tradition: Philosophies of Jewish Law* (New York: Rabbinical Assembly, 2011), 357–78, esp. 370–75.

5. For more on the stance that Jefferson and this author take on the proper limits of religion's influence on national policy, see Elliot Dorff, *To Do the Right and the Good: A Jewish Approach to Modern Social Ethics* (Philadelphia: Jewish Publica-

tion Society, 2002), 96–113, esp. 105; and Elliot Dorff, *Jews and Genes: The Genetic Future in Contemporary Jewish Thought* (Philadelphia: JPS, 2015), 403–19.

11. SEXUAL ORIENTATION AND HUMAN DIGNITY

1. Elliot N. Dorff, "Jewish Norms for Sexual Behavior: A Responsum Embodying a Proposal," https://www.rabbinicalassembly.org/sites/default/files/assets/public/halakhah/teshuvot/19912000/dorff_homosexuality.pdf.

2. Elliot N. Dorff, *"This Is My Beloved, This Is My Friend" (Song of Songs 5:16): A Rabbinic Letter on Intimate Relations* (New York: Rabbinical Assembly, 1996). Now out of print, it is available in a slightly revised form in Elliot N. Dorff, *Love Your Neighbor and Yourself: A Jewish Approach to Modern Personal Ethics* (Philadelphia: JPS, 2003), 73–126.

3. Joel Roth, "Homosexuality Revisited," https://www.rabbinicalassembly.org/sites/default/files/assets/public/halakhah/teshuvot/20052010/roth_revisited.pdf. Elliot N. Dorff, Daniel S. Nevins, and Avram I. Reisner, "Human Dignity, Halakhah, and Homosexuality: A Combined Responsum for the Committee on Jewish Law and Standards," https://www.rabbinicalassembly.org/sites/default/files/assets/public/halakhah/teshuvot/20052010/dorff_nevins_reisner_dignity.pdf.

4. Elliot Dorff, Daniel Nevins, and Avram Reisner, "Rituals and Documents for Marriage and Divorce for Same-Sex Couples," https://www.rabbinicalassembly.org/sites/default/files/assets/public/halakhah/teshuvot/2011-2020/same-sex-marriage-and-divorce-appendix.pdf

5. Dorff, Nevins, and Reisner, "Human Dignity, Halakhah, and Homosexuality."

6. Leonard A. Sharzer, "Transgender Jews and Halakhah," https://www.rabbinicalassembly.org/sites/default/files/public/halakhah/teshuvot/2011-2020/transgender-halakhah.pdf.

7. Dorff, Nevins, and Reisner, "Human Dignity, Halakhah, and Homosexuality." See also the appendix to this rabbinic ruling, approved in 2012: Dorff, Nevins, and Reisner, "Rituals and Documents of Marriage and Divorce for Same-Sex Couples"; and Elliot Dorff and Daniel Nevins, "Dignity: A Jewish Perspective," in *Value and Vulnerability: An Interfaith Dialogue on Human Dignity*, eds. Matthew R. Petrusek and Jonathan Rothchild (Notre Dame IN: Notre Dame University Press, 2020), 92–127.

8. Deut. 21:23–23.

9. M. *Bava Kamma* 8:1.

10. B. *Bava Kamma* 86b.

11. B. *Bava Metzi'a* 58b.

12 *Genesis Rabbah* 24:7.

13 B. *Berakhot* 19b; B. *Shabbat* 81b, 94b; B. *Eruvin* 41b; B. *Megillah* 3b; B. *Bava Kamma* 79b; B. *Menaḥot* 37b, 38a; Y. *Berakhot* 3:1; Y. *Kilayim* 9:1; Y. *Nazir* 7:1, etc.

14. William Shakespeare, *The Merchant of Venice*, act 3, scene 1.

15. That is quite literally the case in the Talmud's discussion of *arakhin* (the market value of humans in the slave market), used to determine the value of a pledge to the Temple; this occupies a full tractate of the Mishnah, following the lead of Leviticus 27. This patriarchal view is even more prominently displayed, if only because it is part of the daily liturgy and therefore more well known, in the blessings in the early morning liturgy that thank God for "not making me a Gentile . . . for not making me a slave . . . and for not making me a woman," for Gentiles are, according to Jewish law, obligated for only the seven laws that God gave, according to the Talmud, to non-Jews; Jewish slaves are exempted from the 248 positive commandments because their status as slaves presumably means that they cannot perform them; and women are exempted from about 20 of the 613 commandments, while free males are subject to all of them. To change the ethnocentrism and sexism involved in these blessings, especially as most people would understand them absent this rubric of increasing obligation to God's commandments, Conservative Jewish liturgy since 1946 has transformed them to thanking God for "making me in God's image . . . for making me a Jew . . . and for making me free"; see *Sabbath and Festival Prayerbook* (New York: Rabbinical Assembly of America and United Synagogue of America, 1946), x, 45.

16. Lev 19:2. See, for example, Rashi's comment to this verse: "You shall be holy. Separate yourself from sexual transgression and other sin, for wherever you find a fence around sexual transgression, you find holiness."

17. The former category includes sexual relations between a man and a woman in *niddah*. The latter category includes rape, incest, adultery, pedophilia, and bestiality.

18. For a summary of research comparing suicide rates among LGBT and other teenagers, see https://www.ncbi.nlm.nih.gov/pmc/articles/pmc1447240/. On smoking and drug and alcohol abuse, see https://nida.nih.gov/research-topics/substance-use-suds-in-lgbtq-populations.

12. PROVIDING REFERENCES WHEN THE TRUTH MAY BE HARMFUL

1. For a discussion of how the Midrash and a number of medieval Jewish thinkers refer to a human being as *ha-midabber*, the speaker, indicative also of the human power to think, see Dvid Mevorach Seidenberg, *Kabbalah and Ecology: God's Image in the More-Than-Human World* (New York: Cambridge University Press, 2015), 43–128, esp. 61–66, in which the human power to speak—and, for some, also to think—is the meaning of being created in God's image.

2. See Rabbis David Booth, Baruch Frydman-Kohl, and Ashira Konigsburg, "Modesty Inside and Out: A Contemporary Guide to Tzniut," https://www.rabbinicalassembly.org/sites/default/files/modesty_final.pdf.

3. Elliot N. Dorff, *For the Love of God and People: A Philosophy of Jewish Law* (Philadelphia: JPS, 2007), 45–130, 211–44.

4. B. *Shabbat* 55a; B. *Yoma* 69b; B. *Sanhedrin* 64a.

5. B. *Pesaḥim* 113b (see also B. *Sotah* 42a, B. *Bava Metzia* 49a); B. *Bava Metzia* 49a.

6. B. *Berakhot* 19b; B. *Shabbat* 81b, 94b; B. *Eruvin* 41b; B. *Megillah* 3b; B. *Menaḥot* 37b.

7. Exod. 23:1, 7; Lev. 19:11.

8 B. *Sanhedrin* 89b.

9. T. *Bava Kamma* 7:3.

10. B. *Berakhot* 4a. See also J. *Nedarim* 10:11 (35b); J. *Ḥagigah* 1:8 (7a).

11. For a good summary of the research on children, see Alex Stone, "Is Your Child Lying to You? That's Good," *New York Times*, January 7, 2018, https://www.nytimes.com/2018/01/05/opinion/sunday/children-lying-intelligence.html. On adults lying, see, for example, Seth Stephens-Davidowitz, *Everybody Lies: Big Data, New Data, and What the Internet Can Tell Us About Who We Really Are* (New York: HarperCollins, 2017).

12. B. *Ketubbot* 16b–17a.

13. Sarah: *Gen. Rabbah* 48:18, based on Gen. 18:11–14. Joseph's brothers and God's advice to Samuel: B. *Yevamot* 65a, based on Gen. 50:16–17 and 1 Sam. 16:2.

14. *Baraita Perek Ha-Shalom.*

15. Isa. 38:1–7; also 2 Kings 20:1–7; *Eccles. Rabbah* on Eccl. 5:6.

16. B. *Mo'ed Katan* 26b; B. *Mo'ed Katan* 26b; see S.A. *Yoreh De'ah* 338:1.

17. For more on how this concern applies to the prognosis that physicians offer patients and how they offer it, as well as what visitors say to patients, see Elliot N. Dorff, *Matters of Life and Death: A Jewish Approach to Modern Medical Ethics* (Philadelphia: JPS, 1998), 245–54; and Elliot N. Dorff, *The Way Into Tikkun Olam (Repairing the World)* (Woodstock VT: Jewish Lights, 2005), 93–98.

18. M.T. Laws of Ethics (*De'ot*) 7:2, 3, 4, 6.

19. *Gen. Rabbah* 24:7.

20. M. *Avot* 2:15 (2:10 in some editions).

21. B. *Berakhot* 19b.

22. Hafetz Hayyim, *Laws of Slurs (Lashon Ha-ra)* 6:2–3, available at http://torah.org/learning/halashon/chapter6.html.

23. Hafetz Hayyim, *Laws of Slurs (Lashon Ha-ra)* 10 and *Laws of Gossip (Rekhilut)* 9, available at http://torah.org/learning/halashon/rchapter9.html.

24. Among the many verses in the Torah that require assistance to others in attaining the basic necessities of life, see, for example, Lev. 19:9–10, 25 and Deut. 15. For a discussion of this obligation, see Elliot N. Dorff, *The Way into Tikkun Olam (Repairing the World)* (Woodstock VT: Jewish Lights, 2005), 107–30; M.T. Laws of Gifts to the Poor 10:7–14; for Maimonides ladder; B. *Bava Metzia* 4:10 [58b].

25. M.T. Laws of Return (*Hilkhot Teshuvah*), chs. 1–2. For an exposition of this process on a personal level, see Elliot N. Dorff, *Love Your Neighbor and Yourself: A*

Jewish Approach to Modern Personal Ethics (Philadelphia: JPS, 2003), 207–30. On a communal level, see Elliot N. Dorff, *To Do the Right and the Good: A Jewish Approach to Modern Social Ethics* (Philadelphia: JPS, 2002), 184–212.

26. B. *Pesaḥim* 22b; B. *Moʾed Katan* 17a; B. Bava *Metzia* 75b.

27. So B. *Pesaḥim* 22b; B. *Moʾed Katan* 17a; B. Bava *Metzia* 75b. So Elliot Dorff ruled in his responsum for the CJLS, "Family Violence," http://www.rabbinicalassembly.org/sites/default/files/public/halakhah/teshuvot/19912000/dorff_violence.pdf.

28. M. *Sanhedrin* 3:4; M.T. Laws of Evidence 13.

29. M. T. Laws of Evidence 15:1.

13. AVOIDING HARMFUL COMMUNICATION

1. On harassment of Jews: Arianne Cohen, "Antisemitism Seeping into the Workplace," *Los Angeles Times*, January 12, 2023, https://www.latimes.com/business/story/2023-01-11/on-the-rise-in-the-u-s-antisemitism-is-seeping-into-the-workplace. On the increased prevalence of hate speech: Zachary Laub, "Hate Speech on Social Media: Global Comparisons," Council on Foreign Relations, June 7, 2019, https://www.cfr.org/backgrounder/hate-speech-social-media-global-comparisons. On physical harm related to hate speech: U.S. Department of Justice, Federal Bureau of Investigation, "2021 Hate Crime Statistics," https://www.justice.gov/hatecrimes/hate-crime-statistics.

2. Other descriptions of these prohibitions include the following: Elliot N. Dorff, *The Way Into Tikkun Olam* (Woodstock VT: Jewish Lights, 2005), 69–106; Alyssa M. Gray, "The Ethics of Speech," in *The Oxford Handbook of Jewish Ethics and Morality*, eds. Elliot N. Dorff and Jonathan K. Crane (New York: Oxford University Press, 2013), 433–44; and Joseph Telushkin, *Words That Hurt, Words That Heal: How to Choose Words Wisely and Well* (New York: William Morrow, 1996).

3. The doctrine: Genesis 1:27; 5:1; 9:6. For a thorough examination of the range of interpretations of this doctrine in rabbinic and kabbalistic literature, see David Mevorach Seidenberg, *Kabbalah and Ecology: God's Image in the More-Than-Human World* (New York: Cambridge University Press, 2015).

4. *Gen. Rabbah* 24:7.

5. For a discussion of the relevant laws, see Elliot Dorff, *The Way into Tikkun Olam* (Woodstock VT: Jewish Lights, 2005), 69–106 (chap. 4, "How We Talk to Each Other"); 171–84 (chap. 8, "Duties of Spouses to Each Other"); 185–200 (chap. 9, "Parental Duties"); and 201–25 (chap. 10, "Filial Duties").

6. M.T. *Laws of Dispositions (Deʾot)* 7:2. In the following sections (7:3–6) Maimonides discusses the severe penalties for engaging in calumny (*lashon ha-ra*) and the nature of "the dust of calumny" (*avak lashon ha-ra*). As the *Kesef Mishneh*, citing Rabbi Abraham ben David of Posquierres, points out in 7:1, Mai-

monides is taking a stringent position here, claiming that this severe penalty applies even if nobody dies as a result. Maimonides also takes a more stringent position than the Talmud on other types of verbal infractions in 2:6, perhaps because his philosophical training, combined with his rabbinic training, made him especially sensitive to the misuse of language.

7. As the New Jewish Publication Society translation of this verse indicates, the meaning of the Torah's phrase here is uncertain, and it may mean "do not deal basely with your countrymen." The Rabbis, though, interpreted it to declare a prohibition on gossip (J. Pe'ah 1:5).

8. This is noteworthy, for the Mishnah asserts that women were much more likely than men to spread gossip (M. Avot 1:5).

9. Benedict Carey, "Have You Heard? Gossip Turns Out to Serve a Purpose," New York Times, August 16, 2005, http://www.nytimes.com/2005/08/16/science/have -you-heard-gossip-turns-out-to-serve-a-purpose.html.

10. Lev. 19:17; see also Prov. 3:11; 9:7–8; 17:10. Sifra, Kedoshim 4:8–9; B. Arakhin 16b; B. Yevamot 65b; B. Bava Metzi'a 31a; M.T. De'ot 6:7–9.

11. B. Pesaḥim 113b.

12. B. Yoma 72b.

13. B. Ḥullin 94a.

14. T. Bava Batra 6:4; B. Ḥullin 94a.

15. T. Bava Batra 6:4; B. Ḥullin 94a.

16. T. Bava Batra 6:4; B. Ḥullin 94a.

17. M.T. Laws of Dispositions (De'ot) 2:6. See also Shai Cherry's penetrating article about how this type of speech can harm family relationships: "Death by Deception," Conservative Judaism 61, no. 3 (Spring 2009), https://www .rabbinicalassembly.org/cj/death-deception.

18. On words: Prov. 3:2; 4:24; 6:12–19; 8:13; 10:10–11, 14, 19–21; 11:11–13; 12: 6, 13–14, 17–22, 25; 13:2–3, 5; 14:5, 25; 15:4; etc. On body language: See esp. Prov. 6:12–19. On stealing a person's thought: T. Bava Kamma 7:3.

19. M. Bava Metzi'a 4:11–12.

20. B. Bava Metzi'a 62a.

21. M. Avot 6:1. See also B. Shabbat 88b.

22. M.T. Laws of the Foundations of the Torah 5:11.

23. For an extended discussion of this process and its limits, including Maimonides' Hilkhot Teshuvah (Laws of Return) and what differentiates pardon, reconciliation, and forgiveness, see Elliot N. Dorff, Love Your Neighbor and Yourself: A Jewish Approach to Modern Personal Ethics (Philadelphia: JPS, 2003), 207–30.

24. B. Bava Metzi'a 58b.

25. On being liable for paying damages: M. Bava Kamma 8:1, 6, and the Talmud thereon.

26. B. Bava Metzi'a 58b.

27. B. *Bava Kamma* 86b. See also B. *Bava Metzi'a* 58b.
28. B. *Arakhin* 16b.
29. M. *Avot* 3:11 (3:15 in some versions).
30. B. *Bava Kamma* 86a.
31. B. *Bava Metzi'a* 58b.
32. M.T. *Laws of Dispositions (De'ot)* 6:8.
33. Elliot N. Dorff, "Family Violence," https://www.rabbinicalassembly.org/sites /default/files/assets/public/halakhah/teshuvot/19912000/dorff_violence.pdf, esp. pt. 3, 31–33.
34. B. *Shabbat* 54b.
35. "What Is Bullying?," U.S. Government, https://www.stopbullying.gov/what-is -bullying/definition/index.html.
36. "What Is Bullying?," U.S. Government, https://www.stopbullying.gov/what-is -bullying/definition/index.html.
37. "Frequency of Bullying," U.S. Government, https://www.stopbullying.gov /what-is-bullying/definition/index.html#frequency; Dorothy Espelage and Erin Reiney, "The Connections between Bullying and Family Violence, Sexual Harassment, and Dating Violence," May 18, 2015, https://www.stopbullying .gov/blog/2015/03/18/connections-between-bullying-family-violence-sexual -harassment-dating-violence.

14. MODESTY IN COMMUNICATION

1. Oddly, as the *Mishneh Berurah* notes, the Shulḥan Arukh omits all the laws governing language developed by the Talmud and Maimonides in M.T. Laws of Dispositions (*De'ot*). See S.A. *Oraḥ Ḥayyim* 156:1 and the *Mishneh Berurah* #4 there.
2. The literature on the relationships between secular law and morality is vast. In modern times, see, for example, the debate between H. L. A. Hart, asserting a positivist legal theory, where the law must be read as it appears in its texts to avoid undermining its authority with any outside considerations, and Lon Fuller, maintaining a natural law theory that bases the law in morality: H. L. A. Hart, *The Concept of Law* (Oxford: Clarendon, 1961); and Lon Fuller, *The Morality of Law* (New Haven CT: Yale University Press, 1964). Another attack on Hart's legal positivism that roots law in moral principles and rights without grounding it in natural law theory was mounted by Ronald Dworkin in his books, *Taking Rights Seriously* (Cambridge MA: Harvard University Press, 1977); *A Matter of Principle* (Cambridge MA: Harvard University Press, 1985); and *Law's Empire* (Cambridge MA: Belknap Press, 1986). The same debate is evident in the conflicting theories of law held by two U.S. Supreme Court justices— Antonin Scalia, who takes a legal positivist view in his book with Bryan A.

Garner, *Reading Law: The Interpretation of Legal Texts* (St. Paul MN: Thomson West, 2012); and Stephen Breyer, who sees law and morality as intertwined in his book, *Making Our Democracy Work: A Judge's View* (New York: Alfred A. Knopf, 2010), where he argues that judges must use not only the texts of the law, but their historical contexts, precedents, and traditions, the law's purpose, and the consequences of potential interpretations in making decisions.

3. David Booth, Ashira Konigsburg, and Baruch Frydman-Kohl, "Modesty Inside and Out: A Contemporary Guide to Tzniut," https://www.rabbinicalassembly .org/sites/default/files/modesty_final.pdf.

4. B. *Shabbat* 30b.

5. B. *Sotah* 49a.

6. Micah 6:8. For a discussion of humility in the Jewish tradition, see Sol Roth, "Toward a Definition of Humility," *Tradition* 14 (1973–74): 5–22.

7. *Webster's New Universal Unabridged Dictionary* (New York: Simon and Schuster, 1983), 1154.

8. M.T. *De'ot* 5:6–7.

9. To speak gently: B. *Yoma* 86a. To avoid carrying a point too far: *Derekh Eretz Zuta* 2:3. To greet people, following the example of Rabban Yohanon ben Zakkai: B. *Berakhot* 17a. To speak well of people, following other Rabbis' examples: B. *Gittin* 67a; B. *Kiddushin* 29b. Not to speak ill of others: B. *Nedarim* 81a. To pursue peace: M. *Avot* 1:12. To say only that which will likely be heard: B. *Yevamot* 65b; see also *Shemot Rabbah* 41. Not to try to appease a person when that person is angry, not to try to comfort a person when a deceased relative has yet to be buried, not to challenge a person when making a vow, and not to intrude on a person suffering a misfortune: M. *Avot* 4:18 (4:23 in some editions). The precedent of none other than God to alter the truth for the sake of peace: B. *Yevamot* 65b, based on the conflict between Genesis 18:12 and 18:13.

10. This is the dominant theme of Kohelet (Ecclesiastes) (e.g., 1:2–4, 9–11; 2:11–17; 3:14–22) and a recurring one in Psalms (e.g., 33:8–11, 16–17; 37:35–36; 39:5–8; 49; 103:14–17; 146:3–4). Similarly, a Yom Kippur prayer (B. *Yoma* 87b) that was reformulated in *Tanna D'vai Eliyahu Rabbah* 21:2 into the form that became part of the early morning daily liturgy asserts, "What are we? What is our life? What is our piety? What is our righteousness? What is our attainment, our power, our might? . . . Compared to You, all the mighty are nothing, the famous nonexistent, the wise lack wisdom, the clever lack reason. For most of their actions are meaningless, the days of their lives, emptiness. Human preeminence over beasts is an illusion when all is seen as futility." Jules Harlow, ed., *Siddur Sim Shalom* (New York: Rabbinical Assembly, 1985), 12–13; Edward Feld, ed., *Siddur Lev Shalem* (New York: Rabbinical Assembly, 2016), 105. See also M. *Avot* 2:7 (2:8 in some editions); 3:1; 5:22 (5:29 in some editions) for other expressions of the importance of seeing life in a humble way.

11. M.T. *De'ot* 5:6–7.

12. *Derekh Eretz Rabbah* 2:29. In some contexts, like this one and in the second quotation from Maimonides immediately following, the term *gass ru'ah* or *gassut ru'ah* clearly means bragging. In other contexts, including some discussed elsewhere in this responsum, it refers to coarse character or behavior.

13. M.T. *Laws of Human Dispositions* (*De'ot*) 2:2.

14. Thomas J. Scheff, Suzanne M. Retzinger, and Michael T. Ryan, "Crime, Violence, and Self-Esteem," in *The Social Importance of Self Esteem*, Andrew M. Mecca, Neil J. Smelser, and John Vasconcellos, eds. (Berkeley: University of California Press, 1989), 165–200, available at http://publishing.cdlib.org/ucpressebooks/view?docId=ft6c6006v5&chunk.id=d0e5821&toc.id=&brand=ucpress. Jim Liske, "Self-Worth Saves Lives: Most People Who Take Lives Have Yet to Value Themselves," *US News and World Report*, October 30, 2014, https://www.usnews.com/opinion/blogs/faith-matters/2014/10/30/prisoners-show-better-self-worth-can-save-lives.

15. B. *Sotah* 5a.

16. Martin Buber, *Tales of the Hasidim: Later Masters* (New York: Schocken Books, 1948), 249–50. "For me the world was created" comes from the Mishnah's description as to why God created only one person first in M. *Sanhedrin* 4:5. "I am but dust and ashes" is from Abraham's speech to God in Genesis 18:27.

17. M.T. *De'ot* 5:6–7.

18. Christine Porath and Christine Pearson, "The Price of Incivility," *Harvard Business Review*, January–February 2013, https://hbr.org/2013/01/the-price-of-incivility.

19. M. *Avot* 1:9, 11.

20. M. *Avot* 2:6 (2:5 in some editions).

21. M. *Avot* 1:15.

22. M. *Avot* 1:12.

23. *Derekh Eretz Rabbah* 2:2. The verse cited is Malachi 3:19. The rabbinic text mentions only the beginning of it, trusting that its readers will know the rest, but here the full verse has been included in order to reveal the author's intention.

24. Jonah Goldberg, "Power Changes the Length of Your Tie," *Los Angeles Times*, August 1, 2017, http://www.latimes.com/opinion/op-ed/la-oe-goldberg-republican-language-20170801-story.html.

25. Reinout E. de Vries, Benjamin E. Hilbig , Ingo Zettler, Patrick D. Dunlop , Djurre Holtrop, Kibeom Lee, and Michael C. Ashton, "Honest People Tend to Use Less—Not More—Profanity: Comment on Feldman et al.'s (2017) Study 1," http://journals.sagepub.com/doi/pdf/10.1177/1948550617714586.

26. Gen. 1:28 (and 9:1); Exod. 21:10. For a discussion of appropriate sexual conduct as defined by the Jewish tradition, see Elliot N. Dorff, *Love Your Neighbor and Yourself: A Jewish Approach to Modern Personal Ethics* (Philadelphia: JPS, 2003), 73–126.

27. Edward Feld, ed., *Siddur Lev Shalem* (New York: Rabbinical Assembly, 2016), 99.

28. An example of this in the classical tradition: the Rabbis insist that when we read the biblical text, every time we encounter the Bible's use of what is clearly foul language to describe sexual intercourse—*tishagalnah*—we are to substitute the apparently cleaner language of *tishakavnah*. See Isa. 13:16; Zech. 14:2.

29. *Derekh Eretz Rabbah* 3:3.

30. The talmudic text actually says, "The youth of the enemies of Israel die." Because the Rabbis could not even utter the words that the youth of Israel should die, they used a euphemism.

31. B. *Shabbat* 33a; see also B. *Ketubbot* 8b.

32. Moshe Hayyim Luzzato, *Mesillat Yesharim: The Path of the Just*, trans. Shraga Zilbershtain (New York: Feldheim, 1987), 126–29. See also Moshe Hayyim Luzzato, *Mesillat Yesharim: The Path of the Upright*, trans. Mordecai M. Kaplan (Philadelphia: JPS, 1966), 164–69. This is the present author's translation.

15. PLAYING VIOLENT VIDEO GAMES

1. Andrew Perrin, "5 Facts about Americans and Video Games," Pew Research Center, September 17, 2018, https://www.pewresearch.org/fact-tank/2018/09/17 /5-facts-about-americans-and-video-games/.

2. An industry-sponsored group, Entertainment Software Rating Board (ESRB), rates video games. You can find their ratings of popular games and their recommendations for parents monitoring their children's use of video games on their website, https://www.esrb.org/.

3. Perrin, "5 Facts about Americans and Video Games."

4. "APA Reaffirms Position on Violent Video Games and Violent Behavior," American Psychological Association, March 3, 2020, https://www.apa.org/news/press /releases/2020/03/violent-video-games-behavior. See also Britannica Procon, "Do Violent Video Games Contribute to Youth Violence," June 8, 2021, https:// videogames.procon.org/ for a good summary of the arguments for and against banning violent video games on consequentialist grounds.

5. See Brian Stetler, "Report Ties Children's Use of Media to Their Health," *New York Times*, December 2, 2008, https://www.nytimes.com/2008/12/02/arts /02stud.html. This study refers to children's use of all media, not just violent video games, but it does indicate what happens when children make media the center of their lives.

6. Peter Grinspoon, "The Health Effects of Too Much Gaming," Harvard Health Publishing, December 22, 2020, https://www.health.harvard.edu/blog/the -health-effects-of-too-much-gaming-2020122221645.

7. Andrew K. Przybylski, et. al, "Internet Gaming Disorder: Investigating the Clinical Relevance of a New Phenomenon," *American Journal of Psychiatry*, March 1, 2017, https://pubmed.ncbi.nlm.nih.gov/27809571/.

8. B. *Shabbat* 32b.

9. B. *Ḥullin* 10a.

10. B. *Pesaḥim* 22b (based on T. Demai 2); B. *Mo'ed Katan* 17a; B. *Bava Metzia* 75b.

11. B. *Shabbat* 129b; B. *Yevamot* 12b, 72a, 100b; B. *Ketubbot* 39a; B. *Niddah* 45a.

12. For sources on this, see Elliot N. Dorff, *Matters of Life and Death: A Jewish Approach to Modern Medical Ethics* (Philadelphia: JPS, 1998), 14–34 (esp. 14–18), 26–29, 245–78.

13. Immanuel Kant, *Fundamental Principles of the Metaphysic of Morals*, trans. T. K. Abbott, from *Kant's Critique of Practical Reason and Other Works on the Theory of Ethics* (London: Longmans, Green, 1898), 9.

14. Kant, *Fundamental Principles of the Metaphysic of Morals*, 46–47.

15. Chris Morris, "Constitution Protects Video Games," CNN *Money*, June 3, 2003, http://money.cnn.com/2003/06/03/technology/games_firstamendment/.

16. For an especially eloquent statement of this balance in American life, see Barack Obama, *The Audacity of Hope: Thoughts on Reclaiming the American Dream* (New York: Crown, 2006), 55.

17. For a comparison of Jewish, Christian, and secular American values and approaches to making moral decisions, see Elliot N. Dorff, *To Do the Right and the Good* (Philadelphia: JPS, 2002), 1–35, 262–82.

18. M. *Avot* 2:11 (2:16 in *Siddur Sim Shalom*).

19. M. *Avot* 4:21 (4:28 in *Siddur Sim Shalom*).

20. M. *Avot* 3:10 (3:14 in *Siddur Sim Shalom*).

21. Elizabeth A. Vandewater, et al., "Linking Obesity and Activity Level with Children's Television and Video Game Use," *Journal of Adolescence*, February 27, 2004, https://pubmed.ncbi.nlm.nih.gov/15013261/. See also Andrew K. Przybylski, et al., "Internet Gaming Disorder: Investigating the Clinical Relevance of a New Phenomenon," *American Journal of Psychiatry*, March 1, 2017, https://pubmed.ncbi.nlm.nih.gov/27809571/.

22. Murder: Gen. 9:6; Exod. 20:13; Lev. 24:17, 21; etc. Assault: Exod. 21:18–19, 22–25; Lev. 24:19–20; etc. Rape: Deut. 22:23–27. Prostitution: Deut. 22:28–29; B. *Yevamot* 110a; B. *Ketubbot* 56b; 33a; etc. The House of Hillel was convinced that no man would want his sexual intercourse to fall to the level of prostitution: B. *Gittin* 81b; see also B. *Yevamot* 107a and B. *Ketubbot* 73a, where the position of the House of Hillel is reported anonymously and without dispute. Women as well as men are created in the image of God: Gen. 1:27; 5:1–2.

23. B. *Ketubbot* 46a; *Avodah Zarah* 20b.

24. M.T. Laws of Forbidden Intercourse (*Hilkhot Issurei Bi'ah*) 21:19 (based on B. *Niddah* 13b). *Tzaphnat Paneah* 1:90 (1900 edition) notes that fantasy is prohibited as *grama*, a predisposing factor to committing the illicit act.

25. Mekhilta, Bahodesh, section 8 (end), interpreting Exod. 20:14. The Talmud (B. *Bava Metzia* 5b, end) interprets this commandment to apply only to longing

for that for which one is not prepared to pay. Maimonides (M.T. Laws of Robbery and Loss 1:9, 12) interprets it to prohibit action that could be the result of coveting, such as pressuring a person to sell you something you desire. Many medieval interpreters (e.g., Ibn Ezra here; Naḥmanides on Exod. 20:12) nevertheless understand Exodus 20:14 to prohibit covetous thoughts alone, lest they lead you to steal. That, however, involves major legal and theological problems, as Ibn Ezra himself notes (even though he seeks to answer them), so we can and should rely on the Mekhilta, the Talmud, and Maimonides to understand the Tenth Commandment to prohibit actions, not just thoughts.

26. S.A. *Orah Hayyim* 60:5; 101:1; see also 63:4; 98:2.

27. David Brodsky, "*Hirhur ke-maʿaseh damei*–'Thought Is Akin to Action': The Importance of Zoroastrianism and the Development of a Babylonian Rabbinic Motif," *Irano-Judaica* 7 (2019), https://www.academia.edu/38676310/_Thought_Is_Akin_to_Action_The_Importance_of_Thought_and_the_Development_of_a_Babylonian_Rabbinic_Motif_in_irano_judaica_VII. The Babylonian sources he cited are these: B. *Berakhot* 20b; B. *Shabbat* 64a–64b; B. *Yoma* 28b–29a; *Gen. Rabbah* 19; *Kallah Rabbati* 1:5, 2:6; B. *Bava Batra* 16a; and especially B. *Bava Batra* 164b, which, he pointed out, is the closest Jewish sources ever get to asserting something akin to President Jimmy Carter's famous admission, in a 1976 *Playboy* interview, that he "lusted in his heart." Even though that source does not make one legally culpable for only thinking of improper sexual relations, nevertheless Rav Amram there says in the name of Rav that "a person is not saved from three sins every day: thought of sin, [the lack of] focusing on prayer, and gossip," thus making thought alone sinful in God's eyes but not legally actionable.

28. The Zoroastrian sources he cited are these: Denkard 6:227, 6:236, 6:1a, and 6:101; Dadestan i Denig 13:3; and Dadestan I Denig.

29. The Tannaʾitic sources he cited are these: *Mekhilta de-Rashbi* 22:7; M. *Bava Metzia* 3:12; M. *Sanhedrin* 8:5–7; M. *Kelim* 25:9; M. *Miqvaʾot* 8:3; M. *Zavim* 2:2; T. *Peʾah* 1:4; T. *Zevaḥim* 5:5 and 5:13.

30. The Palestinian Amoraic sources he cited are these: Y. *Yoma* 45b (8:7) = Y. *Shevuʿot* 33b (1:6); *Lev. Rabbah* 7:3.

31. For example, Jer. 9:23; Mic. 6:8; Ps. 1, 15, 34:13–15, 112; Prov. 31. Isa. 49:6; see also 42:1–4, 51:4–5.

32. Those who do not fulfill their verbal agreements: T. *Bava Metzia* 3:7; B. *Bava Metzia* 48a. Those who disinherit their children: M. *Bava Batra* 8:5 (133b). Those who accept money from a thief or a lender on interest who repented: T. *Shevi'it* 8:12; B. *Bava Kamma* 94b.

33. B. *Kiddushin* 59a. B. *Bava Metzia* 49a; B. *Bekhorot* 13b. Naḥmanides, *Commentary on the Torah*, on Lev. 19:2.

34. Naḥmanides, *Commentary on the Torah*, on Lev. 19:2.

35. "The spirit of the Sages is pleased with him": Naḥmanides, *Commentary on the Torah*, on Lev. 19:2; *kiddush ha-Shem*, a sanctification of the Divine Name: B. *Bava Kamma* 113a; *derekh eretz*, a term sometimes used to mean a job: for example, M. *Avot* 2:2; 3:5; 6:6. As for Rabbi Elazar ben Azariah's comment, "No Torah, no *derekh eretz*; no *derekh eretz*, no Torah" (3:17; 3:21 in some editions), the term may mean gainful employment, but it may mean ethics.

36. *Gen. Rabbah*, Lekh Lekha 44:1; see also *Lev. Rabbah*, Shemini 13:3 and *Midrash Tanḥuma*, Shemini (ed. Buber, 15b).

37. Kohelet 3:12–13; 22; 4:9–12; 5:17–19; 7:15–18.

38. B. *Shabbat* 31a.

39. Elliot N. Dorff, *For the Love of God and People: A Philosophy of Jewish Law* (Philadelphia: JPS, 2007), 207–30.

40. J. O. Urmson, "Saints and Heroes," in *Essays in Moral Philosophy*, ed. Abraham Irving Melden (Seattle: University of Washington Press, 1958), 198–216.

16. A MODERN APPROACH TO WAR

1. Israel Defense Forces: Ruach Tzahal—Code of Ethics, Jewish Virtual Library, https://www.jewishvirtuallibrary.org/ruach-tzahal-idf-code-of-ethics.

2. Elliot N. Dorff, *To Do the Right and the Good: A Jewish Approach to Modern Social Ethics* (Philadelphia: JPS, 2002), 161–83.

3. That Professor Asa Kasher wrote in 1994 and updated in 2001: Mati Wagner, "IDF Ethics Guru Slams High Court Ban on Human Shields," *Jerusalem Post*, October 6, 2010, https://www.jpost.com/israel/idfs-ethics-guru-slams-high -court-ban-on-human-shields#:~:text=Kasher%2c%20a%20professor%20of %20philosophy,the%20co%2dauthor%20with%20maj. The author does not know whether the conference produced any changes in the language of the Code, the way it is explained and justified to soldiers-in-training, or how it is applied to specific cases in which an ethical infraction is alleged.

4. Michael Walzer, "The Ethics of Warfare in the Jewish Tradition," *Philosophia* 40 (September 2012): 633–41, https://link.springer.com/article/10.1007/s11406-012 -9390-5; Elliot N. Dorff, "War and Peace: A Methodology to Formulate a Contemporary Jewish Approach," *Philosophia* 40 (September 2012): 643–61, https:// link.springer.com/article/10.1007/s11406-012-9391-4.

5. Deut. 20:16–18; see also Exod. 23:26–33; Joshua 3:9–10.

6. For example, Isa. 2; Ezek. 35–39; Zech. 14.

7. Exod. 34:6–7. In Numbers 14:18–19, Moses paraphrases this self-description of God in Exodus.

8. *Num. Rabbah* 11:7.

9. Num. 6:22–27. See also Ps. 29:11, 119:165; Prov. 3:1–2, 17–18.

10. Genesis 3 generally, esp. vv. 5, 22.

11. B. Berakhot 58a, 62b; B. Yoma 85b; B. Sanhedrin 72a.

12. B. *Sanhedrin* 72a; similarly, J. *Sanhedrin* 8:8.

13. B. *Bava Metzia* 62a.

14. Elliot N. Dorff, *Matters of Life and Death: A Jewish Approach to Modern Medical Ethics* (Philadelphia: JPS, 1998), 291–99.

15. J. *Terumot* 7:20; *Gen. Rabbah* 94:9.

16. J. *Terumot* 47a.

17. *Sifra* on Deut. 20:10, Shoftim, para. 199.

18. M. *Sotah* 8:7 (44b).

19. B. *Sotah* 44b.

20. B. *Berakhot* 3b; *Sanhedrin* 2a, 16a, 20a. See also B. *Eruvin* 45a; S.A. *Oraḥ Ḥayyim* 339:6.

21. B. *Eruvin* 45a.

22. Joshua 7. The use of that story is recorded in *The Seventh Day: Soldiers' Talk about the Six-Day War*, Avraham Shapira, ed. (New York: Charles Scribner's Sons, 1970), 74–75, 125–29.

23. J. *Pe'ah* 1:1. The verse cited is Psalms 34:15.

24. Isa. 2:2–4. Micah, Isaiah's younger contemporary, quotes these lines verbatim but then adds two lines that portray the Messianic world as one of peace with theological pluralism rather than monotheism (Mic. 4:4–5).

17. DONATIONS FROM ILL-GOTTEN GAIN

1. Elliot N. Dorff, "Donations from Ill-Gotten Gain," http://www
.rabbinicalassembly.org/sites/default/files/public/halakhah/teshuvot/20052010
/Dorff_Donations%20of%20ill-Gotten%20gain.final.062909.pdf.

2. Elliot N. Dorff with Marc Gary, "Donations from Ill-Gotten Gain in Jewish Law and Ethics and in American Law," *The Journal of Jewish Ethics* 2, no. 1 (2016): 1–40.

3. On being allowed to confess to civil liability: B. *Gittin* 40a, 64b; B. *Kiddushin* 65b; B. *Bava Metzia* 3b. Also see B. *Yevamot* 25b; B. *Ketubbot* 18b; B. *Sanhedrin* 9b, 25a. For an extensive treatment of this topic, see Aaron Kirschenbaum, *Self-Incrimination in Jewish Law* (New York: Burning Bush Press, 1970). Confessions in civil law are "like one hundred witnesses": B. *Yoma* 83a; B. *Shevu'ot* 42a. However, "nobody can make himself a criminal": B. *Ketubbot* 18b; B. *Sanhedrin* 9b; M.T. Testimony 3:7; S.A. Ḥoshen Mishpat 34:25.

4. M.T. Laws of Ethics (*De'ot*) 7:2–3.

5. On not rewarding a sinner: B. *Ketubbot* 11a, 36b, 39b; B. *Sotah* 15a; B. *Gittin* 55b; B. *Bava Kamma* 39a; B. *Menaḥot* 6a, 6b; B. *Niddah* 4b. See also the following passages, in which the prospect of a sinner being rewarded serves as an objection to a possible ruling: B. *Yevamot* 92b; B. *Bava Kamma* 38a; B. *Avodah Zarah* 2b. On upholding people's honor: B. *Berakhot* 19b; B. *Shabbat* 81b, 94b; B. *Eruvin*

41b; B. *Megillah* 3b; B. *Bava Kamma* 79b; B. *Menaḥot* 37b, 38a. See the responsum by Rabbis Elliot Dorff, Daniel Nevins, and Avram Reisner, "Homosexuality,
Human Dignity, and Halakhah," section 4 (primarily written by Rabbi Nevins)
at https://www.rabbinicalassembly.org/sites/default/files/assets/public/halakhah
/teshuvot/20052010/dorff_nevins_reisner_dignity.pdf.

6. B. *Bava Kamma* 58b; B. *Sanhedrin* 107a.

7. M. *Bava Kamma* 8:1, 6; B. *Bava Kamma* 83b, 86b.

8. M. Shevi'it 10:8; M. Makkot 2:8. The interpretation in square brackets is based
on the Tosefta (T. *Makkot* 2:2, toward the end).

9. Amos 8:4–8. For other examples of prophets admonishing the Israelites about
their business ethics, see Isa. 26:8–10; Jer. 9:3–8; 21:12–14; Mic. 3:9–12, and, perhaps most famously, 6:8.

10. M.T. Laws of Burglary 5:1; see also S.A. Ḥoshen Mispat 356:1. These citations are
based on B. *Bava Kamma* 118b–119a.

11. M.T. Laws of Robbery and Loss 5:1; see also S.A. Ḥoshen Mispat 369:1. These
citations are based on B. *Bava Kamma* 118b–119a.

12. M. *Bava Kamma* 10:3; B. *Bava Kamma* 115a (and see Rashi there, s.v. *takkanat ha-shuk*); M.T. Laws of Burglary 5:2–3 (cited and translated below); M.T.
Laws of Robbery and Loss 5:7: "For then no person would purchase anything"
(Shakh, S.A. Ḥoshen Mishpat 356, subpar. 4); *Arukh Ha-Shulhah*, Ḥoshen Mishpat 356:2 states the same reason for this enactment.

13. Rabbi Ben Zion Bergman, in an email to this author dated October 27, 2008.

14. B. *Bava Kamma* 66a, 93b.

15. M.T. Laws of Robbery and Loss 1:5, 2:1–2, 10–12. See also S.A. Ḥoshen Mishpat
360:5–6. A Tosefta (T. *Bava Kamma* 10:12), recorded in an expanded form in the
Talmud (B. *Bava Metzia* 21b–22a), says that "a burglar (*ganav*) who stole from one
person and gave to another, and similarly a robber (*gazlan*) who took from one
person and gave to another, and similarly the Jordan River that took from one person and gave to another, what he took, he took, and what he gave, he gave," presumably even without a change in form, on the grounds, apparently, that owners
despair of getting any stolen thing back, but the codes did not follow this position.

16. B. *Bava Kamma* 94b; S.A. Ḥoshen Mishpat 366:2.

17. M.T. Laws of Burglary 5:2.

18. M.T. Laws of Burglary (*Genaivah*) 2:3; S.A. Ḥoshen Mishpat 356:3; 362:3. See B.
Bava Kamma 115a.

19. S.A. Ḥoshen Mishpat 353:3–4.

20. Dr. Neil Spingarn, owner and lab director of S&N Labs, pointed this out to the
author at a session discussing this responsum arranged by Rabbi Elie Spitz of
Congregation B'nai Israel, Tustin, CA.

21. Professor Robert Katz of the Indiana University School of Law made this last
point to the author.

22. M. T. Laws of Burglary, 5:1, 7–9; S.A. Ḥoshen Mishpat 356:1.

23. B. *Pesaḥim* 22b; B. *Moʿed Katan* 17a; B. *Kiddushin* 32b; B. *Nedarim* 62b; B. *Bava Metzia* 5b, 75b. See also B. *Avodah Zarah* 6b and 22a, where it is applied to the theologically blind (i.e., those who worship idols).

24. On this topic generally, see Elliot N. Dorff, "Nonprofits and Morals: Jewish Perspectives and Methods for Resolving Some Commonly Occurring Moral Issues," in David H. Smith, ed., *Good Intentions: Moral Obstacles and Opportunities* (Bloomington: Indiana University Press, 2005), 103–26.

25. On the requirement to judge one's fellow's intentions fairly: M. *Avot* 1:6; see also 6:6.

26. B. *Bava Kamma* 94b; S.A. Ḥoshen Mishpat 366:2.

27. M.T. Laws of Return (*teshuvah*), chaps. 1 and 2 generally, and 3:14 for the power of *teshuvah* even to erase the penalty of egregious sins that deprive a person of a place in the World to Come. For a general description of the nature, scope, and power of these laws, see Elliot N. Dorff, *Love Your Neighbor and Yourself* (Philadelphia: JPS, 2003), 207–30.

18. FINAL THOUGHTS

1. B. *Nedarim* 49b. See also *Avot D'Rabbi Natan* 16; *Leviticus Rabbah* 25:5. For a general description of the Jewish value of work, see Abraham Cohen, *Everyman's Talmud* (New York: E. P. Dutton, 1949), 191–203.

2. Eric Fromm articulated this point elegantly: Eric Fromm, *The Forgotten Language* (New York: Holt, Reinhard, and Winston, 1951), 243–48.

3. Mordecai Kaplan well described this last moral function of the Sabbath, likening it to a painter stepping away from his painting once each week to see it in perspective and thus know how to move forward with it in the week to come: Mordecai Kaplan, *The Meaning of God in Modern Jewish Religion* (New York: Behrman House, 1937), 59–61. As he puts it there, "*The moral implication of the traditional teaching that God created the world is that creativity, or the continuous emergence of aspects of life not prepared for or determined by the past, constitutes the most divine phase of reality. . . . There can hardly be any more important function for religion to keep alive this yearning for self-renewal and to press it into the service of human progress*" (italics in the original).

4. See, for example, Elliot Dorff and Joel Roth, "Shackling and Hoisting," https:// www.rabbinicalassembly.org/sites/default/files/assets/public/halakhah/teshuvot /19912000/dorffroth_shackling.pdf; Pamela Barmash, "Veal Calves," https:// www.rabbinicalassembly.org/sites/default/files/Veal%20teshuvahfinal%2bpic %20%20nb%20%20job%20%20l.pdf; and, more broadly, the Rabbinical Assembly's "*Magen Tzedek*, Shield of Justice" certification for food produced under strict conditions stipulating that the people and animals involved are treated

well: http://www.rabbinicalassembly.org/sites/default/files/public/social_action /magen_tzedek/magen-tzedek-sources.pdf.

5. For a more extensive discussion of the ethical values involved in the dietary laws, see Jacob Milgrom, *The Anchor Bible: Leviticus 1–16* (New York: Doubleday, 1991), 704–42.

6. For more on the moral values involved in study, see Elliot N. Dorff, *Love Your Neighbor and Yourself: A Jewish Approach to Modern Personal Ethics* (Philadelphia: JPS, 2003), 323–37.

7. For more on Jewish norms to protect privacy, see Dorff, *Love Your Neighbor and Yourself*, 33–72.

Bibliography of Works by Elliot Dorff

This bibliography is divided into the four genres of publications that have appeared to date under the byline of Eliot Dorff: books (authored, edited, or coedited), journal articles and book chapters, book reviews, and Rabbinic rulings (responsa, or *teshuvot*, approved by the Conservative movement's Committee on Jewish Law and Standards). Each section is arranged in chronological order of publication, except that book reviews are ordered in alphabetical order of the last names of the authors of the books reviewed and the list of legal rulings is in alphabetical order by subject. To help readers discover the works best suited to them, books and articles for a scholarly audience of academicians and rabbis are marked with (s) for "scholarly."

Some written works never saw the light of day, including a number of articles and one responsum coauthored with Rabbi Elie Spitz on the ways to use musical instruments on Shabbat in accordance with Jewish law, which did not get the requisite six votes in 2011 to become a valid option in the Conservative movement.

The author comments: "Looking back, I am amazed that I have published as much as I have. When I finished my dissertation, in fact, I told my wife, 'I do not want to write another thing in my life!' As the Yiddish proverb says, 'Mann tracht, und Gott lacht' (People plan, and God laughs). What would soon change my mind about writing was the realization that writing can be another form of teaching, and I have loved teaching ever since Miss Burke, my first-grade teacher, asked me to take a friend out to the hallway to help him learn how to read. I subsequently did a lot of tutoring in fifth and sixth grades, and in ninth grade, as president of my junior high school's student body, I established a tutoring program at the school. In high school I was president of the Future Teachers of America club—and, given this background, perhaps it is no surprise that I am still teaching full-time at American Jewish University as I write this at age eighty. Writing has also been a blessing in helping me to sharpen and broaden my thinking. Along the journey I met many new people who challenged me to think in novel ways. Whether any part of the list below is also a blessing for you, my readers, I leave to your good judgment."

BOOKS AUTHORED, EDITED, OR COEDITED

Jewish Law and Modern Ideology. New York: United Synagogue of America, 1970.

Conservative Judaism: Our Ancestors to Our Descendants. 2nd rev. ed. New York: United Synagogue of America, 1977.

A First Course in Hebrew Bible Study, with Sheldon Dorph and Victoria Kelman. Los Angeles: Bureau of Jewish Education, 1977.

A Living Tree: The Roots and Growth of Jewish Law, with Arthur Rosett. Albany NY: State University of New York Press; and New York: Jewish Theological Seminary of America, 1988.

Willing, Learning and Striving: A Course Guide to Emet Ve-Emunah (the official statement of principles of Conservative Judaism). *Sources and Approaches for Teaching Adults.* New York: Jewish Theological Seminary of America, Rabbinical Assembly, and United Synagogue of America, 1988.

Mitzvah Means Commandment. New York: United Synagogue of America, 1989.

Knowing God: Jewish Journeys to the Unknowable. Northvale NJ: Jason Aronson, 1992.(s)

Contemporary Jewish Ethics and Morality: A Reader, with Louis E. Newman. New York: Oxford University Press, 1995.

Conservative Judaism: Our Ancestors to Our Descendants. 2nd ed. New York: United Synagogue of Conservative Judaism, 1996.

Jewish Perspectives on Organ and Tissue Transplantation. New York: Coalition for the Advancement of Jewish Education, 1996.

The Jewish Tradition: Religious Beliefs and Health Care Decisions. Chicago: Park Ridge Center for the Study of Health, Faith, and Ethics, 1996. Rev. and expanded 2nd ed., 2002.

Matters of Life and Death: A Jewish Approach to Modern Medical Ethics. Philadelphia: Jewish Publication Society, 1998.

Contemporary Jewish Theology: A Reader, with Louis E. Newman. New York: Oxford University Press, 1999.

A Guide for the Effective Use of the Film "Prince of Egypt" for Religious Leaders, Lay Leaders, Parents, and Teachers, with contributions by Vicki Kelman and Ronald Wolfson. Los Angeles: DreamWorks Productions, 1999.

"If You Are My Witnesses . . .": Conservative Judaism Special Issue on Theology, edited with Gordon Tucker, 51, no. 2 (Winter 1999). (s)

To Do the Right and the Good: A Jewish Approach to Modern Personal Ethics. Philadelphia: Jewish Publication Society, 2002.

Love Your Neighbor and Yourself: A Jewish Approach to Modern Personal Ethics. Philadelphia: Jewish Publication Society, 2003.

The Unfolding Tradition: Jewish Law After Sinai. New York: Aviv /Rabbinical Assembly, 2005. (s)

The Way Into Tikkun Olam (Repairing the World). Woodstock VT: Jewish Lights, 2005.

For Love of God and People: A Philosophy of Jewish Law. Philadelphia: Jewish Publication Society, 2007. (s)

Jewish Law Association Studies XVI: The Boston 2004 Conference Volume. Liverpool, UK: Deborah Charles, 2007. (s)

The Jewish Approach to Repairing the World (Tikkun Olam): A Brief Introduction for Christians, with Rev. Cory Willson. Woodstock VT: Jewish Lights, 2008.

Jewish Choices, Jewish Voices: Body, with Louis E. Newman. Philadelphia: Jewish Publication Society, 2008.

Jewish Choices, Jewish Voices: Money, with Louis E. Newman. Philadelphia: Jewish Publication Society, 2008.

Jewish Choices, Jewish Voices: Power, with Louis E. Newman. Philadelphia: Jewish Publication Society, 2009.

Jewish Choices, Jewish Voices: Sex and Intimacy, with Danya Rutenberg. Philadelphia: Jewish Publication Society, 2010.

Jewish Choices, Jewish Voices: Social Justice, with Danya Rutenberg. Philadelphia: Jewish Publication Society, 2010.

Jewish Choices, Jewish Voices: War and National Security, with Danya Rutenberg. Philadelphia: Jewish Publication Society, 2010.

The Unfolding Tradition: Philosophies of Jewish Law. Rev. ed. New York: Aviv, 2011. (s)

The Oxford Handbook of Jewish Ethics and Morality, with Jonathan Crane. New York: Oxford University Press, 2012. (s)

Jews and Genes: The Genetic Future in Contemporary Jewish Thought, with Laurie Zoloth. Philadelphia: Jewish Publication Society, 2015. (s)

Modern Conservative Judaism: Evolving Thought and Practice. Philadelphia: Jewish Publication Society; New York: Rabbinical Assembly; and Lincoln: University of Nebraska Press, 2018.

Jewish Medical Ethics: A 21st Century Discussion. Jerusalem: Florence Melton School of Adult Jewish Learning, 2019.

JOURNAL ARTICLES AND BOOK CHAPTERS

"Towards a Legal Theory for the Conservative Movement." *Conservative Judaism* 27, no. 3 (Spring 1973): 65–77. (s)

"The Author Responds." *Conservative Judaism* 28, no. 2 (Winter 1974): 75–78. (s)

"A Response to Richard Rubenstein." *Conservative Judaism* 28, no. 4 (Summer 1974): 33–36. (s)

"A Course Offering in Jewish Law," with Arthur Rosett. *Journal of Legal Education* 27, no. 4 (Winter 1976): 595–98. (s)

"Revelation." *Conservative Judaism* 31, no. 1–2 (Fall-Winter 1976): 58–69. (s)

"Two Ways to Approach God." *Conservative Judaism* 30, no. 2 (Winter 1976): 58–67. (s)

"Conservative Judaism: Response to Lawrence J. Kaplan." *Commentary* 63, no. 2 (February 1977): 7–10.

"God and the Holocaust." *Judaism* 26, no. 1 (Winter 1977): 27–34. (s)

"The Interaction of Jewish Law with Morality." *Judaism* 26, no. 4 (Fall 1977): 455–66. (s)

"Judaism as a Religious Legal System." *Hastings Law Journal* 29, no. 6 (July 1978): 1331–60. (s)

"The Meaning of Covenant: A Contemporary Understanding." In *Issues in the Jewish-Christian Dialogue: Jewish Perspectives on Covenant, Mission and Witness*, edited by Helga Croner and Leon Klenicki, 38–61. New York: Paulist, 1979. (s)

"What It Means to Be a Conservative Jew." *United Synagogue Review* 31, no. 2 (Winter 1979): 1ff.

"Conservative Judaism." *Keeping Posted* 26, no. 3 (December 1980): 8–10.

"Study Leads to Action." *Religious Education* 75, no. 2 (March-April 1980): 171–92. (s)

"Traditional Judaism." *Conservative Judaism* 34, no. 2: (November–December 1980): 34–38. (s)

"Making Our Way into Conservative Jewish Practice." *Direction* 12, no. 3 (November 1981): 1ff.

"A Certain Spice: Sabbath Spirit and Sabbath Law." In *Slow Down and Live: A Guide to Shabbat Observance and Enjoyment*, edited by Stephen Garfinkel, 23–47. New York: United Synagogue Youth, 1982.

"Prayer for the Perplexed." *University Papers*. Los Angeles: University of Judaism, October 1982.

"The Covenant: How Jews Understand Themselves and Others." *Anglican Theological Review* 64, no. 4 (October 1982): 481–501. (s)

"Singles Must Be Accepted By the Community." *Direction* 13:3 (December, 1982): 5ff.

A Hospice Guide for Care of Jewish Patients and Families, with Herman Feifel, Audrey P. Harris, and Maurice Lamm. Los Angeles: Jewish Federation Council of Greater Los Angeles, 1983.

"Pursuing Justice and Peace within Judaism." *Religious Education* 78, no. 4 (Fall 1983): 480–83.

"Rabbi, I'm Dying." *Conservative Judaism* 37, no. 4 (Summer 1984): 37–51. (s)

"A Renewed Understanding of Mission and Method in Jewish Education." *Religious Education* 79, no. 1 (Winter 1984): 78–87. (s)

"Equality with Distinction." *University Papers*. Los Angeles: University of Judaism, March 1984.

"A Jewish Perspective on Living Wills and Withholding Life-Support Systems." *Linkages* (Spring-Summer 1984): 7–9.

"'Choose Life': A Jewish Perspective on Medical Ethics." *University Papers*. Los Angeles: University of Judaism, February 1985. Reprinted in *Jewish News—New Jersey*, September 12, 1985, 11–23.

"A Living Tradition: Ongoing Jewish Exegesis." *Semeia: An Experimental Journal for Biblical Criticism* 34 (1985): 115–21. (s)

Response to "Retribution in the Deuteronomistic History" by Robert M. Voskuhl. In *Church Divinity 1985*, edited by John H. Morgan, 50–52. Bristol IN: Wyndham Hall, 1985. (s)

"Jewish Perspectives on the Poor." In *The Poor Among Us: Jewish Tradition and Social Policy*, 21–55. New York: American Jewish Committee, 1986.

"Medicine in the Jewish Tradition." In *Caring and Curing: Health and Medicine in the Western Religious Traditions*, edited by Ronald L. Numbers and Darrel W. Amundsen, 5–39. New York: Macmillan, 1986. (s)

"The Effects of Science on Jewish Law." *Conservative Judaism* 40, no. 2 (Winter 1987–88): 52–60. (s)

"Honoring Aged Fathers and Mothers." *Reconstructionist* 53, no. 2 (October-November 1987): 14–20.

"'A Time for War and a Time for Peace': A Jewish Perspective on the Ethics of International Intervention." *University Papers*. Los Angeles: University of Judaism, June 1987. Reprinted in part and with revisions as "Defensive War," in *S'vara: A Journal of Philosophy and Judaism* 2, no. 1 (1991): 25–29.

"Training Rabbis in the Land of the Free." In *The Seminary at 100*, edited by Nina Beth Cardin and David Wolf Silverman, 11–28. New York: Rabbinical Assembly and Jewish Theological Seminary of America, 1987. (s)

"Catholic/Jewish Dialogue: A Jewish Perspective on Vatican Documents." *Ecumenical Trends* 17(September 1988): 116–20. Reprinted in *Three Score and Ten: Essays in Honor of Rabbi Seymour J. Cohen*, edited by Abraham J. Karp, Louis Jacobs, and Chaim Zalman Dimitrovsky, 283–91. Hoboken NJ: Ktav, 1991. (s)

"The Covenant: The Transcendent Thrust in Jewish Law." *Jewish Law Annual* 7 (1988): 68–96. (s)

"Judaism and Health." *Health Values* 12, no. 3 (May-June 1988): 32–36. (s)

"A Middle Ground on Abortion." *Jewish News*, August 1989, 14–15. Reprinted, in part, in *United Synagogue Review* 42, no. 2 (Spring 1990): 16–17.

"'This Is My God': One Jew's Faith." In *Three Faiths–One God: A Jewish, Christian, Muslim Encounter*, edited by John Hick and Edmund S. Meltzer, 7–29. London: Macmillan; and Albany: State University of New York Press, 1989. (s)

"Conservative Judaism 1970–1990." *Encyclopedia Judaica, 1990–1991 Yearbook*, 227–31. (s)

"Moral Distinctions." *Sh'ma: A Journal of Jewish Responsibility* 21/401 (November 16, 1990): 6–8.

"Bishops, Rabbis, and Bombs." In *Confronting Omnicide: Jewish Reflections on Weapons of Mass Destruction*, edited by Daniel Landes, 164–95. Northvale NJ: Jason Aronson, 1991. (s)

"The Concept of God in the Conservative Movement." Festschrift in Honor of Dr. Robert Gordis. *Judaism* 40, no. 4 (Fall 1991): 429–41. (s)

"The Covenant as the Key: A Jewish Theology of Christian-Jewish Relations." In *Toward A Theological Encounter: Jewish Understandings of Christianity*, edited by Leon Klenicki, 43–66. New York: Paulist, 1991. (s)

"A Jewish Approach to End-Stage Medical Care." *Conservative Judaism* 43, no. 3 (Spring 1991): 3–51. Reprinted in *Life and Death Responsibilities in Jewish Biomedical Ethics*, edited by Aaron L. Mackler, 292–358. New York: Jewish Theological Seminary, 2000. (s)

Teaching About World Religions: A Teacher's Supplement. Edited by Alfred Wolf (with sections on Judaism and Jews). Boston: Houghton Mifflin, 1991.

"A Time to Live and a Time to Die." *United Synagogue Review* 44, no. 1 (Fall 1991): 21–22.

"Advanced Directive for Medical Care at the End of Life." *United Synagogue Review* 45, no. 1 (Fall 1992): 20–22.

"Conservative Judaism." In *Jewish-American History and Culture: An Encyclopedia*, edited by Jack Fischel and Sanford Pinsker, 114–21. New York: Garland, 1992. (s)

"In Defense of Images." In *Proceedings of the Academy for Jewish Philosophy*, edited by David Novak and Norbert Samuelson, 129–54. Lanham MD: University Press of America, 1992. (s)

"Individual and Communal Forgiveness." In *Autonomy and Judaism: The Individual and the Community in Jewish Philosophical Thought*, edited by Daniel H. Frank, 193–218. Albany: State University of New York Press, 1992. (s)

"A Methodology for Jewish Medical Ethics." In *Jewish Law Association Studies 6: The Jerusalem 1990 Conference Volume*, edited by B. S. Jackson and S. M. Passamaneck, 35–57. Atlanta: Scholars Press, 1992. Reprinted in *Contemporary Jewish Ethics and Morality: A Reader*, edited by Elliot N. Dorff and Louis E. Newman, 161–76. New York: Oxford University Press, 1995. (s)

"No on 161" (California initiative legalizing physician-assisted suicide). *Jewish Journal of Greater Los Angeles* 7, no. 36 (October 30–November 5, 1992): 18–19.

"'No, Thank You, Doctor.'" *Sh'ma: A Journal of Jewish Responsibility* 23/442 (November 27, 1992): 9–11.

"Pluralism." In *Frontiers of Jewish Thought*, edited by Steven Katz, 213–34. Washington DC: B'nai Brith Books, 1992. Reprinted in a different form as "Pluralism: Models for the Conservative Movement," *Conservative Judaism* 48, no. 1 (Fall 1995): 21–35. (s)

Response to Martha A. Ackelsberg's "Jewish Family Ethics in a Post-Halakhic Age." In *Imagining the Jewish Future: Essays and Responses*, edited by David A. Teutsch, 169–74. Albany: State University of New York Press, 1992. (s)

"American Health Care Through Jewish Eyes." *Women's League Outlook* 64, no. 1 (Fall 1993): 12–14, 26.

"'In God's Image:' Aspects of Judaism Relevant to Family Violence." In *Shalom Bayit: A Jewish Response to Child Abuse and Domestic Violence*, edited by Ian

Russ, Sally Weber, and Ellen Ledley, 48–57, 64–66. Los Angeles: Shalom Bayit Committee of the University of Judaism and Jewish Family Service of Los Angeles, 1993. Reprinted in *Resource Guide for Rabbis on Domestic Violence*, edited by Maya Townsend, 93–99. Washington DC: Jewish Women International, 1996.

"A Living Will." In *A Time to Mourn, A Time to Comfort*, edited by Ron Wolfson, 281–91. New York: Federation of Jewish Men's Clubs; and Los Angeles: University of Judaism, 1993.

"Louis Jacobs." In *Interpreters of Judaism in the Late Twentieth Century*, edited by Steven T. Katz, 167–88. Washington DC: B'nai Brith Books, 1993.

"Roundtable: A New Sexual Ethics for Judaism?" *Tikkun* 8, no. 5 (September-October 1993): 61–68, 89.

"Religion at a Time of Crisis." *Quality of Life: A Nursing Challenge* 2, no. 3 (December 1993): 56–59.

"Symposium on Religious Law: Roman Catholic, Islamic, and Jewish Treatment of Familial Issues" (with sections on abortion, *in vitro* fertilization, and contraception). *Loyola of Los Angeles International and Comparative Law Journal* 16, no. 1 (November 1993): 42–46, 55–60, 80–85. (s)

"We Can, But Should We? Philosophical Approaches to the Moral Issues Raised by Technology." In *Technology and Ethics*, edited by E. A. Halevi and D. Kohn, 55–72. Haifa: S. Neaman Institute Press, 1993. (s)

"The Ideology of Conservative Judaism: Sklare After Thirty Years." *American Jewish History* 74, no. 2 (December 1984): 102–17. (s)

"Sex, Values, and the Law." *Jerusalem Report*, August 25, 1994, 54.

"Torah." In *Creating an Environment that Transforms Jewish Lives*, 13–15. New York: Avi Chai, A Philanthropic Foundation, 1994.

"Generating the Next Generation: Problems of Infertility." In *Proceedings of the Rabbinical Assembly 1994*, edited by Amy Gottlieb, 149–66. New York: Rabbinical Assembly, 1995. (s)

"On Giving an Organ for Transplant to an Individual Whose Organ Was Destroyed by His or Her Behavior—Such as Alcoholic Cirrhosis—or to the Very Elderly." *Los Angeles Times*, August 16, 1995.

"On Placing an Elderly Parent in a Nursing Home." *Los Angeles Times*, June 28, 1995.

"On Standing in an Express Check-Out Line behind a Person with an Oversized Shopping Load or a Check." *Los Angeles Times*, November 29, 1995.

"The Tyranny of Technology." *Sh'ma* 25/495 (May 26, 1995): 2–4.

"'This Is My Beloved, This Is My Friend': The Rabbis' Letter on Intimate Relations." *Women's League Outlook* 65, no. 4 (Summer 1995): 7, 8, 20. Response to a letter about this article: *Women's League Outlook* 66, no. 2 (Winter 1995): 29–30.

"Whether Schools Should Accept Grants If the Gifts Require the Use of Names Publicly Linked with Misdeeds." *Los Angeles Times*, September 20, 1995.

"Allocation of Resources to AIDS Research." *Los Angeles Times*, July 17, 1996.

"Artificial Insemination, Egg Donation, and Adoption." *Conservative Judaism* 49, no. 1 (Fall 1996): 3–60. Reprinted in *Life and Death Responsibilities in Jewish Biomedical Ethics*, edited by Aaron L. Mackler, 17–94. New York: Jewish Theological Seminary, 2000. (s)

"Assisted Death: A Jewish Perspective." In *Must We Suffer Our Way to Death? Cultural and Theological Perspectives on Death by Choice*, edited by Ronald P. Hamel and Edwin R. Dubose, 141–73. Dallas: Southern Methodist University Press, 1996. (s)

"Assisted Suicide: A Jewish Perspective." *Sh'ma* 27/517 (September 20, 1996): 6–7.

"Choosing Life: Aspects of Judaism Affecting Organ Transplantation." In *Organ Transplantation: Meanings and Realities*, edited by Stuart J. Youngner, Renee C. Fox, and Laurence J. O'Connell, 168–93. Madison: University of Wisconsin Press, 1996. (s)

"Debate, Not Prophecy: Jewish Law Can Never Be Neatly Defined." *Jerusalem Report*, August 22, 1996, 45.

"Domestic Violence: Curing the Offender vs. Saving the Victims." *Los Angeles Times*, May 8, 1996.

"Family Issues: Spousal Obligations, Parental/Filial Duties, Family Violence." *Proceedings of the Rabbinical Assembly 1995*, edited by Amy Gottlieb, 118–20. New York: Rabbinical Assembly, 1996. (s)

"Family Violence: Our Problem, Too." *United Synagogue Review* 49, no. 1 (Fall, 1996): 15–17, 26–27.

"A Jewish Theology of Jewish Relations to Other People." In *People of God, Peoples of God: A Jewish-Christian Conversation in Asia*, edited by Hans Ucko, 46–66. Geneva, Switzerland: World Council of Churches, 1996. (s)

"Moral Lessons from an Assassination." *Tikkun* 11, no. 1 (January-February 1996): 68.

"'This Is My Beloved, This Is My Friend': A Rabbinic Letter on Intimate Relations." New York: Rabbinical Assembly, 1996. Reprinted in a revised form in *Love Your Neighbor and Yourself: A Jewish Approach to Modern Personal Ethics*, 73–126. Philadelphia: Jewish Publication Society, 2003.

"What Do American Jews Believe?" *Commentary* 104, no. 8 (August 1996): 29–30. Reprinted in *Jewish Political Chronicle* (December 1998–January 1999): 43–44.

"Whether Suicide Is Ever Justifiable." *Los Angeles Times*, January 17, 1996.

"Whether to Say 'We'll See' to a Screaming Child at the Mall When You Really Mean 'No.'" *Los Angeles Times*, November 20, 1996.

"Assisted Suicide." *United Synagogue Review* 50, no. 1 (Fall 1997): 24–26.

"Changing Tax Laws to Support University Tuition Payments." *Los Angeles Times*, May 7, 1997.

"Conservative Judaism," "University of Judaism," "The Historical School," and "Homosexuality." In *The Oxford Dictionary of the Jewish Religion*, edited by R. J.

Zwi Werblowsky and Geoffrey Wigoder, 172–74, 326, 335, 710, respectively. New York: Oxford University Press, 1997.

"Custom Drives Jewish Law on Women." *Conservative Judaism* 49, no. 3 (Spring 1997): 3–21. Response to critics in *Conservative Judaism* 51, no. 1 (Fall 1998): 6–13. Reprinted in *Gender Issues in Jewish Law: Essays and Responsa*, edited by Walter Jacob and Moshe Zemer, 82–106. New York: Berghahn, 2001. (s)

"Family Violence: Halakhic and Programmatic Responses." *Proceedings of the Rabbinical Assembly 1996*, edited by Rahel Musleah, 162–65. New York: Rabbinical Assembly, 1997. (s)

"Hearing God's Voice." *Avar ve'Atid* 4, no. 2 (December 1997): 41–48.

"Human Cloning." *Los Angeles Times*, February 26, 1997.

"The Idea of Redemption in the Siddur." In *Proceedings of the Rabbinical Assembly 1996*, edited by Rahel Musleah, 149–53. New York: Rabbinical Assembly, 1997. (s)

"Jewish Law as Standards." In *American Rabbi: The Life and Thought of Jacob B. Agus*, edited by Steven T. Katz, 195–223. New York: NYU Press, 1997. Reprinted in an expanded form as "'Legislated Spiritual Disciplines: Jacob Agus' Philosophy of Jewish Law," in *Jewish Law Associaton Studies 9: The London 1996 Conference Volume*, edited by E. A. Goldman, 25–56. Atlanta: Scholars Press, 1997. (s)

"Judaism, Business, and Privacy." *Business Ethics Quarterly* 7, no. 2 (March 1997): 31–46. Reprinted in *Spiritual Goods: Faith Traditions and the Practice of Business*, edited by Stewart W. Herman and Arthur Gross Schaefer, 347–66. Bowling Green OH: Philosophy Documentation Center, 2001. (s)

"Judaism's Import for End-of-Life Issues." In *Death and the Quest for Meaning: Essays in Honor of Herman Feifel*, edited by Stephen Strack, 79–108. Northvale NJ: Jason Aronson, 1997. (s)

"Matters of Degree and Kind: An Open Response to Eugene Borowitz's Open Letter to Me." *Conservative Judaism* 50, no. 1 (Fall 1997): 66–71. (s)

"On a Proposed City Council Ordinance Restricting Panhandling." *Los Angeles Times*, February 5, 1997.

"Paying for Medical Care: A Jewish View." 1996 Isaac Franck Distinguished Memorial Lecture at the Kennedy Institute of Ethics. *Kennedy Institute of Ethics Journal* 7, no. 1 (Spring 1997): 15–30. (s)

"Review of Recent Work in Jewish Bioethics." In *Bioethics Yearbook*, vol. 5, edited by B. Andrew Lustig, 75–91. Dortrecht, The Netherlands: Kluwer Academic, 1997. (s)

"Service to Humanity: A Jewish Perspective." *The Ismaili* 2 (July 11, 1997): 52–53.

The Sh'ma and Its Blessings commentator for theological reflections. In *My People's Prayer Book: Traditional Prayers, Modern Commentaries, Vol. 1*, edited by Lawrence A. Hoffman, 29–31, 56, 59, 69–71, 75–77, 87–89, 105, 107–8, 111–13, and 126–27. Woodstock VT: Jewish Lights, 1997.

The Amidah (commentator for theological reflections). In *My People's Prayer Book: Traditional Prayers, Modern Commentaries, Vol. 2*, edited by Lawrence A. Hoffman, 52, 59, 63–65, 72, 75–76, 84, 88, 100, 102, 106, 108, 116, 118, 154, 157–58, 164, 170, and 176. Woodstock VT: Jewish Lights, 1998.

"Formulating Jewish Law for Our Time." *United Synagogue Review* 50, no. 2 (Spring 1998): 21–23.

"Human Cloning: A Jewish Perspective." *Southern California Interdisciplinary Law Journal* 8, no. 1 (Winter 1998): 117–29. (s)

"Introduction" to Naomi Graetz, *Silence Is Deadly: Judaism Confronts Wifebeating*, xv–xxi. Northvale NJ: Jason Aronson, 1998. (s)

"Jewish Law and Lore: The Case of Organ Transplantation." *Jewish Law Annual* 12 (1998): 65–114. (s)

"The Subtleties of the Priestly Blessing." *Moment* 23, no. 3 (June 1998): 62–63, 70.

"*Teshuvah* on Assisted Suicide." *Conservative Judaism* 50, no. 4 (Summer 1998): 3–24. Reprinted in *Journal of Law and Religion* 13, no. 2 (1998–99): 263–87. Reprinted in *Life and Death Responsibilities in Jewish Biomedical Ethics*, edited by Aaron L. Mackler, 403–34. New York: Jewish Theological Seminary, 2000. Reprinted in *Responsa 1991–2000 of the Committee on Jewish Law and Standards of the Conservative Movement*, edited by Kassel Abelson and David J. Fine, 379–97. New York: Rabbinical Assembly, 2002. (s)

"Why We Need Jewish Medical Ethics." *Network—Maimonides: Health in the Jewish World* 4, no. 2 (Spring 1998): 2.

"'Heal Us, Lord, and We Shall Be Healed': The Role of Hope and Destiny in Jewish Bioethics." *Judaism* 48, no. 2 (Spring 1999): 149–64. (s)

"In Search of God." In *Contemporary Jewish Theology: A Reader*, edited by Elliot N. Dorff and Louis E. Newman, 112–21. New York: Oxford University Press, 1999. (s)

"A Jewish Approach to Assisted Reproductive Technologies." *Whittier Law Review* 21, no. 2 (1999): 391–400. (s)

"A Jewish Experience of Religious Pluralism." *Current Dialogue* 34 (February 1999): 6–8.

"Knowing God Through Prayer." *Conservative Judaism* 51, no. 2 (Winter 1999): 37–52. (s)

Letter in response to Rabbi Clifford Librach's article on Conservative Judaism, *Commentary* 107, no. 1 (January 1999): 3–6.

"*P'sukei D'Zimrah* (Morning Prayers)" (commentator for theological reflections). In *My People's Prayer Book: Traditional Prayers, Modern Commentaries*, vol. 3, edited by Lawrence A. Hoffman, 52, 57–59, 78, 84–87, 92, 112, 118, 124, 127, 128, 132, 138, 141, 164, 170–71. Woodstock VT: Jewish Lights, 1999,

"Rabbi, Why Does God Make Me Suffer?" In *Pain Seeking Understanding: Suffering, Medicine, and Faith*, edited by Margaret E. Mohrmann and Mark J. Hanson, 115–25. Cleveland: Pilgrim Press, 1999. (s)

Response to Herbert Bronstein's "Mitzvah and Autonomy: The Oxymoron of Reform Judaism." *Tikkun* 14, no. 4 (July-August 1999): 46.

"Responsibilities for the Provision of Health Care," with Aaron L. Mackler. *United Synagogue Review* 51, no. 2 (Spring 1999): 18–19.

"Another Jewish View of Ethics, Christian and Jewish." In *Christianity in Jewish Terms*, edited by Tikva Frymer-Kensky, David Novak, Peter Ochs, David Fox Sandmel, and Michael A. Signer, 127–34. Boulder CO: Westview, 2000. (s)

"Circumcision," "Divorce," and "Jewish Observance." In *Contemporary American Religion, Vol. 1*, edited by Wade Clark Roof, 131–33, 194–95, 349–50. New York: Macmillan Reference USA, 2000. (s)

"Ethics of Judaism." In *The Blackwell Companion to Judaism*, edited by Jacob Neusner and Alan J. Avery-Peck, 373–92. Oxford, UK: Blackwell, 2000. (s)

"A Jewish Experience of Religious Pluralism." *Current Dialogue* 34 (2000): 6–8.

"A Jewish Ethic of Political and Rabbinic Leadership." In *Proceedings of the Rabbinical Assembly 1999*, edited by David J. Fine, 112–19, 123–24, 125–27. New York: Rabbinical Assembly, 2000. (s)

"Jewish Law and the Family." *Women's League Outlook* 71, no. 1 (Fall 2000): 16–18.

"The King's Torah: The Role of Judaism in Shaping Jews' Input in National Policy." In *A Nation Under God? Essays on the Fate of Religion in American Public Life*, edited by R. Bruce Douglass and Joshua Mitchell, 203–22. Lanham MD: Rowman and Littlefield, 2000. (s)

"Learning about Homosexuality and Taking a New Stand." *New Menorah Journal* 59 (Spring 2000): 3–4.

"Making It Work: The Impact of Jewish Law on Everyday Life." *United Synagogue Review* 52, no. 2 (Spring 2000): 25–27.

"Marriage" and "Mikveh." In *Contemporary American Religion, Vol. 2*, edited by Wade Clark Roof, 418–20, 447. New York: Macmillan Reference USA, 2000. (s)

"Moral Issues in Running a Synagogue." *United Synagogue Review* 52, no. 2 (Spring 2000): 22–24.

"Religious Perspectives on Forgiveness" (responses to five questions about forgiveness on behalf of the Jewish tradition in an interreligious presentation). In *Forgiveness: Theory, Research, and Practice*, edited by Michael E. McCullough, Kenneth I. Pargament, and Carl E. Thoresen, 20, 23–24, 30–31, 32–33, 35–36. New York: Guilford, 2000. (s)

"Religious Views on Biotechnology, Jewish." In *Encyclopedia of Ethical, Legal, and Policy Issues in Biotechnology*, edited by Thomas H. Murray and Maxwell Mehleman, 924–38. New York: John Wiley and Sons, 2000. Reprinted in *Claiming Power Over Life: Religion and Biotechnology Policy*, edited by Mark J. Hanson, 192–214. Washington DC: Georgetown University Press, 2001. (s)

"Responsibilities for the Provision of Health Care," with Aaron Mackler. In *Life and Death Responsibilities in Jewish Biomedical Ethics*, edited by Aaron L. Mackler, 479–505. New York: Jewish Theological Seminary, 2000. (s)

"*Seder K'riat Hatorah* (The Torah Service)" (commentator for theological reflections). In *My People's Prayer Book: Traditional Prayers, Modern Commentaries,*

Vol. 4, edited by Lawrence A. Hoffman, 50, 54, 64, 66–68, 72, 75, 80, 82, 88, 95, 98–99, 104, 106–7, 126, 128–29, 134, 136, 142, 146, 170, 173, 186, 191, 198, 208, 210. Woodstock VT: Jewish Lights, 2000.

"Teaching Jewish Ethics and Morals: Making Sense of Jewish Moral Theory and Practice." In *Academic Approaches to Teaching Jewish Studies*, edited by Zev Garber, 193–212. Lanham MD: University Press of America, 2000. (s)

"*Birkhot Hashachar* (Morning Blessings)" (commentator for theological reflections). In *My People's Prayer Book: Traditional Prayers, Modern Commentaries, Vol. 5*, edited by Lawrence A. Hoffman, 50, 52–53, 56, 59–60, 70, 74–75, 86, 89, 94, 97, 100, 104–5, 108, 111, 122, 129–33, 146, 152, 160, 165, 174, 179–88, 192. Woodstock VT: Jewish Lights, 2001.

"Doing the Right and the Good: Fundamental Convictions and Methods of Jewish Ethics." In *Ethics in the World Religions*, edited by Joseph Runzo and Nancy M. Martin, 89–114. Oxford, UK: Oneworld, 2001. (s)

"The Elements of Forgiveness: A Jewish Approach." In *Dimensions of Forgiveness: Psychological Research and Theological Perspectives*, edited by Everett L. Worthington Jr., 29–55. Philadelphia: Templeton Foundation Press, 1998. Reprinted as *Forgiveness: Theory, Research, and Practice*. Philadelphia: Templeton Foundation Press, 2001. (s)

"The Ethics of Healthcare and Medical Research." *Sh'ma* 31/578 (January 2001): 4–5.

"The Ethics of Pastoral Counseling." *Perspectives on the Professions: A Periodical of the Center for the Study of Ethics in the Professions* 21, no. 1 (Fall 2001): 5–7.

Etz Hayim: Torah and Commentary (co-writer of the *Halakhah Le-Ma'aseh* section and author of "Medieval and Modern Theories of Revelation," "Justice," "Medieval and Modern Halakhah"), edited by David Lieber, 1399–1405, 1427–30, 1474–79. Philadelphia: Jewish Publication Society; and New York: Rabbinical Assembly, 2001.

"Is There a Unique Jewish Ethics? The Role of Law in Jewish Bioethics." *Annual of the Society of Christian Bioethics 2001*, 305–18. Collegeville MN: Society of Christian Ethics, 2001. (s)

"Judaism and Philanthropy." *Sh'ma* (October 2001): 6–7.

Response to Leonard Sharzer's "Artificial Hydration and Nutrition." *Conservative Judaism* 53, no. 2 (Winter 2001): 69–71. (s)

"Stem Cell Research—A Jewish Perspective." In *The Human Embryonic Stem Cell Debate*, edited by Suzanne Holland, Karen Lebacqz, and Laurie Zoloth, 89–94. Cambridge MA: MIT Press, 2001. (s)

"Understanding Election." In *He Kissed Him and They Wept: Towards a Theology of Jewish-Catholic Partnership*, edited by Tony Bayfield, Sidney Brichto, and Eugene J. Fisher, 60–79. London: SCM, 2001. (s)

"Aspects of Judaism and Family Violence." In *Embracing Justice: A Resource Guide for Rabbis on Domestic Abuse*, edited by Diane Gardsbane, 43–51. Washington

DC: Jewish Women's International, 2002. Reprinted in *Healing and Wholeness: A Resource Guide on Domestic Abuse in the Jewish Community*, edited by Diane Gardsbane, 43–51. Washington DC: Jewish Women's International, 2002.

"Challenge Your Child!" *Your Child* (Fall 2002): 1–2.

"Conservative Judaism." In *Religious Traditions and Prenatal Genetic Counseling*, edited by Rebecca Rae Anderson, 1–5. Omaha: Munroe-Meyer Institute at the University of Nebraska Medical Center, 2002.

"Embryonic Stem Cell Research: The Jewish Perspective." *United Synagogue Review* 54, no. 2 (Spring 2002): 29–33.

"Human Cloning: A Jewish Perspective." *Christian Networks Journal* (Summer 2002): 44–45.

"Judaism and Homosexuality." The Swig Lecture, April 21, 2002, San Francisco. In *New Jewish and Christian Approaches to Homosexuality: A Symposium*, 16-21.: San Francisco: Swig Judaic Studies Program at the University of San Francisco, 2002.

"Revenge or Justice? A Test of Our Own Moral Mettle." In *Teaching About Terrorism*, edited by Shoshana Glatzer, 55–58. New York: Coalition for the Advancement of Jewish Education, 2002.

"Setting Moral Limits on Technology." *Health Progress* 83, no. 1 (January-February 2002): 39–43, 54.

Tachanun and Concluding Prayers (commentator for theological reflections). In *My People's Prayer Book: Traditional Prayers, Modern Commentaries, Vol. 6*, edited by Lawrence A. Hoffman, 40, 48–50, 64, 66, 72–73, 75–76, 82, 85, 88, 90, 96, 102, 105–6, 112, 117, 134, 138, 150, 154–55, 164, 170. Woodstock VT: Jewish Lights, 2002.

"Conservative and Reconstructionist Judaism." In *The Jewish Hospice Manual: A Guide to Compassionate End-of-Life Care for Jewish Patients and Their Families*, edited by Maurice Lamm, 78–80. New York: National Institute for Jewish Hospice; and Miami: Vitas, 2003.

"Jewish Law and Tradition Regarding Sexual Abuse and Incest." In *Shine the Light: Sexual Abuse and Healing in the Jewish Community*, edited by Rachel Lev, 46–60. Boston: Northeastern University Press, 2003.

"A Jewish Perspective on Human Rights." In *Human Rights and Responsibilities in the World Religions*, edited by Joseph Runzo, Nancy M. Martin, and Arvind Sharma, 209–32. Oxford: Oneworld, 2003. (s)

"Judaism Influencing American Public Policy." In *Religion as a Public Good: Jews and Other Americans on Religion in the Public Square*, edited by Alan Mittleman, 231–48. Lanham MD: Rowman and Littlefield, 2003. (s)

Meshaneh Ha-Briyyot: Gishah Yehudit Hadashah L'ba'alei Mum ("Who Made People Different: A New Jewish Approach to the Disabled"), *Hado'ar* 83, no. 1 (Fall 2003): 46–50. Hebrew. (s)

"Responsibilities for the Provision of Health Care," with Aaron Mackler. *Sh'ma* 33/599 (March 2003): 7–8.

"The Role of Rabbis, Cantors, and Educators in Preventing Abuse and Repairing Its Consequences." In *Shine the Light: Sexual Abuse and Healing in the Jewish Community*, edited by Rachel Lev, 177–89. Boston: Northeastern University Press, 2003.

"Stem Cell Research." *Conservative Judaism* 55, no. 3 (Spring 2003): 3–29. (s)

"The Tainted Legacy of Hans Reiter," with Richard S. Panush and Diana Parashiv. *Seminars in Arthritis and Rheumatism* 3, no. 4 (February 2003): 231–36. (s)

"Applying Traditional Jewish Law to PVS." *NeuroRehabilitation: An Interdisciplinary Journal* 19, no. 4 (2004): 277–84. (s)

"Conservative Judaism." In *Encyclopedia of Religion and War*, edited by Gabriel Palmer-Fernandez, 242–44. New York: Routledge, 2004. (s)

"Judaism, Money, and Health Care." *Sh'ma* 34/608 (February 2004): 20.

"Judaism." In *Tobacco in History and Culture: An Encyclopedia*, 281–85. New York: Charles Scribner's Sons, 2004.

"Judaism." In *Visions of Service*, edited by Linda A. Chisholm, 173–262. New York: International Partnership for Service-Learning and Leadership, 2004.

"The Passionate Encounter: The Ethics of Affirming Your Own Faith in a Multireligious World." In *After "The Passion" Is Gone: American Religious Consequences*, edited by J. Shawn Landres and Michael Berenbaum, 255–66. Walnut Creek CA: Alta Mira, 2004.

Shabbat at Home (commentator for theological reflections). In *My People's Prayer Book: Traditional Prayers, Modern Commentaries, Vol. 7*, edited by Lawrence A. Hoffman, 42, 44–45, 58, 60–61, 66, 69–70, 76, 81–82, 92, 96–98, 118, 121–22, 128, 132, 136, 140, 148, 151–52, 156, 159–60, 166, 169–70. Woodstock VT: Jewish Lights, 2004.

"Spirituality, Religion, and Healing in Palliative Care," with Christina M. Puchalski and Imam Yahya Hendi. *Clinics in Geriatric Medicine* 20, no. 4 (November 2004): 689–714. (s)

"Embryonic Stem Cell Research—A Jewish Perspective." *Initiative* 13 (2005): 36–37.

"End-of-Life: Jewish Perspectives." *Lancet* 366 (2005): 862–65. (s)

"The Jewish Family in America: Contemporary Challenges and Traditional Resources." In *Marriage, Sex, and Family in Judaism*, edited by Michael J. Broyde, 214–43. Lanham MD: Rowman & Littlefield, 2005. (s)

"*Kabbalat Shabbat* (Welcoming Shabbat in the Synagogue)" (commentator for theological reflections). In *My People's Prayer Book: Traditional Prayers, Modern Commentaries, Vol.8*, edited by Lawrence A. Hoffman, 50, 53–55, 66, 69–71, 78, 81, 100, 110, 112, 118, 122–23, 140, 143, 156, 161. Woodstock VT: Jewish Lights, 2005.

"Making Your Child a Martyr." In *Murder Most Merciful: Essays on the Ethical Conundrum Occasioned by Sigi Ziering's "The Judgment of Herbert Bierhoff,"* edited by Michael Berenbaum, 135–52. Lanham MD: University Press of America, 2005. (s)

"Nonprofits and Morals: Jewish Perspectives and Methods for Resolving Some Commonly Occurring Moral Issues." In *Good Intentions: Moral Obstacles and*

Opportunities, edited by David H. Smith, 103–26. Bloomington: Indiana University Press, 2005. (s)

"*Welcoming the Night: Minchah and Ma'ariv* (Afternoon and Evening Prayer)" (commentator for theological reflections). In *My People's Prayer Book: Traditional Prayers, Modern Commentaries, Vol. 9*, edited by Lawrence A. Hoffman, 38, 48, 50–52, 58, 61, 68, 72–74, 84, 87–88, 96, 106, 109, 114, 117, 122, 125, 132, 138, 141, 160, 166–67, 180, 184, 192, 197, 202, 205, 210, 212. Woodstock VT: Jewish Lights, 2005.

"God-Talk: The Implications of Theology for Rabbinic Practice." *Proceedings of the Rabbinical Assembly* 64 (2006): 264–67, 269. (s)

"Jewish Models of Leadership." In *Traditions in Leadership: How Faith Traditions Shape the Way We Lead*, edited by Richard J. Mouw and Eric O. Jacobsen, 4–40. Pasadena CA: De Pree Leadership Center of Fuller Theological Seminary, 2006. (s)

"A Clarion Call to Fixing the World." In *Celebrating the Jewish Year: The Fall Holidays*, edited by Paul Steinberg, 53–55. Philadelphia: Jewish Publication Society, 2007.

"God in Modern Jewish Thought." In *Walking with God*, edited by Bradley Shavit Artson and Deborah Silver, 95–106. Los Angeles: Ziegler School of Rabbinic Studies, 2007.

"Jewish Law in the Conservative Movement." *Periodica de re Canonica* 96, no. 3–4 (2007): 639–52. (s)

"A Jewish View of Embryonic Stem Cell Research." In *Righteous Indignation: A Jewish Call for Justice*, edited by Or N. Rose, Jo Ellen Green Kaiser, and Margie Klein, 110–19. Woodstock VT: Jewish Lights, 2007.

"Judaism and Ethical Issues in End of Life Care." In *Science, Religion, and Society: An Encyclopedia of History, Culture, and Controversy, Vol. 2*, edited by Arri Eisen and Gary Laderman, 712–19. Armonk NY: M. E. Sharpe, 2007.

"Judaism and Marijuana." In *Pot Politics: Marijuana and the Costs of Prohibition*, edited by Mitch Earleywine, 208–27. New York: Oxford University Press, 2007. (s)

"Judaism and the Disabled: The Need for a Copernican Revolution." In *Healing and the Jewish Imagination: Spiritual and Practical Perspectives on Judaism and Health*, edited by William Cutter, 107–20. Woodstock VT: Jewish Lights, 2007. (s)

"Moral Freedom and Responsibility." In *Celebrating the Jewish Year: The Fall Holidays*, edited by Paul Steinberg, 99–102. Philadelphia: Jewish Publication Society, 2007.

Response to Carl Braaten's interpretation of the Seventh of the Ten Commandments in "Sexuality and Marriage." In *The Ten Commandments for Jews, Christians, and Others*, edited by Roger E. Van Harn, 148–56. Grand Rapids MI: William B. Eerdmans, 2007. (s)

"*Shabbat Morning: Shacharit and Musaf* (Morning and Additional Services)" (commentator for theological reflections). In *My People's Prayer Book: Traditional*

Prayers, Modern Commentaries, Vol. 10, edited by Lawrence A. Hoffman, 24, 30–31, 44, 53–54, 70, 74–75, 80, 83, 88, 91, 94, 98–99, 106, 110–11, 122, 134, 138, 148, 151–52, 156, 158–59, 164, 168. Woodstock VT: Jewish Lights, 2007.

"Theories of Jewish Law and Movement Borders." In *Jewish Law Association Studies 16: The Boston 2004 Conference Volume*, edited by Elliot Dorff, 56–77. Liverpool, UK: Deborah Charles, 2007. (s)

"'These and Those Are the Words of the Living God': Talmudic Sound and Fury in Shaping National Policy." In *Handbook of Bioethics and Religion*, edited by David E. Guinn, 143–68. New York: Oxford University Press, 2007. (s)

Untitled. In *A Dream of Zion: American Jews Reflect on Why Israel Matters to Them*, edited by Jeffrey K. Salkin, 158–60. Woodstock VT: Jewish Lights, 2007.

"Educating Moral Guides and the Consequences of Theory." In *A New Agenda for Higher Education: Shaping a Life of the Mind for Practice*, edited by William M. Sullivan and Matthew S. Rosin, 26–31, 157–61. San Francisco: Jossey-Bass, 2008. (s)

"The Ethical Impulse in Rabbinic Judaism." In *Walking with Justice*, edited by Bradley Shavit Artson and Deborah Silver, 30–40. Los Angeles: Ziegler School of Rabbinic Studies, 2008.

"Homosexuality: A Case Study in Jewish Ethics." *Journal of the Society of Christian Ethics* 28, no. 1 (Spring-Summer 2008): 227–31. (s)

"Judaism and Stem Cells." In *Controversies in Science and Technology: From Climate to Chromosomes*, Vol. 2, edited by Daniel Lee Kleinman, Karen A Cloud-Hansen, Christina Matta, and Jo Handelsman, 80–89. New Rochelle NY: May Ann Liebert, 2008. (s)

"Judaism and Germline Modification." In *Design and Destiny: Jewish and Christian Perspectives on Germline Modification*, edited by Ronald Cole-Turner, 29–50. Cambridge MA: MIT Press, 2008. (s)

"Making Marriages Stronger: A Multi-Tiered Approach Based on Traditional Jewish Understandings of Marriage." *University of St. Thomas Law Journal* 5, no. 2 (Winter 2008): 580–94. (s)

"Moral Character and Dilemmas in Leadership." *Contact* 11, no. 1 (Autumn 2008): 12–13.

"The Practice of Marriage and Family Counseling in Judaism." In *The Role of Religion in Marriage and Family Counseling*, edited by Jill Duba Onedera, 135–52. New York: Routledge, 2008. (s)

Response to Peter Pettit's "Covenants Old and New." In *Covenantal Conversations: Christians in Dialogue with Jews and Judaism*, edited by Darrell Jodock, 40–41. Minneapolis: Fortress, 2008. (s)

"Some Comparative Thoughts on Worship in the Library Minyan." In *Many Ways into God's Palace: Essays in Honor of the 36th Anniversary of the Library Minyan*, edited by Michael Berenbaum and Mitchell Malkus, 88–101. Los Angeles: Temple Beth Am, 2008.

"Becoming Yet More Like God: A Jewish Perspective on Radical Life Extension." In *Religion and the Implications of Radical Life Extension*, edited by Derek F. Maher and Calvin Mercer, 64–74. New York: Palgrave Macmillan, 2009. (s)

"Judaism and Children in the United States." In *Children and Childhood in American Religions*, edited by Don S. Browning and Bonnie J. Miller-McLemore, 71–84. New Brunswick NJ: Rutgers University Press, 2009. (s)

"Forward." In *Tempest in the Temple: Jewish Communities and Child Sex Scandals*, edited by Amy Neustein, ix–xiii. Waltham MA: Brandeis University Press, 2009. (s)

"Forward." In *There Shall Be No Needy: Pursuing Social Justice through Jewish Law and Tradition*, edited by Jill Jacobs, xi–xv. Woodstock VT: Jewish Lights, 2009.

"Homosexuality, Human Dignity, and Halakhah," with Daniel Nevins and Avram Reisner. In *Das Judische Eherecht*, edited by Walter Homolka, 186–241. Berlin: De Gruyter Recht, 2009. (s)

"How Flexible Can Jewish Law Be? *Parashat Acharei Mot* (Leviticus 16:1–18:30)." In *Torah Queeries: Weekly Commentaries on the Hebrew Bible*, edited by Gregg Drinkwater, Joshua Lesser, and David Shneer, 151–56. New York: New York University Press, 2009.

"A Jewish Perspective on Birth Control and Procreation." In *The Passionate Torah: Sex and Judaism*, edited by Danya Ruttenberg, 152–68. New York: NYU Press, 2009. (s)

"Shelach Lecha: Our Personal Minority Report." In *The Modern Men's Torah Commentary*, edited by Jeffrey K. Salkin, 214–18. Woodstock VT: Jewish Lights, 2009.

"To Fix the World: Jewish Convictions Affecting Social Issues." *Journal of Ecumenical Studies* 44, no. 1 (Winter 2009): 57–69. (s)

"Applying Jewish Law to New Circumstances." In *Teferet Leyisrael: Jubilee Volume in Honor of Israel Francus*, edited by Joel Roth, Menahem Schmelzer, and Yaacov Francus, 189–99. New York: Jewish Theological Seminary, 2010. (s)

"Jewish Law in the Conservative/Masorti Movement Since 1970." In *Jewish Law Association Studies 20: The Manchester 2008 Conference Volume*, edited by Leib Moscovitz, 16–33. Liverpool, UK: Deborah Charles, 2010. (s)

"Jewish Perspectives on Death and Dying." In *Religion, Death, and Dying: Perspectives on Dying and Death, Vol. 1*, edited by Lucy Bregman, 91–114. Santa Barbara CA: Praeger, 2010. (s)

"Teaching Ethics." *Jewish Educational Leadership* 8, no. 3 (Summer 2010): 64–65. (s)

"Capital Punishment," "Courts," "Medical Ethics," "Sexual Ethics," and "Halakhah." In *The Cambridge Dictionary of Judaism and Culture*, edited by Judith R. Baskin, 94–95, 119–20, 162, 164–65, 212–13. Cambridge: Cambridge University Press, 2011.

"Conservative Judaism," "Historical Movement," "United Synagogue of Conservative Judaism," and "University of Judaism." In *The Oxford Dictionary of the Jewish Religion*, second edition, edited by Adele Berlin, 184–85, 350, 758–59. New York: Oxford University Press, 2011.

"Donations from Ill-Gotten Gain: A Jewish Legal Perspective," Indianapolis: The Center on Philanthropy at Indiana University, 2008 (published as a separate monograph as part of the Lake Institute on Faith and Giving). (s)

"Aspiring to Godliness." In *On Sacred Ground: Jewish and Christian Clergy Reflect on Transformative Passages from the Five Books of Moses*, edited by Jeff Bernhardt, 110–11. New York: Blackbird, 2012.

"Biblical Law and Rabbinic Precedent in Hard Cases: The Example of Homosexual Relations in Conservative/Masorti Halakhah." In *Wisdom and Understanding: Studies in Jewish Law in Honour of Bernard S. Jackson*, edited by Leib Moscovitz and Yosef Rivlin, 44–59. Liverpool, UK: Deborah Charles, 2012. (s)

"Caring for the Needy." In *The Observant Life: The Wisdom of Conservative Judaism for Contemporary Jews*, edited by Martin S. Cohen, 806–30. New York: Rabbinical Assembly, 2012.

"Charitable Giving." In *The Observant Life: The Wisdom of Conservative Judaism for Contemporary Jews*, edited by Martin S. Cohen, 391–411. New York: Rabbinical Assembly, 2012.

"Jews." In *Religion: A Clinical Guide for Nurses*, edited by Elizabeth Johnston Taylor, 171–80. New York: Springer, 2012.

"Questions of Legal Competency." In *Broken Fragments: Jewish Experiences of Alzheimer's Disease through Diagnosis, Adaptation, and Moving On*, edited by Douglas J. Kohn, 47–56. New York: URJ Press, 2012.

"Same-Sex Relationships." In *The Observant Life: The Wisdom of Conservative Judaism for Contemporary Jews*, edited by Martin S. Cohen, 657–72. New York: Rabbinical Assembly, 2012.

"War and Peace: A Methodology to Formulate a Contemporary Jewish Approach." *Philosophia: Philosophical Quarterly of Israel* 40, no. 4 (December 2012): 643–61. (s)

"A Case on the Border Between Jewish Law and Morality: Violent and Defamatory Video Games." In *Jewish Law Association Studies 24: The Netanya Conference Volume*, edited by Yuval Sinai, 75–99. Liverpool, UK: Deborah Charles, 2013. (s)

"Forward." In *Judaism and Health: A Handbook of Practical, Professional, and Scholarly Resources*, edited by Jeff Levin and Michele F. Prince, xi–xiv. Woodstock VT: Jewish Lights, 2013.

"Jewish Images of God." In *Personal Theology: Essays in Honor of Neil Gillman*, edited by William Plevan, 18–41. Boston: Academic Studies Press, 2013. Reprinted in a slightly different form in *Models of God and Alternative Ultimate Realities*, edited by Jeanine Diller and Asa Kasher, 111–24. New York: Springer, 2013. (s)

"The Limits of Tikkun Olam." *Jewish Political Studies Review* 25, nos. 3 and 4 (Fall 2013): 99–107. (s)

"Stories, Kashrut, and Passover." In *Slavery, Freedom, and Everything Between: The Why, How, and What of Passover*, edited by Aaron Alexander and Menachem Creditor, 65–68. Los Angeles: Mazon, 2013.

"Applying Jewish Law to New Circumstances." *The Muslim World*, special edition 104, no. 4 (September 2014): 418–23. (s)

"Gaining Moral Guidance from the Jewish Tradition: Four Examples to Test David Ellenson's Approach and Mine." In *Between Jewish Tradition and Modernity: Rethinking an Old Opposition*, edited by Michael A. Meyer and David N. Myers, 35–50. Detroit MI: Wayne State University Press, 2014. (s)

"Judaism—The Body Belongs to God: Judaism and Transhumanism." In *Transhumanism and the Body: The World Religions Speak*, edited by Calvin Mercer and Derek F. Maher, 101–20. New York: Palgrave Macmillan, 2014. (s)

"A Perspective on the Ethics of Fertility Treatments." *Sh'ma: A Journal of Jewish Ideas* 45/712 (October 2014): 7–8.

"When Alzheimer's Turns a Spouse into a Stranger: Jewish Perspectives on Loving and Letting Go," with Laura Geller. In *The Sacred Encounter: Jewish Perspectives on Sexuality*, edited by Lisa J. Grushcow, 549–64. New York: CCAR Press, 2014. (s)

"'To Work It and Preserve It': A Jewish Response to Mudge's Covenantal Humanism and Stakeholdership." In *We Can Make the World Economy a Sustainable Global Home*, edited by Lewis S. Mudge, 107–19. Grand Rapids MI: William B. Eerdmans, 2014. (s)

"Borowitz on *Halakhah, Aggada*, and Ethics." *Journal of Jewish Ethics* 1, no. 1 (2015): 59–76. (s)

"A Conservative Jewish Approach to Family Violence." In *Religion and Men's Violence Against Women*, edited by Andy Johnson, 117–32. New York: Springer, 2015. (s)

"Contemporary Jewish Religious Movements: Conservative." In *The Oxford Encyclopedia of the Bible and the Law, Vol. 1*, edited by Brent A. Strawn, 116–20. New York: Oxford University Press, 2015. (s)

"Ethnicity, Humility, Revelation, and Action: A Jewish Response to Marvin Wilson." *Evangelical Interfaith Dialogue* 6, no. 1 (Spring 2015): 15–18. (s)

"A Jewish Perspective on the Ethics of Care." In *Intercultural and Interreligious Pastoral Caregiving*, edited by Karl Federschmidt and Daniel Louw, 235–50. Norderstedt, Germany: Society for Intercultural Pastoral Care and Counseling, 2015. (s)

"What Is *Tikkun Olam*, and Why Does It Matter? An Overview from Antiquity to Modern Times." In *Tikkun Olam: Judaism, Humanism, and Transcendence*, edited by David Birnbaum and Martin S. Cohen, 11–38. New York: New Paradigm Matrix, 2015. (s)

"Donations from Ill-Gotten Gain in Jewish Law and Ethics and in American Law," with Marc Gary. *Journal of Jewish Ethics* 2, no. 1 (2016): 1–40. (s)

"Why the Priestly Blessing Is Not Redundant: Three Relationships with God, Three Distinct Blessings." In *Birkat Kohanim*, edited by David Birnbaum and Martin S. Cohen, 19–30. New York: New Paradigm Matrix, 2016. (s)

"Havdalah: Distinctions that Provide Identity and Meaning." In *Havdalah*, edited by David Birnbaum and Martin S. Cohen, 31–36. New York: New Paradigm Matrix, 2017. (s)

"Jewish Surrogate Motherhood." In *Motherhood in Historical and Contemporary Jewish Thought, Volume* 2, edited by Shumuly Yanklowitz, 143–50. Phoenix AZ: Valley Beith Midrash, 2017.

"Moden Ani: Awaking with Gratitude." In *Modeh Ani: The Transcendent Prayer of Gratitude*, edited by David Birnbaum and Martin S. Cohen, 71–76. New York: New Paradigm Matrix, 2017. (s)

"Moses, the Prophets, and the Rabbis." In *Christianity and Family Law: An Introduction*, edited by John Witte Jr. and Gary S. Hauk, 16–35. New York: Cambridge University Press, 2017. (s)

"How Do I Find Meaning in Life?" In *Search for Meaning*, edited by David Birnbaum and Martin S. Cohen, 9–20. New York: New Paradigm Matrix, 2018. (s)

"Jewish Philosophy and Public Policy." In *The Future of Jewish Philosophy*, edited by Hava Tirosh-Samuelson and Aaron W. Hughes, 115–30. Leiden, The Netherlands: Brill, 2018. (s)

"The Limits of Choosing Life, Theologically and Medically." In *U-Vacharta Ba-Chayim*, edited by David Birnbaum and Martin S. Cohen, 195–214. New York: New Paradigm Matrix, 2018. (s)

Comments. In *Text Me: Ancient Jewish Wisdom Meets Contemporary Technology*, edited by Jeffrey Schein with Brian Amkraut, 44, 71, 75, 102. Lanham MD: Hamilton, 2019.

"Jewish Perspectives on End-of-Life Decisions." In *Death and Dying: An Exercise in Comparative Philosophy of Religion*, edited by Timothy D. Knepper, Lucy Bregman, and Mary Gottschalk, 145–68. Cham, Switzerland: Springer, 2019. (s)

"Judaism on the Body and the Practice of Medicine." In *Treating the Body in Medicine and Religion: Jewish, Christian, and Islamic Perspectives*, edited by John J. Fitzgerald and Ashley John Moyse, 44–63. London: Routledge, 2019. (s)

"Judaism and Neonatology." In *Religion and Ethics in the Neonatal Intensive Care Unit*, edited by Ronald M. Green and George A. Little, 11–36. New York: Oxford University Press, 2019. (s)

"Planning for What You Don't Want to Plan For." In *Getting Good at Getting Older*, edited by Richard Siegel and Laura Geller, 180–87. Millburn NJ: Behrman House, 2019.

"A Sign Between Me and the People Israel." In *V'shamru*, edited by David Birnbaum and Martin S. Cohen, 185–200. New York: New Paradigm Matrix, 2019. (s)

"Becoming Yet More Like God: A Jewish Theological, Institutional, and Legal Perspective on Radical Life Extension." In *Jewish Law Association Studies 39: The Impact of Technology, Science, and Knowledge*, edited by Elisha S. Ancselovits, Elliot N. Dorff, and Amos Isarel-Vleeschhouwer, 125–38. Liverpool, UK: Deborah Charles, 2020. (s)

"Conservative Judaism." In the *Encyclopedia of Jewish-Christian Relations* (online). Berlin: De Gruyter, September 2020. (s)

"Dignity: A Jewish Perspective," with Daniel Nevins. In *Value and Vulnerability: An Interfaith Dialogue on Human Dignity*, edited by Matthew R. Petrusek and Jonathan Rothchild, 92–127. Notre Dame IN: Notre Dame University Press, 2020. (s)

"Divine Command Theory in Jewish Law and Ethics." In *Swimming Against the Current: Reimagining Jewish Tradition in the Twenty-First Century, Essays in Honor of Chaim Seidler-Feller*, edited by Shaul Seidler-Feller and David N. Myers, 188–203. Boston: Academic Studies Press, 2020. (s)

"Halakhah (Jewish Law) in Contemporary Judaism." In *Judaism 3: Culture and Modernity*, edited by Michael Tilly and Burton L. Visotzky, 44–71. Suttgart, Germany: W. Kohlhammer, 2020. (s)

"Jewish and Hindu Perspectives on Dignity: Responses," with Christopher Key Chapple. In *Value and Vulnerability: An Interfaith Dialogue on Human Dignity*, edited by Matthew R. Petrusek and Jonathan Rothchild, 165–72. Notre Dame IN: Notre Dame University Press, 2020. (s)

"Conservative Judaism on Abortion and Related Topics." In *Abortion: Global Positions and Practices, Religious and Legal Perspectives*, edited by Alireza Bagheri, 9–22. New York: Springer, 2021. (s)

"Providing References for Schools or Jobs," with Marc Gary. In *Hakol Kol Yaakov: The Joel Roth Jubilee Volume*, edited by Robert A. Harris and Jonathan S. Milgram, 28–66. Leiden, The Netherlands: Brill, 2021. (s)

"Triage in the Time of a Pandemic: The Sanctity of Saving as Many Lives as Possible." In *Ra'u Or: Essays in Honor of Dr. Ora Horn Prouser*, edited by Joseph Prouser, 29–42. Teaneck NJ: Ben Yehuda Press, 2021. (s)

"The Use of All Wines." In *Wine Law and Policy: From National Terroirs to a Global Market*, edited by Julien Chaisse, Fernando Dias Simoes, and Danny Friedman, 682–709. Leiden, The Netherlands: Brill/Nijhoff, 2021. (s)

"A Philosopher Explains What Belief in God Means." In *A God We Can Believe In*, edited by Richard Agler and Rifat Sonsino, 51–56. Eugene OR: Wipf and Stock, 2022. Reprinted in an expanded form in *Masorti: The New Journal of Conservative Judaism* 67, no. 1 (Winter 2022–23): 104–12. https://masortijournal.org/ds/. (s)

"Triage in the Time of the Pandemic: The Sanctity of Saving as Many Lives as Possible." In *American Jewish University's Scholar Symposium: Reflections on Post-Covid-19 Judaism*, edited by Michael Berenbaum, 1–16. Los Angeles: American Jewish University, 2022. (s)

"Applying Jewish Theology to Issues in Mental and Physical Health." *Dialog: A Journal of Theology*, January 27, 2023. https://doi.org/10.1111/dial.12778. (s)

"Epistemological Humility in Jewish Law and Ethics." *Journal of Jewish Ethics*, special issue honoring Louis E. Newman. University Park: Pennsylvania State University Press, forthcoming (s).

"Gamete Donation and Surrogacy." In *The Oxford Handbook on Religious Perspectives in Bioethics*, edited by Dena Davis. Oxford University Press, forthcoming (s).

"Health and Medicine in the Rabbinic Tradition." In *The Oxford Handbook of Households in the Biblical World*, edited by Eric Myers. New York: Oxford University Press, forthcoming (s).

"Jewish Law." In *Building Bridges among Abraham's Children: A Celebration of Michael Berenbaum*, edited by Edward Gaffney, Marcia Sachs Littell, and Michael Bayzler. Boston: Academic Studies Press, forthcoming (s).

"The Role of Religion in Shaping Public Policy." In *Commemorating Herbert Morris*, edited by George Fletcher. Jerusalem: Mazo Publishers, forthcoming (s).

"'Within Judaism' in Contemporary Jewish Life." In *What Does "Within Judaism" Mean? Perspectives from the New Testament to the Present*, edited by Karin Hedner Zetterholm and Anders Runesson. Lanham, MD: Rowman and Littlefield, forthcoming (s).

BOOK REVIEWS

Review of Elieser Berkovits, *Major Themes in Modern Philosophies*; and William E. Kaufman, *Contemporary Jewish Philosophies*. In *Conservative Judaism* 30, no. 4 (Summer 1976): 86–90.

Review of Gilmer W. Blackburn, *Education in the Third Reich: Race and History in Nazi Textbooks. Holocaust and Genocide Studies* 3, no. 1 (1988): 317–18.

Review of Eugene B. Borowitz, *Renewing the Covenant: A Theology for the Postmodern Jew*, "Autonomy vs. Community: The Ongoing Reform/Conservative Difference." *Conservative Judaism* 48, no. 2 (Winter 1996): 64–68.

Review of Eugene B. Borowitz and Frances Weinman Schwartz, *The Jewish Moral Virtues*; Aaron Levine, *Case Studies in Jewish Business Ethics*; and Byron Sherwin, *Jewish Ethics for the Twenty-First Century: Living in the Image of God. AJS Review* 26, no. 1 (April 2002): 198–202.

Review of *Central Conference of American Rabbi Yearbook 1981. Religious Studies Review* 8, no. 4 (October 1982): 391.

Review of Dena S. Davis and Laurie Zoloth, eds., *Notes from a Narrow Ridge: Religion and Bioethics*; and Laurie Zoloth, *Health Care and the Ethics of Encounter: A Jewish Discussion of Social Justice*, "A Narrow Ridge, a Larger Vision." *Hastings Report* 31, no. 3 (May-June 2001): 44–46.

Review of Leon Wiener Dow, *The Going: A Meditation on Jewish Law. Jewish Law Association Studies 39: The Impact of Technology, Science, and Knowledge*, edited by Elisha S. Ancselovits, Elliot N. Dorff, and Amos Isarel-Vleeschhouwer, 196–98. Liverpool, UK: Deborah Charles, 2020.

Review of Ze'ev Falk, *Law and Religion: The Jewish Experience. Association of Jewish Studies Review* 9, no. 2 (Fall 1984): 295–97.

Review of four books in medical ethics: *Caring and Curing: Health and Medicine in the Western Religious Traditions*, Ronald L. Numbers and Darrel W. Amundsen; *Jewish Values in Bioethics*, edited by Levi Meier; *Health and Medicine in the Jewish Tradition* by David M. Feldman; and *When Life Is In the Balance: Life and Death Decisions in Light of the Jewish Tradition*, by Barry D. Cytron and Earl

Schwartz, "Modern Medicine and Jewish Values." *Conservative Judaism* 40, no. 4 (Summer 1988): 73–80.

Review of Neil Gillman, *Sacred Fragments: Recovering Theology for the Modern Jew*; and David Wolpe, *The Healer of Shattered Hearts: A Jewish View of God*, "Groping for God." *Judaism* 42, no. 1 (Winter 1993): 114–22.

Review of John Glad, *Jewish Eugenics. Journal of Bioethical Inquiry* 9, no. 4 (2012): 499–502 (review coauthored with Israel Berger).

Review of Robert Gordis, *Jewish Ethics for a Lawless World. Ethics* 99, no. 3 (April 1989): 663–64.

Review of Simon Greenberg, *A Jewish Philosophy and Pattern of Faith. Conservative Judaism* 37, no. 2 (Winter 1983–84): 70–74.

Review of Jerome Groopman, *The Anatomy of Hope: How People Prevail in the Face of Illness*, "The Place of Hope in Patient Care." In *Quality of Life in Jewish Bioethics*, edited by Noam J. Zohar, 67–74. Lanham MD: Rowman and Littlefield, 2006.

Review of Joshua O. Haberman, *Philosopher of Revelation: The Life and Thought of S. L. Steinheim. Moment* 15, no. 6 (December 1990): 56–57.

Review of Eugene Korn, *To Be a Holy People: Jewish Tradition and Ethical Values. Journal of Jewish Ethics* 8, no. 2 (November 2022): 246–53.

Review of David Novak, *Halakhah in a Theological Dimension. Religious Studies Review* 12, no. 3–4 (July-October 1986): 276.

Review of David Novak, *The Image of the Non-Jew in Judaism: An Historical and Constructive Study of the Noahide Laws. Journal of Religion* 67, no. 1 (January 1987): 120–22.

Review of Edmund D. Pellegrino and Alan I. Faden, eds., *Jewish and Catholic Bioethics: An Ecumenical Dialogue. Second Opinion* (October 2001): 77–79.

Review of Lawrence Perlman, *Abraham Heschel's Idea of Revelation. Religious Studies Review* 17, no. 2 (April 1991): 173.

Review of Nathan Rotenstreich, *Jews and German Philosophy: The Polemics of Emancipation. Religious Studies Review* 14, no. 2 (April 1988): 169.

Review of Elijah J. Schochet, *Amalek: The Enemy Within. Jewish Spectator* 57, no. 4 (Spring 1993): 55–56.

Review of Joseph B. Soloveitchik, *Halakhic Man. Modern Judaism* 6, no. 1 (February 1986): 91–98.

Review of Meir Tamari, *"With All Your Possessions": Jewish Ethics and Economic Life. Ethics* 99, no. 3 (April 1989): 678.

Review of The Assembly of Rabbis of the Reform Synagogues of Great Britain, *Forms of Prayer for Jewish Worship*, vols. 1 and 3. *Judaism* 38, no. 1 (Winter 1989): 112–19.

Review of *The Jewish Law Annual*, vol. 10. *Hebrew Studies* 35 (1994): 158–60.

Review of Michael Wyschogrod, *The Body of Faith. Journal of Reform Judaism* 33, no. 1 (Winter 1986): 95–97.

Review of Noam J. Zohar, *Alternatives in Jewish Bioethics. Medical Humanities Review* 12, no. 1 (Spring 1998): 83–86.

LEGAL RULINGS FOR THE COMMITTEE ON
JEWISH LAW AND STANDARDS

Accessible at https://www.rabbinicalassembly.org/rabbinic-resources/committee
-jewish-law-and-standards

Annual and Triennial Systems for Reading the Torah (1987).

Artificial Insemination, Egg Donation, and Adoption (1994).

Assisted Suicide/Aid in Dying Revisited (2021).

Assisted Suicide, and CJLS Statement on Assisted Suicide (1997).

Chanting Psalm 118:1–4 in Hallel, with Aaron Alexander and Reuven Hammer (2015).

Computer Privacy and the Modern Workplace, with Elie Kaplan Spitz (2001).

Donations of Ill-Gotten Gain (2009).

Family Violence (1995).

Harmful Communication (2019).

"Hazak, Hazak" in the Triennial Cycle (2015).

Homosexuality, Human Dignity, and Halakhah, with Daniel Nevins and Avram
Reisner (2006).

A Jewish Approach to End-Stage Medical Care (1990).

Jewish Businesses Open on Shabbat and Yom Tov (1995).

Jewish Norms for Sexual Behavior: A Responsum Embodying a Proposal (1992).

Joint Conservative-Reform Religious Schools (1988).

Loneliness, Family, and Community during the Pandemic (2020).

Modest Communication (2019).

Providing References for Schools or Jobs, with Marc Gary (2014).

Rabbinical Assembly Ketubbah Translation (1987).

On Recording Shabbat and Yom Tov Services, with Gordon Tucker (1989).

Responsibilities for the Provision of Health Care, with Aaron Mackler (1998).

Rituals and Documents for Same-Sex Couples, with Daniel Nevins and Avram
Reisner (2012).

A Second Wedding Ceremony (2021).

Shackling and Hoisting, with Joel Roth (2000).

Stem Cell Research (2002).

Triage in the Time of a Pandemic: The Sanctity of Saving as Many Lives as Possible
(2020).

The Use of All Wines (1985).

Use of Synagogues by Christian Groups (1990).

Wearing Face Covering, Physical Distancing, and Other Measures to Control the
COVID-19 Pandemic, with Susan Grossman (2021).

Index

ability to speak, 25–26
abortion, 93–95
Abraham, 14, 48, 107, 202n16
abstraction(s), 15; first level of, 7, 9, 11; second level of, 9–12; third level of, 11
acquiring stolen property from a thief, 168–69
action(s), 12, 20, 23, 42, 147–48, 150–51
active euthanasia, 70, 193n25
Adam, 26
Adonai, 10, 19
Adonai elohei tz'va'ot (the Lord, God of armies), 154
Adonai tz'va'ot (Lord of armies), 154
adult Jews-by-conversion, 34
agnostic or atheist, 11
aid in dying, 58–70; and active euthanasia, 70, 193n25; factors in prohibiting, 61–65; terminology used in, 59–60, 59–60; through a Jewish lens, 68–70; and use of aid-in-dying laws, 65–67
AIDS epidemic, 96–97
Akiba, Rabbi, 109, 117, 156–58
Albo, Joseph, 5
allegorical interpretation of religious images, 16
alleviation of boredom, 62
altruistic instincts, 28, 155
Amalek, 154, 161
American ideology, 24–25, 29, 31–38
American Jewish University, 103
American Jews, xxiii, 35, 38

American law, 36–38, 90, 94–95, 103, 114–15, 146, 165, 166
American Medical Association, 64, 70
American Psychological Association, 143–44
Americans with Disabilities Act, 37, 110–11
Amidah, xxviii, xxxiv, 11, 148, 162
Amos, 168
anthropomorphic images of God, 10, 15, 16
antisemitism, 127–28, 176
appreciation of the world, 20
appropriate speech, 146
Aquinas, 145
arakhin (market value of human slaves), 196n15
Aristotle, 8, 145
arrogance, 26, 135
art, music, literature, and dance, 9, 179
artwork stolen by the Nazis, 171
aspirational modes of behavior, 12, 132–33. See also *middat ḥassidut* (person is exemplifying)
aspirations for holiness, 12
assisted dying or suicide. *See* aid in dying
assumptions, 31–33, 47–48
assur (forbidden), 148
Austin, J. L., 6
authority: of images, 20–23; of Jewish law, 86–87; of rabbis, 56, 89–90
autonomy, 53–54, 76–90; and the autonomous Jewish self, 77–79, 81–84; and autonomous will, 87

Avtalyon, 136
Ayer, A. J., 6

Babylonian sources, 148
Bag-Bag, Ben, 51–52
Bagwell, Eric, xxxiii–xxxv
Bahya ibn Pakuda, 150
ban: against thinking about violating a commandment (*hirhur davar ha-asur*), 147; on verbal oppression, 111–12
Bardin, Shelomo, 179
bar or bat mitzvah, 28
baseball as metaphor of prayer, 72–74
before those who are blind (*lifnei ivair*). *See* stumbling block before the blind
behavior of a cheat (*minhag rama'ut*), 149
Belgium, 59, 193n20
belief, 3–12; and levels of experience, 7–8; and religions of the world, 7–11; and what belief in God means, 11–12
Ben Bag-Bag, Rabbi, 51–51
Ben Petura, 156, 158
Berenbaum, Michael, 6
Bergen, Benjamin, 137
Bergman, Ben Zion, 169
Berner, David, 93
beyond the letter of the law (*lifnim m'shurat ha-din*), xxxiii, 43, 149, 180
bias, positive and negative, 112
Bible, 6, 10–11, 13, 15, 17, 20–21, 32, 36, 43, 151, 154–55, 160–61
bioethics, xxvi, 60, 93, 96, 193n25
Bleich, J. David, 83, 88
Board of Nechama: Jewish AIDS Services, 96
body and soul, 47, 189n2
book of Ruth, 54
boredom, 62
born Jews, 34
Borowitz, Eugene, 53–54, 76–90
boshet (shame), 100, 108–9, 167
bragging, 133–35

Brodsky, David, 148
Buber, Martin, 12, 82
bullying (*iyyum*), 116, 126–27
burden, sense of being a, 62–63
business norms, 43

California, 58, 60, 65–70
Camp Ramah, 3, 48–49, 71–72, 116, 165–75
Canaanite nations, 154, 159
Canada, 59, 67–70
candidate who poses known risks, 115
Carey, Benedict, 118–19
Catholic position on abortion, 93–95
CCAR (Central Conference of American Rabbis), 76, 82
Centennial Perspective of the Reform Movement, 77
Central Conference of American Rabbis (CCAR), 76, 82
"Challenge to Orthodoxy" (Rackman), 88
"The Champion Who Picked a Date to Die," 67
change in form (*shinnuy ma'aseh*), 170–71, 174
change of ownership (*shinnuy reshut*), 171, 175
character, 136, 148–51
characteristics of God, 16, 18, 179
charities, 168, 169–70, 173
children, effects of media consumption on, 144
Christian communities, 29–31
Christianity, 5, 12, 25, 29–31, 34, 59, 189n2; and just war theory, 153
civility, requirement to be, 136
civil laws, 67–69, 103, 105
CJLS (Committee on Jewish Law and Standards), 58, 84, 93, 96–98, 103, 165
classical Jewish tradition, 38, 52, 87, 89, 101, 145–46, 150, 153
classical Rabbis, 11, 21, 87
classical sources, 101, 153

code(s): of ethics, 152, 154; of Jewish law, 168–69

cognitive content, 15

Cohen, Steven M., 54

Colombia, 59

Colorado, 58

commandments, xxiv, 27–28, 32, 147–48, 196n15

Committee on Jewish Law and Standards (CJLS), 58, 84, 93, 96–98, 103, 165

communication, harmful, 116–28; and bullying (*iyyum*), 116, 126–27; and enticement, incitement, and rabble-rousing (*hasatah*), 127–28; and gossip (*rekhillut*), 118–19; and insulting others (*pi'gi'ah b'khvod aharim*), 121–23; and prohibitions of harming others, 117–27; and purposely misleading others (*g'naivat da'at*), 119–21; and shaming others, 123–26. *See also* modesty (*tzini'ut*) in communication; references

community, 76–90; and autonomy, 53–54, 76–80; and community standards, 167, 173; and conceptions of law, 85–90; and differences between Jewish and American ideology, 31–35; and family, 176–77; and human dignity, 100–102; and images, 19, 20–22, 24–25; and the individual, 29–31; and interaction between rabbis and laypeople, 56; of rabbis, 89–90; and Reform Judaism, 82–84; and similarities between Jewish and American ideology, 35–38; and text study, 44

comparative religion. *See* religions

complicity in illegal actions, 168

concrete language, 16

concrete level of experience, 7, 11

conditions, limits that warrant aid in dying, 69

conferring ownership, 170, 171

conquest of Canaan, 152, 164

consequentialist issues, 143–45

Conservative movement, 58, 78–80, 83–84, 96–99. *See also* Camp Ramah

Conservative rabbis, 84, 97–99

constitutive text, 21

constructive criticism, 122

continuity and authority, 52–53, 56

conversion, 6, 34, 77

convictional community, 19

Covenantal relationship with God, 32–34, 37, 48, 77–78, 81–84, 176–77

creedal religions. *See* religions

Crescas, Hasdai, 5

crude speech. *See* incivility (*gassut, boorut, hoser nimus*)

customs (*minhagim*), 56, 90

Danto, Arthur, 71

death with dignity terminology, 60

deception, 106. *See also* lies (*sheker*); lying

decision-making process, 53–54, 56, 78–79, 82–84, 88–90

deism, 9

dementia, 67

demographic crisis, 94

deontology, 145–48

depression, 61–62

depth theology, 55, 153

derekh eretz, 149

Deuteronomy, 161, 168

Dewey, John, 18

dietary laws, 3, 13, 50, 178

differences in Jewish and American ideology, 31–35

"Dignity: A Jewish Perspective," 99–100

disability/disabled people, 26–27, 37, 64–65, 69, 110–11

discernment, ethical, xxv–xxvi

discretionary wars (*milhamot reshut*), 159–60

District of Columbia, 58

divine image. *See* image of God

Divine self, 154

divrei nevailah (obscenities), 7, 136–38

Dobbs v. Jackson Women's Health Organization, 94

doctors, and aid in dying, 64, 69–70

donations, 171–75

Dorff, Tanya, 66

Dosa, Rabbi, 146–47

duty: to the community, 31–32; to give negative information, 110, 112–13; to pray, 148; to protect others, 122; to protest, 34, 126, 138; to relieve pain, 61; to tell the truth, 112–13

Eck, Diana, xxvi

economic transactions, 173

e-faith, 12

Eighth Circuit Court of Appeals, 146

Ein Sof, 16

Einstein, Albert, 19

eisegesis, 53

Eisen, Arnold, 54

Eleazar, Rabbi, 146

Eliezer, Rabbi, 109

Ellenson, David, 53–54

Emmett, Dorothy, 17

emotional functions of language, 6

emotions, 17, 23

enactment for those who repent (*takkanat ha-shavim*), 170

enactment of the market (*takkanat ha-shuk*), 169, 171, 173

encountering God's transcendence, 20

End of Life Option Act, 60

Enlightenment, 33–35, 79–80, 81, 87

enticement, incitement, and rabble-rousing (*hasatah*), 127–28

epikorsut, 83

epistemological humility, xxvii

Establishment clause, 95

Ethics Committee, UCLA Medical Center, 96

Etzioni, Amitai, 80

euthanasia. *See* aid in dying

Evangelical Christians, 75, 95

exegesis, 53

existentialists, 9

existential suffering, 62–63

Exodus from Egypt, 42, 48

experience(s), 7–12, 15, 19–20, 23; of God, 16–17, 22, 178

expletives. *See* foul language (*nivlut peh*)

fake news, 121

false centers of loyalty. *See* idolatry

family, 8, 176–77

fantasies, 62, 146, 147

feticide, 94

Finkelstein, Louis, 87

First Amendment, 95

First Temple, 88, 152, 159

Fishbane, Michael, 52

Florence Melton School of Adult Jewish Learning, 60

folkways, 13

the forbidden (*assur*), 148

forgiveness, 122–23

For the Love of God and People (Dorff), 46

foul language (*nivlut peh*), 136–38

foundational Jewish concepts and values, 55–56

freedoms, 104, 146

free speech, 126, 146

free will, 27–29, 155

ganav me'fursam (known thief), 171, 173

Garden of Eden story, 155

Gary, Marc, 103–4, 165

gassut, boorut, hoser nimus (incivility), 135–36

gay and lesbian people, 96–102

speech (*ona'at devarim*), 111; ownership under, 171; and relatives ineligible to serve as witnesses, 112; and the requirement to be civil, 136; and returning donated money that had already been used, 168–70; and the ruling (*p'sak halakhah*) on providing references, 112–15; and shame (*boshet*), 100, 167; and similarities in Jewish and American ideology, 36–38; and slurs (*lashon ha'ra*), 108–9, 118; and the sociality of Jewish spirituality, 80; theory of, 46–49; and virtue ethics, 148–51; and war and peace, 158–62

Jewishness, 77, 81–82

Jewish nonprofit organizations, 105

Jewish prayer, 71–75

Jewish response, 55–56

Jewish scholars, 102, 135

Jewish self, 81–83, 85, 90

Jewish sources, 55–56, 119, 125–26, 152–54, 155, 161, 164

Jewish spiritualtiy, sociality of, 80

Jewish Theological Seminary, New York, 98

Jewish tradition and moral values, 41–45; and abortion, 93–95; and aid in dying, 58–70; and authoritative law and moral standards, 86–87; and the autonomous Jewish self, 77–79, 81–84; and belief in God, 3–12; and bullying, 127; and the Conservative movement, 78–80; and the demand to tell the truth, 113; and duties to the community, 31–32; and the duty to give negative information, 110; and ethical discernment, xxv–xxvi; and family and community, 176–77; and freedoms, 104; and free speech, 126; and free will, 27–29; and gossip (*rekhillut*), 118; and holidays and rituals, 177–78; and honor of all God's

creatures (*kevod ha-briyyot*), 105; and human dignity, 96–102, 109; and human worth, 25–27; and the ideal person, 149–50, 189n2; and Jewish law, 46–49, 50–57, 179–80; and lies (*sheker*), 106–8; and modesty (*tzini'ut*) in communication, 129–40; and moral leaders, 43; and music, dance, and art, 179; and oppressive speech (*ona'at devarim*), 111–12; and physical and sexual assault, 150; and prayer, 71–75; and prohibitions against harming others, 117–27; and saving yourself at the expense of other people, 156–57; and sexual and excretory functioning, 138; and sexual orientation, 97; and shaming, 125; and study, 178–79; and *teshuvah* (returning to the proper path), 172–74, 209n27; and theology, 178; and war, 153–54, 158–64

Jews and Genes (Dorff and Zoloth), 93

Jews in the Middle Ages, 161

Jews working for non-Jewish employers, 115

The Jew Within (Eisen and Cohen), 54

Jose ben Judah, Rabbi, 105

Joshua, 154

Joshua, Rabbi, 146

Judah the Prince, Rabbi, 130

Judaism, as applied to contemporary circumstances, 50–57

judgment(s), xxv, 25, 49, 107, 112

justice, xxxiii–xxxiv, 7–8

justifications for going to war, 163

just laws, 29

just war theory, 152–53

kabbalistic image of God, 22

Kagan, Israel Meir Ha-kohen, 109–10

Kant, Immanuel, 81, 145

Kaplan, Mordecai, 13, 82

Kasher, Asa, 152
kavvanah (proper intention), 148
kevod ha-briyyot (honor of all God's
    creatures), 105
kiddush ha-Shem (sanctification of the
    Divine Name), 149
King Saul, 154, 161
Knowing God (Dorff), 4–5, 14, 20, 46, 72
known thief (ganav me'fursam), 171, 173
Kohelet (Ecclesiastes), 149, 155
Kohlberg, Lawrence, 41
Konvitz, Milton, 34–35

laity, 56, 89–90
language, 6, 19
Language, Truth, and Logic (Ayer), 6
lashon ha'ra (slurs), 108–10, 118
laypeople, 56–57
legal and moral norms, 9, 29, 42–43, 46,
    87, 104–5, 128, 130, 179–80
legal contracts, 168
legal precedents, 54–56
letters of recommendation. See references
level of the crime, 167
levels of experience, 7–8
Levinas, Emanuel, 80
Leviticus, 172
liberation theology, 31
liberty, 32
lies (sheker), 106–8, 121, 133
lifnei ivair (before those who are blind), 112
lifnim m'shurat ha-din (beyond the let-
    ter of the law), xxxiii, 43, 149, 180
Locke, John, 80
Los Angeles, 36–37
Los Angeles Times, 67, 137
love, Jewish law as expression of, 47–49
Love Your Neighbor and Yourself
    (Dorff), 24, 41, 50
Luxembourg, 59
Luzzato, Moses Hayyim, 42, 139–40, 150

lying, social consequences of, 106. See
    also lies (sheker)

Maccabean period, 152, 160–61
Maccabees, 161
Maimonides: and Abraham, 48; on
    change of form confers ownership,
    170; on charity funds to support
    the poor, 36; on duty to give nega-
    tive information, 110; and epikorsut,
    83; and fantasies, 147; and forgive-
    ness, 122–23; and gossip (rekhillut),
    118; and haughtiness and bragging
    (ravrevanut, hitpa'arut, hitya'ahrut,
    gassut ru'ah), 202n12; and the ideal
    person, 150; and the image of God,
    25–26; and laws against shaming
    others, 124; and the Messianic Era,
    33; and misuse of words, 198–99n6;
    and the nature of God, 15; and pur-
    posely misleading others (g'naivat
    da'at), 119–20; and religious images,
    16; and the requirement to be civil,
    136; and slurs (lashon ha'ra), 108; and
    the Tenth Commandment, 205n25;
    thirteen beliefs of, 5; on the Torah
    was given in the language of human
    beings, 88–89; and tzini'ut (modesty)
    in communication, 131, 133–35
Maine, 58
martyrs, 161
Masorti, 5
Matters of Life and Death (Dorff), 50,
    87–88, 93
media consumption, 144
medical ethics, 87–88, 93
medically induced comas, 66
medications: for depression, 62; for
    pain, 63, 66, 68–70
Meir, Rabbi, 122
membership, 34, 38

process of return. *See* returning to the proper path (*teshuvah*)

process theology, 9

profanity and honesty, 137

Prohibition, 85–86

Promised Land, 42, 48

proper conduct of war, 163–64

proper intention (*kavvanah*), 148

prophets, 168

protecting and saving life, 26, 160

protecting the reputation of the non-profit agency, 175

Protestants, 30–31, 41

Proverbs, 42, 120, 148

p'sak halakhah (ruling), 112–15

Psalmist, 14, 57, 68

Psalms, 144, 148, 161–62

psychological disorders, 62

public harm, 125–26

public policy, 70

purposely misleading others (*g'naivat da'at*), 119–21

Rabbinical Assembly, 58, 97. *See also* Committee on Jewish Law and Standards (cjls)

rabbinical schools, 97–99, 103

rabbinic image of God, 22

rabbinic Judaism, 21, 36, 88–90

rabbinic law, 100, 160–61

rabbinic literature, 15, 28, 106–8, 131, 149–50, 151

rabbinic method for defining Jewish law, 89

rabbinic texts, 101–2

rabbinic tradition, 147, 161

Rabbis: and abortion, 93–94; attitudes of toward non-Jews, 36; and authority of images, 21; and bans on forms of speech, 105–12; and conduct, 149; and covetousness, 147–48; and forgiveness, 122; and foul language (*niv-lut peh*), 136–37; and free will, 27–29; and gossip (*rekhillut*), 118–19; and Hebrew phrase for shaming, 123; on how Jews should conduct war, 159; and human nature, 155; and human worth, 26–27; and the image of God, 26–27; and interpretation of the Torah, 88–89; and levels of abstraction, 11; and medical aid in dying, 70; and peace, 161–62; and the power of images, 19; and prayer, 11; and the prohibition against accepting further donations, 172; and putting ourselves in danger, 144; and religious images, 17; and sexual and excretory functioning, 138; and the social consequences of lying, 106; and tact, 107; and *takkanat ha-shuk* (enactment of the market), 169; on before those who are blind (*lifnei ivair*), 112; and the Torah, 51–53; and war and peace in the nature of God, 154–55

rabbis and laity, 56, 89–90

Rackman, Emanuel, 88

rationalists, 9, 16

Rav, 148

Rava, 135, 148

Ravina, 148

ravrevanut, hitpa'arut, hitya'ahrut, gassut ru'ah (haughtiness and bragging), 133–35, 136–37, 202n12

reality, 10, 17–19, 22

recipients of evaluations, 114

references, 103–15; and misuse of words, 105–12; and positive or negative bias, 112; and ruling (*p'sak halakhah*), 112–15; when to refuse to provide, 113–14

references to God, 3, 6, 13

Reform Jewish Ethics and the Halakhah (Borowitz), 82

Reform Judaism, 77–85

Reform rabbis, 53–54, 76

Reisner, Avram, 65, 97–98, 101
rekhillut (gossip), 118–19
relating to God, 10, 16
relatives ineligible to serve as witnesses, 112
religions, 8–11; comparative, xxvi; creedal, 5; East Asian, 19. *See also* belief
religious images, 16–20
religious language, 9, 17
religious obligations, 78
Renewing the Covenant (Borowitz), 81–84, 85
repentance, 20. See also *teshuvah* (returning to the proper path)
Republic (Plato), 8
reputation, 136
required (*hayyav*), 148
requirement to be civil, 136
respect, 29, 99–102, 109, 117, 125, 127, 136, 164, 177, 178, 179. *See also* human dignity
responsibility for making moral decisions, 53
returning to the proper path (*teshuvah*), 29, 44, 111, 170, 172–74, 209n27. *See also* forgiveness
revelation, 78–79, 83, 88–89
revelation at Mount Sinai, 34, 42, 48, 52
reward a sinner (*shelo yeheh hoteh niskar*), 167
rights, 24, 25, 31–32, 33–34, 35–38
rights movements, 100–101
right to defend. *See* self-defense
Ritba, 156
rituals, xxiv, 9, 13, 177–78. *See also* Jewish tradition and moral values
Roe v. Wade, 93–94
Roman Catholics, 21, 30–31, 41
Romans, 43–44
Rosett, Arthur, 46
Ross, W. D., 145

Roth, Joel, 97
ru'ah hakhamim 'aina nohah haymenu (spirit of the Sages is not pleased with him), 149
ru'ah hakhamim nohah heimenu (spirit of the Sages is pleased with him), 149
rudeness, 136
ruling (*p'sak halakhah*), 112–15

Sages, 101, 124, 139, 149
salacious talk (*z'nut ha-peh v'ha-ozen*), 139–40
Salanter, Israel, 150
same-sex weddings, 97–99
sanctification of the Divine Name (*kiddush ha-Shem*), 149
sanctity, 79
Sanhedrin, 160
saving yourself at the expense of other people, 157–58
Schechter Rabbinical School (Jerusalem), 98
scientific propositions, 17
scoundrel within the bounds of the Torah (*naval b'reshut ha-Torah*), 149, 180
Second Temple, xxxiii
Securities and Exchange Commission, 172
self-defense, 150, 155–58, 160–61, 163
self-esteem, 134–35
selfhood, 81
self-respect, 136, 177
self-serving instincts, 28, 155
self-worth, 134–35
Seminario Rabbinico Latin Americano (Buenos Aires), 98
separation of church and state, 94
sexual and excretory functioning, 138
sexual attraction, 139
sexual orientation, 96–102
sexual urges, 28
Shabbtai Tz'vi, 43
shame (*boshet*), 100, 108–9, 123–26, 167

text study, 44, 178–79

theological convictions. *See* morality and theological convictions

theology, 178; and aid in dying, 65

thievery, 170, 171, 172–73

thirteen beliefs of Maimonides, 5

"This Is My Beloved, This Is My Friend" (*Song of Songs 5:16*), 97

Tillich, Paul, 16

Tisha b'Av, 49

To Do the Right and the Good (Dorff), 24, 50

Torah: and aid in dying, 68; on concerns of character, 149; and a Covenantal relationship with God, 48; and duty to protest, 126; everything is in it, 51–53; and forgiveness, 123; and gossip (*rekhillut*), 119; and human dignity, 109; and human worth, 25–26; and idolatry, 43; and images, 22; and impulses, 27–28; and insulting others (*pi'gi'ah b'khvod aharim*), 122; and lies (*sheker*), 106, 121, 133; and moral precepts, 41, 42; and oppressing others (*ona'ah*), 121; and public harm, 125; and putting ourselves in danger, 144; and the Rabbis, 88–89; requires the king to own a copy of the, 37; and salacious talk (*z'nut ha-peh v'ha-ozen*), 139; and self-defense, 156; and sexual and excretory functioning, 138; and truthfulness, 104; and war and peace in Jewish law, 158–59

Tosefta, 36, 120

tradition and modernity, 51, 77–79

transcendence, 11, 20

transgender issues, 98

trust, 106, 108, 121, 133

truthfulness, 104–5, 106–8, 112–13, 121, 126, 133

truth-functional language, 6–8

truth of images, 17–20

UCLA Medical Center, 96

ultimate reality, 8, 10, 18–19, 75

The Unfolding Tradition (Dorff), 76

United States Conference of Catholic Bishops, 30

United Synagogue of Conservative Judaism, 97

University of Judaism (Los Angeles), 96. *See also* American Jewish University

untrustworthiness, dishonesty (*yesh bahem mishum mehusarai emunah*), 149

Urban, Wilbur, 16

Urmson, J. O., 151

U.S. Constitution, 93–95

U.S. Supreme Court, 93–95, 121

Value and Vulnerability, 99–100

verbal bullying, 127

verbal inflation, 137–38

verbal oppression, 111–12

verifiability criterion, 6

Vermont, 58

Vervoort, Marieke, 67

video games, 141–51

violence, 143–45

virtue ethics, 148–51

vulgar language. *See* foul language (*nivlut peh*)

Walzer, Michael, 152, 153, 164

war, 152–64; commanded by the Torah (*milhamot mitzvah*), 159–60; in Jewish law, 155–62; justifications for going to, 163; modern Jewish theory of, 162–64; and peace in the nature of God, 154–55

Washington DC, 58

Western theories of ethics. *See* character; consequentialist issues; deontology
Wittgenstein, Ludwig, 6
World to Come, 36, 167, 209n27
worship, 13, 20, 75
Written Torah, 52

yesh bahem mishum mehusarai emunah (untrustworthy, dishonest), 149
yetzer ha-ra, 27, 29, 146, 155
yetzer ha-tov, 27, 29, 155

Yose, Rabbi, 37
your life comes first (*hayyekha kod'min*), 29, 122
Yudoff, Judy, 97

Zechariah, 104
Ziegler School of Rabbinic Studies (Los Angeles), 98
z'nut ha-peh v'ha-ozen (salacious talk), 139–40
Zoloth-Dorfman, Laurie, 54
Zoroastrian sources, 148

To order or obtain more information on these or other Jewish Publication Society titles, visit jps.org.

www.ingramcontent.com/pod-product-compliance
Lightning Source LLC
Chambersburg PA
CBHW020348100426
42812CB00035B/3396/J